Kirsty Sword (Gusmão) … in 1966. She grew up in Melbour… lbourne University where she c… onours), majoring in Indonesian and Italian, and a Diploma of Education.

In 1991, after working as an administrative secretary with the Overseas Service Bureau (Australian Volunteers International), she joined the Refugee Studies Program at Oxford University. During 1991 she travelled to East Timor as the researcher/interpreter on the Yorkshire Television documentary film *In Cold Blood: The Massacre of East Timor*.

From 1992 to 1996 she lived and worked as a teacher and human rights campaigner in Jakarta, Indonesia. It was during these years that her work for the East Timorese independence cause intensified and brought her into contact with the independence leader Xanana Gusmão, who was serving a twenty-year sentence in a Jakarta jail and whom she married in July 2000.

She has lived in East Timor since October 1999 and is the founding director of the Alola Foundation, which she established in 2001 to address the needs of East Timorese women and their families. She has two sons, Alexandre and Kay Olok.

Information about the work of the Alola Foundation can be found on the website: http://www.alolafoundation.org

A WOMAN OF INDEPENDENCE

Kirsty Sword Gusmão

WITH

Rowena Lennox

MACMILLAN
Pan Macmillan Australia

First published 2003 in Macmillan by Pan Macmillan Australia Pty Ltd
St Martins Tower, 31 Market Street, Sydney

National Library of Australia
Cataloguing-in-Publication data:

Gusmão, Kirsty Sword.
A woman of independence.

ISBN 0 7329 1197 4.

1. Gusmão, Kirsty Sword. 2. President's spouse – East Timor – Biography. 3. Women – Australia – Biography. 4. East Timor – History – Autonomy and independence movements. 5. East Timor – Politics and government. 6. East Timor – Biography. I. Title.

959.87092

Set in 13/15 pt Granjon by Post Pre-press Group, Brisbane, Queensland
Printed in Australia by McPherson's Printing Group

This book is dedicated to the memory of my father, Brian Sword, who taught me a lot about dragons and to never shy away from the difficult.

There is one thing stronger than all the armies of the world,
and that is an idea whose time has come.

Victor Hugo

And if only we arrange our life in accordance with the principle which tells us that we must always trust in the difficult, then what now appears to us as the most alien will become our most intimate and trusted experience. How could we forget those ancient myths that stand at the beginning of all races, the myths about dragons that at the last moment are transformed into princesses? Perhaps all the dragons in our lives are princesses who are only waiting to see us act, just once, with beauty and courage. Perhaps everything that frightens us is, in its deepest essence, something helpless that wants our love.

Rainer Maria Rilke, Letters to a Young Poet

CONTENTS

ACKNOWLEDGEMENTS

My heartfelt thanks to Rowena Lennox for her companionship and for helping to concentrate my thoughts on events of the past at a time when the demands of the present are so all-consuming. Thanks, too, to my darling mother, Rosalie, and to the women of Balibar for being mother to my children and for attending to the needs of my body and soul during the long months of writing. I am also grateful to Don and Fiona Clarke for the use of the quiet haven of their home.

But thanks, most of all, to my East Timorese friends, the fence-jumpers, the refugees, the students, the political leaders. Thank you for taking your country, and me along with it, to the place where we stand today: on the hearth of a new beginning.

ORGANISATIONS

ABRI	Armed Forces of the Republic of Indonesia
ASDT	Timorese Association of Social Democrats
ASEAN	Association of South-East Asian Nations
BAIS	Indonesian Strategic Intelligence Agency
BIA	Indonesian Military Intelligence Agency
BRTT	East Timor People's Front
Canvisti	East Timorese Non-Violent Solidarity Committee
CDPM	Commission for the Rights of the Maubere People
CNRM	National Council of Maubere Resistance (formerly CRRN)
CNRT	National Council of Timorese Resistance (formerly CNRM)
CRRN	Revolutionary Council of the National Resistance
Falintil	National Liberation Army of East Timor
Fretilin	Revolutionary Front for an Independent East Timor
ICRC	International Committee of the Red Cross
Interfet	United Nations International Force in East Timor

JAKER	People's Culture Network
LBH	Legal Aid Institute
LPHAM	Institute for the Defence of Human Rights
NAM	Non-Aligned Movement
NC	National Council (formerly NCC)
NCC	National Consultative Council (of East Timor)
OSB	Overseas Service Bureau (later Australian Volunteers International)
PDI	Democratic Party of Indonesia
PKB	National Awakening Party
PPBI	Centre for Indonesian Workers' Struggle
PRD	People's Democratic Party (Democratic People's Alliance until 1998)
Renetil	National Resistance of East Timorese Students
SMID	Student Solidarity for Democracy in Indonesia
SPRIM	Indonesian–Maubere Peoples' Solidarity Struggle
STN	National Farmers' Union
TAPOL	Indonesia human rights campaign
TNI	Indonesian Armed Forces (from 1999)
UDT	Timorese Democratic Union
UNAMET	United Nations Mission in East Timor
UNHCR	United Nations High Commissioner for Refugees
UNTAET	United Nations Transitional Administration in East Timor

Chapter one

THE NEWEST NATION
19 May 2002

I HAD BEEN waiting for this moment for almost twenty years – the party celebrating East Timor's independence – but somehow it came around too fast. I wasn't ready. The Portuguese President's bathroom was missing a towel rail, I hadn't yet wrapped the gift for Indonesian President Megawati Sukarnoputri's husband, and as for what I was going to wear to the airport to greet the VIP guests later in the day, well I really hadn't had time to give it much thought. My husband, Xanana Gusmão, was butting out a cigarette on the concrete landing outside the back door of our house and about to get into his car to head for Dili.

'Shouldn't you at least put on a tie?' I called to him as one of the bodyguards flung open the door of the car. It was 9 am on 19 May 2002 and he was about to go and receive the first of the foreign dignitaries at the airport. In exactly fifteen hours time he would be sworn in as the first President of the Democratic Republic of East Timor. Not only had he refused to don a suit for the occasion, he wasn't even wearing a tie! 'It's here in my pocket,' he answered from the back seat of the car, withdrawing a length of crumpled red silk from the pocket of his shirt. 'If I need to use it,' he added. There was a squeal of tyres and he and his convoy of minders disappeared behind a cloud of dust.

It seemed that we had been racing against time for months. While the official organisation and protocol relating to the Independence Day celebrations were in the hands of a National Steering Committee chaired by the Senior Minister of Foreign Affairs and Cooperation, Dr José Ramos-Horta, there were bits of the schedule and arrangements for the big day that were intensely personal and which it seemed I couldn't avoid being involved in – the invitations, for example.

The Chief Minister, Dr Mari Alkatiri, and the UN Special Representative of the Secretary-General, Dr Sergio Vieira de Mello, had both signed letters inviting heads of state and senior government officials from around the world to witness the birth of the newest nation of the third millennium and the twenty-first century. These invitations bore the insignia of the United Nations (UN), which at midnight on 19 May would ceremonially transfer its authority over the territory to the speaker of East Timor's National Parliament.

Earlier in the year, around March, however, I began to receive some disgruntled emails from longstanding friends of East Timor in Australia and other countries – activists, the staff of non-government organisations (NGOs) and trade unions, and some people of goodwill without any particular affiliation. Most politely intimated that they were interested to know more about the planned celebrations. Others were less bashful and demanded an explanation as to why they had not received an invitation to be present. They weren't expecting to have an expenses-paid trip; it was the thought that counted, the courtesy of being remembered, appreciated and included.

And so I discussed the problem with Xanana. It was decided that he would issue invitations to the members of solidarity groups and other friends who hadn't figured on anyone's guest list. He would do so in a private capacity, signing off on each letter as president-elect.

Xanana's office was made up of a handful of hardworking and dedicated volunteers who had coordinated the work related to his campaign for the presidency a month earlier. Although weary after the weeks on the hustings, they had stayed by Xanana's side to help him through the busy pre-independence period. No one received salaries, and the very unglamorous My Field Hotel and Restaurant in an inner suburb of Dili, which had functioned as Xanana's campaign headquarters, was now transformed into the office of the nation's president-to-be. With all that had to be done to prepare for the arrival of fourteen heads of state and the ninety-odd official delegations expected for Independence, no one had the time to take on the task of sending out individualised invitations to the friends of East Timor. Before long it became clear that if this job were to be done, I would have to do it myself.

And so I somewhat begrudgingly set about drafting a letter and compiling a list of invitees, trawling through three or four years worth of emails to gather their addresses. With everything I had on my plate already – my work for the Alola Foundation, an NGO I had established; the routine barrage of media interviews; preparations for a trip to South Korea later in May; not to mention caring for our nineteen-month-old son, Alexandre – I would have dearly loved just to delegate this job to someone else. However, there were delicate considerations regarding forms of address. Some of Timor's oldest and most faithful allies were also close personal friends of ours, and it would have been inappropriate, perhaps even rude, for them to be addressed in a formal way. And so, each evening for two weeks leading up to 20 May, I would settle Alexandre down for the night and then get another batch of letters printed off or queued up for sending by email the next day. The satellite phone rigged up at our home delivered the letters into the ether at the excruciatingly slow rate of approximately one per ten minutes. After fifty or so invitations, my patience and sanity were in short supply. Nevertheless, I was satisfied that an important gesture of recognition had been extended. After all, I myself had begun my East Timor journey as a member of the huge worldwide network of supporters of this little nation's right to be free.

To make matters more chaotic, building work was underway at our home in the hills of Balibar, ten kilometres south of Dili. The house we were living in was one of several buildings on the site. Other pavilions housed an office, Alexandre's playroom and some guest accommodation. Up the hill about fifty metres from our house a sizeable area had been levelled, and in February 2002 construction of a new structure began.

'What exactly are they building up there?' I had asked Xanana one morning. I had noticed builders sleeping on site, cooking their breakfast on an open fire and getting started on their work in the cool of the early morning. The deafening sound of earthmoving equipment and trucks coming and going with cement and rocks commenced at 7 am each morning and ceased about twelve hours later.

'Another house, of course,' said Xanana, as if the project had been the subject of numerous conversations between us. The reality was that Xanana had issued instructions to a building contractor friend of his to commence work on the building and, as tends to happen around my husband, the former guerrilla commander, orders were executed at once, with few questions asked.

Given that our family was about to expand with the birth of our second child in August, I presumed that the dwelling under construction would be bigger than our present rather tiny one and that, sooner or later, we would move into it. 'Great,' I thought. But we were not to be its first inhabitants.

One morning in early May, as I flitted between the office and the main house, I noticed that a coat of rose-pink paint was being applied to the external wall of the new building. Surely it was just the undercoat. However, when a week later it had still not been painted over with another colour, I decided to investigate. Until that point, I had not had a minute spare even to lay foot inside the new building, let alone take stock of the plan, the configuration of the house, the layout of its rooms. And while there was no time for a thorough inspection on this particular day either – I had a journalist waiting to interview me on the verandah of our house – I did ask the builders about the colour scheme. They confirmed my suspicion that the house was indeed to be painted pink.

'So who exactly was it that chose this colour?' I enquired of the foreman.

'Katuas [the old man],' he answered matter-of-factly.

There were times that I deemed it wise not to question my husband's judgement – on matters political and cultural, for example. However, on this occasion there was nothing for it but to overrule him. 'White, I think, would be far more appropriate, don't you? Do you think you can arrange that?' I asked.

'Sim, Senhora,' came the reply.

When I challenged Xanana later about his colour tastes, he tried to cover himself by saying he hadn't meant that particular birthday cake–icing pink but rather an attractive salmon.

Some time after the building works commenced, José Ramos-Horta paid his first visit to our house. He had come to quiz Xanana on whether or not he intended to stand in the presidential elections, which were looming. Only a week remained for Xanana to register himself as a candidate and people were beginning to get jittery about his continued insistence that he did not wish to be president.

'The East Timorese people demand it of you,' said José, glancing about at the sun setting on the orange, light-filled hills below us. 'You mustn't let them down.' The beauty of Balibar temporarily distracting him from his serious mission, he turned to me. 'Wow, this is a really beautiful place you have here.'

Xanana, who was keen to direct the subject of the conversation away from the delicate question of his candidacy, offered to take José on a little tour of the premises.

Later, over coffee, José blithely put to Xanana and me the possibility of our putting up the President of Portugal and his family when they visited for the Independence celebrations. José was grappling with the problem of where he was going to accommodate the heads of state and the thousands of other VIP guests scheduled to fly in to Dili for East Timor's big day. It was only two years since the entire country had been shattered – in September 1999 – by pro-autonomy militias (those who had wanted Timorese autonomy within Indonesia) following the vote for independence, and only a handful of hotels and guesthouses had been built on the ashes of the devastation. They had all been booked out months in advance. A floating hotel had even been brought in to Dili Harbour from Thailand in response to what could only be described as the accommodation crisis. In answer to José's proposal, we didn't say no. After all, we had nothing but the highest regard for the Portuguese leader, and had become quite friendly with him and his family in recent years. But nor did we feel superbly confident about the idea, given our inexperience in such matters and the fact that our accommodation was, by presidential standards at least, extremely basic. And so the question was left hanging.

The lead-up to Independence was feverishly active but exciting. In addition to the extensive program of festivals, fairs, workshops, performances, exhibitions and tributes planned in Dili, a host of cultural and sporting events were to take place in each of the district centres. All over the country, people were busy and brimming with anticipation, happy to be temporarily distracted from the extreme hardship and poverty they faced in their day-to-day lives.

The Alola Foundation, which I had set up in March 2001 to support the work of women's organisations across East Timor, was contributing to preparations for a Women's Fair which was to take place the week before Independence. From the tiny storeroom at the rear of the World Bank that functioned as the Alola Foundation office, we convened meetings with the other members of the Rede Feto Timor Lorosa'e – the East Timorese Women's Network – to organise our participation in the fair. The foundation decided to present an award to about thirteen women who had fought alongside East Timor's national liberation army, known as Falintil, throughout the war. In addition to the framed tribute to the women's courage and self-sacrifice, we presented each awardee with a monetary gift and a hamper containing practical offerings such as soap, candles, towels and washing powder. It was nothing more than a gesture, but the women were moved and appreciative of the recognition of their contribution – and in spite of the demands on his own time during this frenetic period, Xanana agreed to make the presentations to the women.

In the week prior to the celebrations, a meeting of donor countries was held in Dili. Its aim was to discuss the budgetary needs of the new government in the first year of independence. For months Xanana had been drafting and revising the structure for the office of the president, making important decisions relating to staffing requirements and budgets. There was much speculation as to whether or not the new government would allocate resources to an office of the first lady. In the expectation that there would indeed be some limited support provided to facilitate my work, I set about preparing a structure and a budget for presentation to the government and its donors.

Of course I was pretty clueless when it came to anticipating what the role of first lady would entail, and so was grateful when Xanana's staff organised a briefing for me with a visiting American woman working under contract to the International Republican Institute. She had worked in the White House in Washington and so knew a thing or two about the roles of presidents and of first ladies. Patiently and thoughtfully, the distinguished-looking white-haired woman talked to me about everything from the management of schedules and events to the preference of some first ladies for outdoor marquees to host their state banquets.

'I think it is quite essential that you have a press secretary to handle requests for media appearances and an events manager who can take charge of organising gala dinners and the like,' she said.

Hmmm. I wasn't quite sure how many banquets we would be hosting, given that the building it was rumoured would become the 'presidential palace' was currently nothing more than a pile of rubble in the foothills of Dili. I thanked the well-meaning American and went back to contemplating whether it would be considered excessive to ask the state for a car.

As it turned out, my lobbying for official recognition of the role of first lady was unsuccessful. A decision was taken somewhere that given East Timor's other huge and pressing needs, the spouse of the president would have to strike out on her own. It seemed that, for the time being at least, I would have to get by on my wits and the smell of an oily rag. Fortunately, the preceding ten years of work for East Timor had prepared me well for this challenge.

When 19 May came around, hot on the heels of a string of official and not-so-official receptions, dinners and cocktail parties, it seemed that the whole world had converged on Dili. Xanana looked exhausted before the day had even begun. Having seen him off to Dili, where he was to welcome Australian Prime Minister John Howard, among other important visitors, my mother, Rosalie, and I slipped into a pair of thongs each and trudged through the red mud to inspect the new house. In spite of our misgivings and insecurities, Xanana had bitten the bullet and formally extended an invitation to the President of Portugal, his wife, and his daughter Vera, to spend the night of 19 May in our new house.

Our faithful band of household helpers were hard at work already, mopping the workmen's muddy footprints from the tiled verandah. The work on the house had literally been completed that morning; there was the smell of fresh paint on the interior walls, and wood shavings, nails and cement dust still littered the floor of the living room and kitchen. At least the beds were made up with fresh white linen and the fridge was stocked with food for the president and his family's breakfast the next morning. Fortunately, the Portuguese diplomatic mission had taken pity on our inexperience in these intimate matters of state, and had kindly helped us out by providing bed linen, towels and some of the other comforts of home. We were lucky, too, that a friend of the builder had a large quantity of furniture in storage and was able to lend it to us for the duration of the president's stay. Having been stored for some time in Dili's humid climate, the bases of the beds were mouldy, so we improvised, using double-bed sheets as valances to cover the marks.

Things had gone from bad to worse in the ensuite, however. Not only had I discovered that there was nowhere for the president to hang his towel, but the shower head had sprung a leak and water was escaping in all directions.

'Where are we going to find a plumber at this late hour?' I complained to Regina, the former resistance cadre who managed the affairs of our household.

'I'll deal with it,' she answered.

She would have to. I was due to leave for the airport in five minutes and I still hadn't decided what to wear for the day of meeting and greeting. As I rummaged through my wardrobe for something appropriate, Rosalie got back to drafting replies to the hundreds of emails and letters of congratulation that Xanana had received following his victory at the polls on 14 April. A few minutes later, my arms draped with the plastic-covered outfit I would wear for the evening ceremony, I kissed Alexandre goodbye and dived into the waiting car.

'Don't forget to dress Alexandre in something swanky!' I cried out to Rosalie as the car swung down the driveway. She, Alexandre and members of Xanana's family, including his old and frail mother, would join us at Taci Tolu, where the celebrations would take place later that evening.

A month before, I had emailed my measurements to Nelson Leong, a Timorese fashion designer based in Sydney, who had made two stunning outfits for me to wear that evening and the following day. It was a complicated exercise. In the middle trimester of pregnancy, I was rapidly expanding, and my measurements were changing at a rate of knots. Nevertheless, the finished products were extremely beautiful and sat perfectly in spite of my ample waistline.

The airport was abuzz with excitement and tension. Timorese protocol officers from the Ministry of Foreign Affairs darted in and out of the crowds of guests, which included traditionally dressed dancers and members of the guard of honour, passing copies of the schedule of arrivals back and forth and shouting instructions to one another. 'It's Bill Clinton next and then Kofi Annan just before three,' I heard one of them bark.

Out on the little pathway leading from the terminal to the tarmac, Xanana stood smoking and poring over the text of his inaugural presidential speech.

'Thank God you're here,' he exhaled heavily, as I reached his side. 'Help me with this wording, will you?'

Knowing that it was a rhetorical question, I sighed and took the document and pen he was thrusting into my hand. Agio Pereira, Xanana's chief of staff, leant over with a manila folder open on his back while I stood, pen poised, working on the translation of the parts of Xanana's speech directed to the Indonesian President and the people of Indonesia. Xanana was insistent that in his speech he address each of the significant guests present at the ceremony in their own language. So the text he was preparing featured not only Tetum (the native East Timorese lingua franca), but also English, Portuguese and Bahasa Indonesia. I had managed to translate two sentences from Portuguese to Bahasa Indonesia when Clinton descended from his plane and we had to rush out onto the tarmac to shake his hand. I had completed an entire paragraph by the time Kofi Annan and his wife stepped off their jet half an hour later. Every minute counted.

The meeting and greeting parade over, we headed for Xanana's 'official' office back in the centre of town. The government had allocated space to him on the first floor of the huge, white government palace on the waterfront, and he also retained his campaign headquarters at the My Field Hotel in Bairropite. The spacious, elegant office still had a bare, unoccupied feel to it; the large wooden desk opposite the door was scattered with unopened gifts and an assortment of unread official communiqués. It was here that I changed into my knee-length cream silk skirt and coat, and Xanana fastened his red necktie around the collar of his favourite white shirt. A hairdresser friend of mine was on hand and quickly replaced my ponytail with something more in keeping with the significance of the occasion and the elegance of my outfit. A dozen pins and half a can of hairspray later, my hair was thoroughly lacquered to the side of my head. Not even a gale force wind could have budged it. By the time we had made it past the queue of guests and friends who were clamouring at the door of the office to shake Xanana's hand, it was just after 6 pm and we were already late for the VIP reception getting underway up the road in Lecidere.

By the time we pulled up at the curb alongside the outdoor reception site, Sergio Vieira de Mello, the Special Representative of the UN Secretary-General, was leaping into his car. 'The Mass is about to begin in Taci Tolu,' Sergio shouted in our direction. We decided to skip the reception and make our way immediately to Taci Tolu.

The huge dry plain of Taci Tolu, a couple of kilometres west of Dili, is reputed to be the site on which victims of atrocities committed by the Indonesian military during its twenty-four-year occupation of East Timor had been buried in mass graves. It was also the place where Pope John Paul II had celebrated mass during his visit to the territory in 1989. So it was fitting that Taci Tolu was now to host an event that would usher in a new era of peace and reconciliation. Also significant was the fact that a team of Japanese military engineers had been responsible for preparing the ground on which the stage and VIP stands were built. The Japanese military had joined the UN peace-keeping force amidst bitter controversy regarding the role Japanese troops had played in subjugating Timor during the Second World War. Their contribution to the celebrations marking East Timor's entry into the community of nations helped to close the book on a painful chapter in Timor's history and in relations between the two countries.

Huge crowds of East Timorese and foreign guests had already begun to mass in Taci Tolu. The expanse of dusty ground set aside to accommodate the 100,000 expected visitors to the site stretched as far as the eye could see. Mass was already underway as we found our way to our seats on the raised platform, which was one of four VIP stands clustered around the circular performance arena. Sitting either side of us were the Portuguese President and his wife. Behind us was a sea of familiar faces. Mass was a sombre affair, dedicated to the memory of all those who had died in the heroic struggle for independence, but the voices of the choir were uplifting and the predominant sentiment was one of thanksgiving and rejoicing, not of mourning. This was to be the tenor of the entire evening.

I smiled to myself as I noticed that the stage area was covered with a length of blue material. It was the same hue as the tarpaulins that had been issued by the United Nations High Commission for Refugees (UNHCR) to the destitute and the homeless at the height of the humanitarian crisis two and a half years earlier. The ubiquitous blue plastic had become part of the East Timorese landscape; here it was a shelter for a family, there the roof of a school, and throughout Timor, passengers crowded on the back of open trucks held it above their heads to protect them from the elements.

Following Mass, the guests were treated to a traditional welcome by elders and 'keepers of the word' (oral historians and guardians of traditional law) from each of East Timor's thirteen districts, and then a troupe of dancers and traditional warriors riding Timor ponies stormed onto the arena to take their turn in the colourful pageant. At around 9 pm, I glanced at my watch. Rosalie and Alexandre must have arrived by now, I thought, but there was no sign of them anywhere. I guessed they must have been seated in another stand, since there were few vacant places remaining in our own.

Later Rosalie was to share with me how she was moved to tears by the sight of hundreds of lit candles, each one symbolising a life lost, floating onto the arena as if on a slow-moving tide. And how Alexandre had been transfixed by the sight of the giant crocodile of Timor's creation myth being paraded by hundreds of children. Sadly, we missed these and a number of other spine-chilling items on the program, since at 10 pm we were due back at the airport to collect Indonesian President Megawati Sukarnoputri, her husband, Taufik Kiemas, and their daughter. Since we had ten minutes to spare, we swung by the My Field Hotel for a cheese sandwich and a can of Coke – midway through the Mass, Xanana had leant over me and whispered, 'I'm starving!' He wasn't the only one. I hadn't had time to eat anything since breakfast.

There had been months of speculation regarding Megawati's attendance at the Independence Day celebrations. Would she come or wouldn't she? There was some opposition to her visit from within the Indonesian parliament and sections of the military. When this opposition appeared to have swayed her, Xanana made a special visit to Jakarta to personally extend the invitation to her and members of her government. It was testimony to the importance he attached to good relations with Indonesia.

The airport was now without the frantic protocol officers but crawling with a dozen or more poker-faced men in black suits with wires protruding from their ears. They were Indonesian intelligence officers who had come with the advance party to guarantee the security of their president. In spite of Xanana's assurances that the East Timorese people would welcome Megawati warmly, as they had done the former Indonesian president, Abdurrahman Wahid, two years earlier, there were understandably some anxieties in the ranks of the security forces about her safety. Megawati and her daughter were dressed in black. According to the demands of protocol, I travelled in the car with her husband, Taufik, whom I had met on a previous visit to Jakarta and who sported a cheerful red tie. Along the way to the Indonesian heroes' cemetery, where Megawati would lay a wreath on the graves of fallen Indonesian soldiers, we chatted about all sorts of things, including Taufik's background. He came from very humble beginnings but had carved out a successful career for himself in the business world.

With time ticking on, I was itching to get back to Taci Tolu. José Ramos-Horta was midway through his speech when Xanana guided Megawati to her seat in the front row of our stand. Noticing our arrival, José interrupted his address and invited the crowds to welcome the Indonesian President. A spontaneous and deafening cheer erupted from below us, and Xanana took Megawati's hand in his own and raised it high above their heads. There could have been no more unequivocal evidence of the political maturity of the East Timorese people. Megawati looked a little taken aback. Perhaps it was relief that caused a small, satisfied smile to play on her lips as she took her seat at my husband's side.

Shortly before midnight, the UN Secretary-General, Kofi Annan, took to the stage. The audience whooped and cheered when he prefaced his comments with the promise that he would not speak for long as East Timor's new day was about to dawn. In his address he congratulated the people on their tenacious struggle and their hard-won freedom, imploring them to approach self-rule with 'compromise, discipline, unity and resolve'. Minutes later, the UN flag was lowered, and as it came down, Barbara Hendrix, the soprano, sent the strains of the negro spiritual 'Oh Freedom' shimmering out into the night sky. The power of her voice and the sentiments expressed in the words of her song caused me to break out in a rash of goose bumps.

And then came the moment I had looked forward to with unimaginable longing. I wanted nothing better than to share it with my family: my mother, Alexandre and Xanana, the people who had lived with me all the collective emotion, pain and sacrifice that had culminated in this glorious day. But just then Xanana was ushered to the stage and the flag of the Democratic Republic of East Timor was made ready to begin its journey up the flagpole. Rosalie and Alexandre were still nowhere to be seen. Even Xanana was now lost from view, as the seats of the stand stood at right angles to the stage. Fortunately, huge TV screens had been erected at the edges of the arena, and onto them were projected the figures of those occupying the stage. As the orchestra commenced playing the national anthem, the camera – which was now my eye – homed in on the gloved hands of the two soldiers who were slowly hoisting the red, black and yellow flag.

The eyes of the performers squatting in the dust at the foot of the stand were wet with tears as they followed the progress of the flag, *their* flag. Out of the darkness of the memories of every East Timorese present loomed the faces of dead friends or family members, recalling the tragic loss of over 200,000 lives in the course of the war. In every heart was a glowing ember of pride and hope, reflected now in the smiles of the upturned faces. How I wished I could be down there among them! How I wished I were free to give expression to my own emotion, to the smiles and tears welling up inside me as the final strains of the anthem rang out and the flag reached its destination at the top of the flagpole. But to my right was the President of the World Bank and on my left a line of prime ministers and government officials. It didn't do to cry. Xanana's face, superimposed on the fluttering flag, betrayed nothing of his own feelings. Perhaps he was too weary to feel anything very much; perhaps foremost in his mind was the heavy weight of responsibility that he would bear as leader of the poorest nation in Asia.

Minutes later, Xanana was sworn in as President of the Democratic Republic of East Timor. I didn't congratulate him. I couldn't. He had to give priority to receiving the handshakes and smiles of the heads of state and members of their delegations. In any case, he had never desired to be president, and the only appropriate words, really, were not words of congratulation at all but those which for twenty-four years had spurred Xanana and the resistance on. 'A luta continua [the struggle goes on],' I whispered into his beard as finally he reached my side and the sky erupted in colourful bursts of fireworks.

Before long the race against time resumed. We had to accompany Megawati and her family back to the airport, locate Rosalie and Alexandre, and get home to Balibar ahead of the Portuguese President.

The world watched East Timor's Independence celebrations from near and far. For every international guest at Taci Tolu there were dozens more spectators at home in Australia, the Americas, Asia, Europe and elsewhere. The East Timorese were masters of their own destiny at last. Newspapers devoted pages to the festivities. Television programs broadcast the images. The new nation of East Timor had a place in people's hearts and minds.

But Timor wasn't always the focus of international attention, a place on the itineraries of senior government officials and heads of state, a nation wished well by the world's leaders. When I first visited East Timor, in 1990, it was an abandoned and almost forgotten half-island.

Chapter two

UNWILLING COLONY 1990

'BOA TARDE,' I ventured a little half-heartedly. The two nuns in habits who stood before me replied with a smile and a welcoming gesture. It was difficult to know what nationality they were – Portuguese or Italian perhaps – and therefore which language to opt for. They soon introduced themselves as Sister Clementina and Sister Luigia. By the time I had made my introduction in a faltering combination of Portuguese, Bahasa Indonesia and English, I had established that they were Italian. Ah, there was some sense to be found in my odd choice of university majors after all. Most people, when I told them that I was a student of Indonesian and Italian, had looked at me askance. And I must admit that there, on the doorstep of a convent in Dili, East Timor, I was marvelling myself at how, within the space of half an hour, I had managed to put the two unrelated languages to practical use.

Twenty minutes earlier, as I had waited for a taxi at Dili's Comoro Airport, my Indonesian language skills had allowed me to spin an elaborate tale of love and longing for a Javanese officer ('stationed somewhere out beyond Manatuto') which was sufficient distraction for the Intel (intelligence) agent who had accompanied me to the door of my clapped-out blue taxi – he forgot to ask me which hotel I was staying at. And now, in the cool of the whitewashed convent, I was making polite conversation in Italian with two Canossian nuns while sipping sweet black Timorese coffee and wondering how I was going to broach the subject of my accommodation.

I had been warned that Dili's hotels were teeming with spies whose mission it was to keep a close eye on the activities and movements of foreign guests. The assumption was that outsiders were either friends of the resistance (and therefore troublemakers) or human rights activists bent on uncovering the facts of Indonesia's fifteen-year reign of terror. These assumptions were not ill-founded. After all, East Timor had been open to outsiders for only one year, and 'genuine' tourists rarely ventured further east than the holiday isles of Bali and Lombok.

The hospitality of the East Timorese clergy was famous, so I enquired whether a bed might be available for the night. Mother Superior had just woken from her afternoon nap and was summoned to join us. Madre Carla greeted me with a kiss on both cheeks. It was impossible not to feel entirely comfortable and at home among these smiling women in their crisp, white habits, so it was disappointing to learn that the convent was hosting a large number of guests from Jakarta and that there was not a single bed vacant. Madre Carla was most apologetic and offered to write me letters of introduction to the sisters in Baucau when I mentioned that I was keen to visit East Timor's second largest town.

There was nothing for it but to head for the Hotel Turismo. I drained my cup of Timorese coffee while Sister Luigia called a boy to assist me with my luggage. A taxi appeared out of nowhere and my bag was placed on the back seat. I kissed each of my new friends goodbye and promised to return the following day to collect the letters for Baucau.

The sun was starting to set as the old blue taxi lumbered along the foreshore in the direction of the infamous Hotel Turismo. A group of boys were kicking a soccer ball among the driftwood and rubbish washed up on the narrow strip of beach. The rumble and splutter of the taxi as we passed caused them to look up momentarily, but I resisted the temptation to raise my hand in greeting. I was all too aware of the consequences for East Timorese of knowing a foreigner, even in the most casual sense. It would be assumed that they were passing on information on the human rights situation in the territory, the price for which was intimidation or possibly interrogation at the hands of the military.

The reception desk was empty. The only person in sight was a bare-chested Timorese youth balancing a newly bathed and overfed Chinese infant on one hip. The child was covered from head to toe in talcum powder. The contrast of the child's fleshy, white thighs against the dark torso of the teenage boy was stark. 'Pedro,' barked a woman's voice from a distant place in the hotel. The youth was gone, and in his place appeared a tall, wiry figure with a moustache and a sneer. I recognised him as the man who had offered to carry my luggage at the airport earlier that day. I had managed to avoid him then by pretending not to understand his heavily accented English. But now there was no getting away from him. He was Mr Carlos, the Turismo's resident spook; he doubled as receptionist and would check me into my room.

He asked me for my passport and proceeded to note down all the details on a coffee-stained hotel registration form and on a second, white paper which he informed me was for police records. The fact that the police, and indeed Mr Carlos himself, were in possession of my name and passport details made me feel decidedly uneasy. Throughout the whole process, which seemed never-ending, Mr Carlos quizzed me as to the reasons for my visit to East Timor ('fed up and bored with Bali'), the length of my stay ('just a few days') and the places I intended to visit in East Timor. When my answer to the last question failed to satisfy him, he seemed to delight in announcing that permission for all travel beyond Dili must be sought – from him!

The inquisition over and my passport safely back in my hip pocket, I was finally led across the garden and up a flight of stairs to my room. The two Chinese gents nursing bottles of beer on the porch of the neighbouring room sized me up, unsmiling, as I passed. It was a relief to close the door of my room firmly behind me.

The room was airless and shabby, but private enough. With the flick of a switch, the air-conditioner roared to life on the wall, but within minutes it was dripping water onto the warped linoleum floor. I settled for an open window and the fan instead, and then set about unpacking my bag, reorganising its contents so that nothing of a potentially compromising nature – a letter to a member of the clergy or a human rights report, for instance – was left within view of curious hotel staff or other possible visitors to my room.

I was starving, and after a quick bath in the half-bucket of water that was the most I could extract from the bathroom tap, I headed down to the small restaurant that opened onto the courtyard garden below. Apart from one table of diners and two Timorese waiters lurking in the dark corners of the restaurant, the place was deserted. As I approached the occupied table, one of the diners, whom I recognised from the airport, motioned to me to join them. I didn't hesitate, despite the presence of an Indonesian among them (he turned out to be the interpreter and 'fixer' of the Italian geologist who'd called me over). 'Buona sera,' I greeted the Italian and then waited for the third member of the party to introduce himself. He was an American agricultural extension officer who had lived in East Timor for close to nine months. To have negotiated and survived such a long stay he must be pro-integration, I assumed, and I therefore decided not to trust him. He remarked flippantly on the local custom of phone-tapping. A warning to me perhaps?

The waiters appeared to be afraid to approach us, and when they finally brought our meals, I noticed that their eyes kept darting back nervously over their shoulders in the direction of the kitchen. Not even my best, most reassuring smile seemed to help them feel at ease.

When dinner was over, I paid for my meal and retreated to my room. To my surprise, I burst into tears and spent the next fifteen minutes crying in front of my reflection in the bathroom mirror. I knew that the tears were the result of the emotion associated with being, finally, in East Timor and of the discomfort of my subterfuge. I was not used to having to lie so assiduously, and the strain was beginning to show after only one day. If someone had told me then that my interest in East Timor was to make me, in the years to come, a skilful and effortless liar for the cause, I would not have believed them.

I slept soundly in spite of the heat and the whirring of the fan, which seemed to get progressively louder as the night wore on. In the morning Motael Church loomed through the haze from the opposite side of Dili's sleepy little bay. This morning the soccer-playing youths had been replaced on the foreshore in front of the hotel by a band of hungry pigs rooting about noisily. They seemed to be the only creatures oblivious to the presence of my tourist's video camera.

I knew that Mr Carlos was watching me from the shadows of the hotel's portico, no doubt attempting to detect the mark of a professional in my use of the camera, a sure sign that I was a journalist and therefore to be subject to the closest scrutiny. Crossing the road again, I disarmed Mr Carlos with the most cheerful 'Selamat pagi' I could manage and then trained the lens on his weasel-like features, smiling and cajoling him to play along with the tourist's charade. He disappeared from view in a flash, as if it were the sights of an M-16, not a Sony Handycam, that I had pointed in his direction. I guess spies are as touchy about their identities as subversives are.

Back in my room, I stuffed everything compromising into my day pack, then headed out in the direction of Motael Church. I had correspondence and some other reading material to deliver to the parish priest. It was only nine o'clock, but already the sun was biting. By the time I reached the curve in the road and the tree-lined stretch of elegant old colonial buildings, I was wet through with sweat. The shade of the last two blocks was a welcome relief. I attempted to regain my composure by mopping up as much sweat as I could with a single tissue, and plucking at my skirt, which was clinging to my damp legs.

I found Father Domingos da Cunha emerging from what must have been the residence at the rear of the church. Two or three young men with serious expressions, who gave the impression of being minders, accompanied him as far as the verandah of the church. This is where we sat and where I introduced myself – 'I'm Kirsty Sword from Melbourne' – and told him my intentions in visiting East Timor and him: 'I've come with greetings and news from friends in Australia and letters for the bishop.' I felt the same calm and trust as I had in the presence of the Canossian sisters. When I came to extract the mail from my bag, Father Domingos quickly rose and urged me to follow him into the residence.

The sitting room was large and a little gloomy. The sofa on which we sat was draped with finely embroidered cloths, some with images of the cross-stitched in lilac. A tea set painted in the blues and whites of the Portuguese *azulejo* (tiles) had pride of place at the centre of the coffee table. It was odd. There was a woman's touch in every corner, and yet not a woman to be seen anywhere.

I didn't want to stay long, knowing that my visit would not have gone unnoticed by the ubiquitous Intel. I refused a cup of coffee and began to haul from my bag the letters to Bishop Belo from various friends and supporters in Australia, some correspondence for members of the Timorese clergy, and some current affairs magazines I had purchased in the airport lounge in Melbourne. As I prepared to leave, Father Domingos told me that the youth were united and well organised. He referred to the demonstration they had staged to coincide with the recent visit to Dili of the American Ambassador to Jakarta, John Monjo. Apparently the youths I had spotted earlier had been involved in the demonstration and were now seeking refuge in the church. No doubt the boys' protective attitude towards Father Domingos was their way of reciprocating the protection that he and his parish were offering them.

On the way back to the Turismo I stopped at a small barber's shop I had seen on the way. I needed a trim, it was true, but was more interested in the experience than in the results. The sign, produced in a flurry of spray paint above the open door, read in Bahasa Indonesia 'hair cut here'.

The owner was from Surabaya and had come to East Timor seven years ago in search of the kind of prosperity which was unattainable on overcrowded Java. He spoke with nostalgia of his home as he went about his business with my hair. All the while his Timorese assistant, a young man of about twenty, looked on in silence, a mixture of resentment and curiosity in his eyes. He wore a brightly coloured shirt emblazoned with the image of Bob Marley and a large wooden crucifix. I decided to direct a few words to him in Portuguese, knowing that he was likely to speak the language as badly as I did. His eyes flashed, and it was as if I had declared my allegiance to Timor, to the cause of independence! Up until that point he had only heard me speak Indonesian. He sidled up to my chair in his own chair, and, with his eyes flitting constantly between my face and that of his boss, began to fish for hints of solidarity in imperfect Portuguese. I could see that the barber was feeling uncomfortable – after all, he couldn't understand a word we were saying. He kept on snipping.

The youth, who was called Roque, answered my query about ownership of the shop with 'the Timorese are too poor to own anything here'. I felt obliged to interrupt his periodic outbursts ('the Javanese came and have dominated everything') and make polite conversation with the barber, who seemed to be growing resentful that his prize foreign client was being monopolised by his side-kick. In answer to Roque's increasingly animated declarations, I could do little but nod and sigh wistfully. He must have understood my predicament because, as I paid my 10,000 rupiah for the haircut, he asked whether he could visit me at the Turismo. I discouraged him. As I was leaving, he asked me for my address in Australia, and as I wrote it for him in a tiny address book the size of a matchbox, I whispered 'cuidado' (be careful) and told him that for his sake it would be best if he didn't show his face at the hotel.

The next morning I was up at 5 am in anticipation of my departure for Baucau. I had collected the correspondence from Madre Carla and purchased my ticket for Rp 3000 the afternoon before. I even had a freshly stamped 'surat jalan', or travel pass, ready to show to whoever was interested. Ever since the episode with the Handycam, Mr Carlos had given me a wide berth and was surprisingly cooperative when I had approached him for the travel pass. Perhaps I had uncovered a new use for my video camera!

At the Bele Batu Terminal, I boarded a dilapidated old minibus along with roughly thirty other passengers and a dozen or so tethered chickens. The coastal road leading east out of Dili offered stunning views back in the direction of the town and then, beyond the fishing village of Hera, it rose again to snake through the barren, sun-scorched hills which overlooked picture-pretty coves and the endless blue of the ocean.

Next to me on the bus sat a girl of about seven and her mother. When the little girl started nodding off, her head bobbing precariously towards my shoulder, with my free arm I helped her to nestle into my armpit. There she slept for the duration of the trip to Baucau, to the slight embarrassment of her mother, who periodically giggled in my direction, flashing a mouthful of teeth stained bright betel-red. The driver kept his other passengers entertained with a selection of sixties' tunes ('Put Your Sweet Lips'), all of which were preceded by a different animal noise – the bleating of a lamb, the crowing of a cock, the quacking of a duck. I had never heard anything quite so bizarre.

I asked to be dropped at the convent and, after three and a half hours on the bus, it was a joy to stretch my limbs again. At the entrance to the building stood three shy young girls – novices, I presumed. They seemed relieved when I addressed them in Indonesian. I asked to see the two sisters named in the letter prepared by Sister Carla in Dili. One of the three took me by the hand and led me through a breezy corridor into a small waiting room.

I smiled and thanked the girls and settled down to wait for Madre Elsa. I heard doors slamming, names being called, the excited babble of the three girls as they spread the word about the arrival of a guest. Madre Elsa appeared shortly after, wiping her hands on the front of her pristine habit and then embracing me warmly. She was a small woman who, in her manner, resembled more an efficient headmistress than a nun. I liked her immediately.

After presenting her with the letter from Sister Carla and being assured that there was a bed for me, I was taken on a tour of the convent. We were joined at that point by Sister Celeste, a delicate, gentle young nun who walked by my side, her protective and guiding arm linked through mine all the way. In the refectory, ninety pairs of eyes looked up from their morning tea and a cheer spontaneously erupted. I tried hard not to blush. Obviously visitors were quite a novelty here.

After lunch, Celeste enquired whether I would like to see the beach and take a swim. With my appetite already whetted by the sight earlier in the day of a thousand inviting swimming holes, I responded enthusiastically. The panorama of Baucau, with its rocky slopes and view of the sea through the palms and bougainvillea, was quite spectacular. We caught a lift in a passing car the last kilometre or so, since the beach was further than it looked from the centre of town and our heads were pounding with the heat.

The cove we finally arrived at was a little oasis. After the tales Celeste had told me during our long descent to the beach – stories of intimidation, of young people joining the guerrilla struggle just to be free of the daily fear and oppression – it occurred to me that there was something incongruous about the existence of such natural beauty as the backdrop to an unsightly human drama like the one being played out in East Timor. But for the next hour we put all unhappy thoughts behind us and simply enjoyed the pleasure of the salt air in our noses, the shouts of delight from the local children, the sting of the sun on our backs.

On our return, the steep ascent forced us to make regular stops. Timorese hospitality prevailed, in spite of the known consequences of being seen with a foreign visitor, and we found ourselves being plied with glasses of water, freshly fried slices of bread-fruit, sweet finger-thin bananas and the surprising *kue rambo*, or hair biscuit, which resembled a nest of crispy spaghetti coated with syrup.

We stopped to visit old Mr Guterres, who cradled his bony, chafed hands in his lap and answered Celeste's cheerful greeting by raising only his eyes. He seemed not to have the energy or the will to stand or even to extend a hand. As Celeste said my name and explained that I was from Melbourne, where his son resided, I stepped forward and crouched before him so that he didn't have to strain to see my face. A woman in a faded print dress, who could have been a neighbour or perhaps a niece, explained that *Tio* (Uncle) was partially paralysed. The story went that he pushed himself too far and too hard on the construction of the stone house he sat in front of. With the Indonesians plundering and destroying his land, murdering and imprisoning the young people, the rocks and stones were the only things he felt would still obey him, the only things he still had control over, and yet even they had got the better of him in the end.

Our walk back to the convent took us past two candle-filled grottoes at which a dozen or so people were praying. Their prayers were a monotone whisper, the repetition both reassuring and haunting as the dusk muddied the air around us. Back at the convent, it felt good to wash the sand and salt off my body. As I savoured my bath, the novices sang 'Ave Maria' in the next wing. The beauty of the harmonies gave me goose bumps.

After dinner a group of senior novices gathered around the television set and enjoyed a supper of sweet biscuits and home-made grape spirits. There was the air of a special occasion, and even the most straight-laced of the sisters joined the young ones in a glass or two of *grappa*. On the television, Indonesia was playing South Korea in badminton. The girls were clearly and noisily behind Korea!

When the others had gone to bed, Celeste and an elderly Italian nun, Madre Giuseppina, drew their chairs up close to mine and told me stories of the church, the clergy and their work in East Timor. The Canossians first established a mission in East Timor in 1879. They recounted how, at the time of the Indonesian invasion in 1975, the Italian priest Father Locatelli and three other priests, thought to be Australians, were tied up by members of the Indonesian armed forces and taken hostage in a car bound for Baucau. What saved them was the fact that, close to Baucau, the car overturned – the priests were helped to safety by the people. The story goes that when the Indonesians discovered that the men were members of the clergy, they were allowed to go free and were not harmed. Celeste and Giuseppina told me that for all the brutality of the Indonesian military, they had respect for religious leaders, members of the Catholic clergy and the sanctity of the church as a place of worship.

Although it was tempting to spend another few days in the peaceful environment of the convent in the company of my gracious hosts, I needed to return to Dili because I had a plane to catch to Bali. The nuns and novices gathered at the side of the road to farewell me as I joined the other passengers on the overcrowded bus that would take me back. It was with a mixture of sadness and relief that I later left Dili: my first visit to East Timor had been accomplished without incident but I was concerned for the people I had met, people I admired, who may have suffered ill consequences as a result of being seen with me. I wondered whether I would see them again.

I arrived in Bali where João, my Timorese boyfriend from Melbourne, was waiting to meet me. He plied me for news of Timor in general and particularly his home town, Baucau. He had not been able to travel to Timor with me because of his involvement in the underground movement working for East Timor's independence. João and I had met a couple of years earlier at Melbourne University, where we were both students of Indonesian language. My connection with João and his personal tale of struggle brought East Timor's sad story to life for me and spurred me to make that first visit to his country. I needed to satisfy my curiosity, to see and experience East Timor for myself.

I had learnt my first words of Indonesian at the tender age of four when my father was a mature-age student of the language at Monash University. In the evenings he would return home to teach my brother and me some basic greetings: 'Apa kabar?', 'Baik baik saja'. When, many years later, at Golden Square High School in Bendigo, Victoria, Indonesian was offered as an elective, I chose the language on the strength of this childhood connection. I was too young to appreciate the geographical logic of the choice, the other options being French and German. Despite being a fairly typically insular Australian country town, Bendigo had developed something of a reputation as a centre for Indonesian language studies, and lessons were frequently supplemented with cooking classes and visits to our classroom by gamelan orchestras and traditional dance troupes.

As a student of Indonesian studies at Melbourne University in the 1980s I came across an edition of *Inside Indonesia* magazine. It was a low-budget publication that prided itself on its hard-hitting reportage of a range of 'uncomfortable' social, economic and political issues, including labour disputes, the role of ABRI (as the Indonesian armed forces were then known), human rights, environmental devastation and the plight of minority groups, particularly those brought unwillingly under Indonesian control. I wrote a letter to the magazine's editor, Mrs Pat Walsh, and received a reply from Mr Pat Walsh. He encouraged me to take on some voluntary administrative and editorial work for the magazine.

This was the beginning of an involvement with the 'real' Indonesia that I was not encouraged in by my lecturers at Melbourne University. It was through my ongoing contact with Pat Walsh and the other contributors to the magazine, and its broad network of Indonesian and Australian friends, including academics and NGOs, that I gained a well-rounded understanding of sociopolitical life in Indonesia and of the facts of the Indonesian invasion of East Timor in 1975.

While *Inside Indonesia* took a highly critical stance on hot topics (we used to have to send issues into Indonesia in plain, unmarked brown paper bags), the people who worked on the magazine, and others whom I met through my involvement, all had their own unique love affair with Australia's beguiling northern neighbour. Indonesia and Indonesians were never the enemy. The enemy was repression and ignorance, including the ignorance of our own Australian community about conditions in Indonesian society.

At the request of João and his Timorese colleagues, I began translating reports from the clandestine resistance movement and helped to make public the tales of the appalling human rights abuses these documents told. My conscience was pricked. As Australians and as neighbours, it seemed to me that we had a duty to speak out in defence of a martyred people.

Indonesia's invasion and the ensuing occupation of East Timor were thought to have resulted in the annihilation of over 200,000 East Timorese, or one-third of the population. Portugal, which had administered the territory for 400 years, could do little in the face of the full-scale military invasion that Indonesian President General Suharto launched on 7 December 1975. The fragile independence, which had been declared by the left-leaning Fretilin (Revolutionary Front for an Independent East Timor) party on 28 November 1975, was short-lived. The United States, nervous about the prospect of 'communism' taking root in Southeast Asia, gave its blessing to Indonesia's illegal and brutal military action. Australia followed suit, and the rest of the developed world simply looked the other way.

My love for Indonesia was neither diminished nor compromised by my growing awareness of conditions inside East Timor, however. My first few visits to Indonesia in the mid 1980s taught me that the enemy of East Timor – oppression and military abuse of power – was also the scourge of Indonesian society.

From Bali, following my return from East Timor, João and I travelled to Jakarta. My first experience of the big, dirty Indonesian capital was a bit of an initiation: not only into the sights and sounds of this overcrowded melting pot of humanity, but also into the way of life of members of East Timor's clandestine resistance. Many were friends of João; he was particularly keen to seek out his old *companheiro* João Freitas da Camara, with whom he had studied at the Atmajaya Catholic University in Jakarta.

We managed to track João down in the suburb of Menteng, at the comfortable home of his girlfriend Victoria, a German-born Australian language teacher. Her blonde hair was cut in a bob and she exuded a warmth and energy that were instantly appealing. Like me, Victoria had developed a strong interest in the East Timorese cause, and also like me, her firm belief in the justice of this cause and the depth of her feeling for João had created undercurrents in her relationship with Indonesia. She had an abiding affection for the people of the country she had chosen to live in, but at the same time her distaste for the shameless lies and whitewashing of the Suharto regime put her at odds with her political environment. Moreover, I sensed that Victoria's solidarity with the East Timorese had isolated her from other members of Jakarta's expat community. By taking East Timor's struggle to heart and drawing back the curtain on what was happening there – by becoming an informant for human rights groups and a conduit for the delivery of financial and material assistance – she had incurred the displeasure of many friends. Knowing her was something of a liability. While the two Joãos reminisced and shared tales of their recent activities, Victoria and I delighted in the opportunity to compare notes on our experiences of travelling in East Timor. For both of us it was a chance to debrief and swap stories about the difficulties associated with befriending a people the world had deliberately turned its back on.

Like many other Timorese in Jakarta, João Freitas da Camara was attempting to juggle a university education with the demands of the independence struggle. These students worked as couriers and disseminators of documents to and from East Timor's national liberation army, Falintil, who operated from hide-outs in East Timor's mountainous interior. They also coordinated the collection of financial and material contributions to support the work of the guerrilla fighters and fellow members of the clandestine resistance who were active in the urban centres.

They, particularly the scholarship recipients, knew that their efforts for the cause of independence put them at risk of having their studies, if not their lives, terminated. Many had scholarships provided by the provincial government of Timor Timur (East Timor) cut off when it became known that they had links with the resistance inside or outside East Timor. They lived a precarious existence, not only because of the hostility of the government and military apparatus, but also because the average Indonesian citizen had no knowledge, no understanding, of East Timor's story. The government propaganda – that Indonesia had been invited by the Timorese to unite and liberate them from the shackles of Portuguese colonial rule – was swallowed whole. It was just easier that way. The Indonesian people knew all too well what the consequences of challenging the New Order regime's version of history were – the stigma of being branded a 'subversive' and a communist at best, and life imprisonment at worst.

In the early 1990s, the Indonesian student and NGO movements had yet to take up the cause of the East Timorese as part of their own struggle to challenge the dominance of the military in Indonesian sociopolitical life. The expatriate community, too, had other preoccupations, and largely chose to accept the government's line on matters pertaining to the nation's 'hot spots'. So the East Timorese in Indonesia derived little support and sympathy from their host community and for that reason tended to keep to themselves. Like other minorities, they found strength and security in numbers and chose to live in close proximity to other East Timorese. This also made them vulnerable, since certain areas of the city soon came to be known to the military as East Timorese ghettos. This knowledge greatly facilitated the raids and campaigns of intimidation the government authorities periodically launched.

A number of remarkable Indonesian individuals and organisations were sticking their necks out for the East Timorese, however, and I had the good fortune to meet some of them on this visit to Jakarta. The first and best known of them was Haji Princen, the founder of an NGO called LPHAM (Institute for the Defence of Human Rights). As a Dutchman by origin, but a citizen of Indonesia, his work in defence of the rights of Indonesia's poor and oppressed attracted a good deal more attention – both negative and positive – than it otherwise would have. On the day I first visited him in his small office in Jalan Menteng Kecil, Central Jakarta, he was joking with his Indonesian staff about their 'efficient inefficiency' and how it was a national trait. I noticed that only his personal assistant, Hamid, showed signs of being amused.

Princen was unable to move around his office with ease. His advanced age and recent poor health had physically incapacitated him. So he relied heavily on the hands and feet of his office staff and gave the impression of being something of an autocrat as he barked orders from behind his desk. Despite his physical handicaps, he was a formidable human rights advocate who managed to make his voice heard above the din of the New Order propaganda machine. He commanded a strange sort of respect, even from the government, perhaps because of his personal history, which he recounted for me. After trying hard to avoid conscription into the Dutch army and fleeing to France, Princen arrived in Indonesia in 1947. When he deserted from the Dutch army (his avoidance had failed) to join the Indonesian independence fighters, the Dutch government put a price of 40,000 guilders on his head (around US$1 million today). The Indonesians, however, were reluctant to surrender him. He joked that nowadays they would be only too glad to be rid of him!

Through Princen I met the staff of two other organisations that had begun to do some limited work on documenting human rights violations in East Timor. Skephi (the Indonesian Network for Forest Conservation) was principally an environmental NGO; its sister organisation Infight (Indonesian Front for the Defence of Human Rights), with which it shared an office, focussed its attention on issues of political detainees and the promotion of human rights.

On the afternoon I visited Princen, the Skephi/Infight office was full of movement; people coming and going, passing papers to one another, making cups of coffee, sitting chatting or sharing a clove-scented *kretek* cigarette in a corner of the floor. Two or three computer printers were noisily churning out documents in an adjoining room. The atmosphere was relaxed and welcoming and I immediately felt at home.

The staff were mainly young, recent graduates, who had deliberately foregone the lure of a highly paid career in the private sector to do their bit for democracy and human rights in their country. It was easy to see that they were a close-knit and mutually supportive group. They needed to be. Their work on behalf of Indonesia's 'little people' meant that they frequently incurred the wrath of individuals and companies close to the Suharto family. Office raids and even the arrest of members of staff were fairly regular occurrences.

Over a coffee, Princen and the Infight coordinator, Saleh Abdullah, talked to me about the difficulties and frustrations of heading a human rights NGO. For the sake of the longevity of the organisation, it was imperative that the government did not perceive it to be involved in politics or supportive in any way of self-determination for the 'renegade provinces' of East Timor and West Papua. The upshot of this was that human rights groups found themselves unable to tackle anything other than the symptoms of problems requiring a political solution. Nevertheless, they found strength and courage in the knowledge that their work was contributing to a movement and a momentum which would, sooner or later, bring the old dictator, Suharto, to his knees.

Chapter three

TURNING POINT 1991

IN EARLY 1991 I moved to England, where I worked in the Refugee Studies Programme at Oxford University. João had been offered a place as a Visiting Fellow in the Programme and, being a twenty-four-year-old citizen of the Commonwealth, I was entitled to a working holiday visa in the United Kingdom. I decided to go along. Living in Oxford I felt a long way away from Indonesia's democracy movement and East Timor's struggle, but later that year I had the opportunity to visit Indonesia and its reluctant province once again. With great enthusiasm I had accepted a job on an English television documentary. The crew would travel to East Timor and film for a number of weeks in an attempt to open the eyes of the British public and TV audiences around the world to the reality of life in occupied East Timor. It was a small team – it had to be, given the sensitivity of the project. Peter Gordon was the producer, Max Stahl the cameraman and I was the researcher/interpreter. When I signed the contract with Yorkshire Television I had no idea that

Max was about to capture on film an event that marked a turning point in East Timor's fate.

Bali was our stepping stone to Timor. On Kuta beach we honed our skills with the recording and other equipment we carried with us. Max designed a number of bags in which to conceal his camera, and which allowed him to film subjects without their knowledge. The Aussie surfers and beer-swilling tourists were completely foiled by our ruse. We made our move to Dili with a mixture of excitement and trepidation, decked out in the Bali tourist garb that we hoped would disguise the true nature of our mission.

There was fear and determination in the voice of the young man we interviewed in the darkened taxi: 'We are living in this situation where we are putting our lives at risk just by talking to you.' We had purposely chosen to film this interview in a taxi at night, to conceal the identity of our informant. During the filming, in September and October 1991, we interviewed people from all walks of life. Most of them told us about the actions taken by the military to silence them in anticipation of a long-awaited visit from a Portuguese parliamentary delegation. They hoped that this visit would afford them an opportunity to make their aspirations for independence known to the Portuguese and the world.

Father Domingos da Cunha kept watch for us while we interviewed youths who were taking refuge at the Motael Church. One of them showed us his scars, razor blade slashes and cigarette burns, proof of his torture at the hands of the Indonesian military. Before we left Dili for the southern coastal town of Suai we entrusted our tapes to the safekeeping of Father Domingos. In Suai we hoped to talk to Father Domingos Soares, who was well known for his sympathy towards the pro-independence cause.

By that stage we realised that graveyards and burial sites were a feature of the Timorese landscape. On the road between Dili and Maubisse we stopped on numerous occasions to film these stark reminders of the brutality of the occupation. And we tested the patience of the public bus driver when we repeatedly requested that he stop, 'just for five minutes', so that we could film the beauty of the mountainous terrain north of Maubisse.

It was already getting dark by the time we reached Ainaro, some twenty-five kilometres south of Maubisse. There, local police pounced on us like cats. They shook their heads and wrinkled their brows when we told them that we intended to continue south to Suai. I whispered to Peter that it was perhaps best that I pretend not to understand Indonesian so they would feel free to discuss any interesting plans they had for us. We were obliged to stay at an official guesthouse that night.

Having spent the early evening eavesdropping on the police and learning of the plan they were putting in place to prevent us from reaching Suai, I left Max in charge of public relations and went to bed in disgust. From my musty, mozzie-ridden room I listened to him use the Spanish he had learnt in Central America to good effect, perhaps hoping to charm the local constabulary into granting us our wish of visiting Suai. But for some reason unknown to us, they seemed determined to thwart our efforts.

The next morning the police plan swung into action: our helpful hosts diverted traffic to prevent us from boarding any Suai-bound vehicles. We were frustrated with the impasse and then surprised when a young Englishman accompanied by a nervous-looking Timorese youth appeared in our midst. The cats had caught some more mice. We had no idea whether these two were to be trusted, and from the whispers they exchanged we understood that the feeling was mutual.

After a long and uncomfortable silence the Englishman stepped forward and introduced himself, Steve Cox, and his interpreter, Domingos Segurado. It turned out that Steve was a photographer who, like us, was running the gauntlet of intelligence operatives and their lies in order to record the atmosphere in the lead-up to the Portuguese parliamentary delegation's visit. After Peter's fifth game of chess with the local police chief our patience was wearing thin and we announced our intention to return to Dili. A bus appeared out of nowhere and our police friends assisted us all in boarding with our luggage.

Steve and Domingos travelled back to Dili with us. Steve had met up with Domingos, an English teacher from the Externato São José (a Portuguese secondary school), in Dili. Later, when we interviewed Domingos for the film, he told us that he and his two younger siblings, for whom he was responsible, were the only survivors of his family. It was hard to comprehend how someone who had lived with such unimaginable violence could be so softly spoken and seemingly so at peace with the world. 'They've killed my whole family. They can kill me too if they want to. Our struggle will go on.'

Peter Gordon and I had left East Timor – and I had returned to England – by 12 November 1991, the day the Indonesian military opened fire on a peaceful demonstration at the Santa Cruz cemetery in Dili. More than 200 people were killed. With the knowledge that something big was afoot, after a brief respite in Darwin, Max Stahl and Steve Cox had returned to Dili. At great risk they managed to capture images of the carnage, which were reproduced around the world. The Yorkshire Television documentary – *In Cold Blood* – and Steve's bloody photographs helped turn the tide of public opinion against Suharto's regime. Bloodshed of this kind had not been uncommon in East Timor, but this was the first time that foreign eyewitnesses were present and able to record the events on film.

For me it took some time for the events of 12 November to sink in. At work I found myself having to rush off to the bathroom to weep privately on quite a few occasions. It was so difficult, at a time like this, to find myself on the other side of the world. While my work colleagues at the Refugee Studies Programme were concerned and sympathetic, I felt isolated and unable to share the depth of my fears and sadness with them. My full-time job also prevented me from involving myself actively in efforts to inform the British public of what had happened at Santa Cruz and to denounce the bloodshed.

So I was pleased when, a week or so after the Dili massacre, Carmel Budiardjo, director of TAPOL, the Indonesia human rights campaign, phoned to ask whether I would travel to London to meet Steve Cox at the airport and help organise a series of press conferences and meetings with politicians for him. Being a citizen of Great Britain, Steve's testimony and personal tales of the brutality meted out to the Timorese were likely to rouse the interest of the British media and politicians in a way the words of an East Timorese survivor could never hope to do.

I took a day off work and caught the train to London. I slept the night on the floor of the lounge room of Carmel's house, which doubled as the office of TAPOL. Carmel suggested that I was likely to get a better night's sleep in the lounge than in the study, since I would be kept awake in the latter by the fax machine and the offerings it was continuously spewing forth. Among the documents coming in from East Timor was a list of names of those confirmed dead as a result of the massacre. Looking through the list, I came across the misspelt name of Domingos Segurado, Steve's interpreter.

The following morning the alarm jolted me awake at 4:30 am. I braced myself against the cold and drizzling rain and caught the train to Heathrow Airport to meet Steve. When he finally came through customs he looked pretty well but exhausted by the flight and the non-stop media and solidarity work he had done in Darwin. He wasn't aware of the TAPOL plans to whisk him away to interviews and press conferences, and in fact was supposed to get on another plane to Lisbon to deliver his photos and story to the newspaper he was under contract to. He seemed happy to be hijacked, however, and was able to phone the paper once we got back to TAPOL in Thornton Heath. In the space of about half an hour we had to organise interviews with the BBC, the press conference, flights to Portugal and the processing of Steve's slides. In order to meet his deadline he had to make a 6 pm flight for Lisbon. The poor guy only just managed a quick shower before we had to head out into the pouring rain for the BBC interview.

While Steve was at his interview at the BBC, he left me to select the best of his slides and have them copied for use in other mainstream media, such as *Time* and *Newsweek*. Scouring through the ten or so rolls of film at the photo studio, I came across images of Domingos Segurado among the demonstrators. He looked jubilant in his bright white shirt, striding out with the other young people participating in the procession, oblivious to the fate awaiting him at the cemetery. Among the pictures I chose for reproduction was one of Domingos looking directly into the lens of the camera – on his lips was a smile clearly meant for his friend Steve.

The girl on duty in the photo studio calculated the cost of the processing and gave me the figure of £600. I rushed off to the press conference, which was just about to commence at the House of Commons, and managed to convey this information to Steve. We both concluded that there must have been some sort of mistake – the cost could not possibly be so high. Returning to the photo studio after the press conference we discovered to our horror that there had been no mistake. Steve had arrived in London with very little money – it had been stolen by the Indonesian military, who had also beaten him up on the day of the massacre.

Since the girl in the photo studio was threatening Steve with the non-return of his film if we did not at least come up with the processing fee, we tried to explain the situation to her, the importance of these photos to the fate of the East Timorese. But she knew nothing about where East Timor was, let alone what had happened there less than two weeks earlier. Finally we reached an agreement that we would pay £100 and take the processed film without the prints. I gave the girl £20 on the spot and promised to send her a cheque for the remainder the following day.

It was 4:15 pm when we got out of the photo lab and hailed a cab to take Steve to the airport. Before parting, I told Steve that I had seen Domingos' name on the list received by TAPOL. In spite of being numb with jet-lag and exhaustion, Steve's eyes filled with tears as he told me: 'He kept appearing in front of me as I took photographs. A few times he winked at me and pushed people aside so that I could get a better view of the action. He looked so proud of what he and the other demonstrators were doing, happy almost.'

That image of Domingos and his triumphant smile stayed with me as I made my way through the rain to Victoria Station to catch the bus back to Oxford. I was swept up in the tide of homeward-bound workers who, like me, clutched their overcoats and scarves around them against the icy wind. Suddenly I became aware of being tremendously tired and hungry. I had not eaten anything all day. I stopped at a burger van, but when I opened my wallet to pay, remembered that I had given most of my remaining money to Steve to pay for his taxi fare to Heathrow. I could go another two hours without food, but how was I going to get back to Oxford? Thanks to the understanding of a good-humoured bus driver, I was allowed to get on the bus even though what I was able to scrape together from the loose change in my wallet fell short of the full fare. I was so exhausted by the time I had walked the two and a half kilometres from central Oxford to Summertown, where I lived, that I flopped into bed without bothering to fix myself something to eat. Somehow, in the context of the day's happenings, an empty belly was an irrelevance.

Two weeks later I received a distraught letter from Victoria in Jakarta. Started on 25 November, it related the story of the protest action of a large number of Java-based East Timorese students, in which João Freitas da Camara had participated. They had peacefully demonstrated on the streets of Jakarta as a means of drawing local and international attention to what had happened at Santa Cruz and to demand punishment of those responsible.

> . . . Almost the whole clandestine network has been caught! They have practically disappeared from the face of the earth and may actually never be seen again. This probably goes especially for João. He agreed to be the spokesperson, because his English is best and because he is articulate. He was nervous and didn't really want to do it . . . [H]e has

now been singled out as the leader of the demonstration, the 'mastermind' behind it all by BAIS [the Strategic Intelligence Agency]. It is apparently very likely that he will be charged under the anti-subversion law from 1963, which carries as a maximum penalty the death penalty. And all seventy have been charged with Article 154/155 (threat to the state), which carries imprisonment of between seven and ten years.

They have been kept at Polda Metro Jaya on Jalan Sudirman (the women, nine, in Kebayoran) for a whole week without access to a lawyer or a humanitarian organisation like the Red Cross. In fact, LBH (Legal Aid Institute) has been thoroughly prevented from seeing them, and when the lawyers and Princen [who had also been arrested then released] turn up there, trying to see the students, they are being mocked in the most cynical, despicable way: Colonel Wagiman who is in charge of this case sent the human rights men and lawyers home again with the excuse that today (Monday) he did not have time, since in the morning he had to take the visiting Police Commissioner from Singapore around the golf course and afterwards he would be having lunch with him, and if there was any time left, maybe the students could be seen then . . .

Friday, 29 November

In the meantime, I am in danger myself. I think our phone may be tapped and I cannot get rid of the idea that I am being followed. There are strange cars outside my house, my office, with mysterious antennae on the car roof, military-looking vehicles driving up close to my taxi, men with walkie-talkies moving around the Hilton Coffee Shop, while I am meeting up with friends for a coffee. I should be lying low, but I can't. I am going to LBH daily, talking to groups of human rights lawyers, or to see the journalists. Particularly helpful is Luhut Pangaribuan, but

> he needs details of the disappeared students, identity, name, age, location of university etc . . . We use crazy names on the phone, because everyone is convinced their phone is bugged. They probably are. Students who had managed to escape rang me in the first week, with timid voices, worrying about where to stay the night. There has been a subsequent wave of detentions of Timorese students all over Java . . . The embassies are almost useless . . .
>
> One of the saddest, heart-rending events took place last night. João, after ten full days without a lawyer, a Red Cross person, a change of clothes or toiletry, was led out of his cell to speak to some LBH lawyers, Luhut and Rini, Frans and, I think, Princen. He looked very depressed, but said in the presence of two accompanying policemen, that he was fine (no bruises, it seems, good!), but needed some soap and toothpaste and clothes. The door to his own house has been barricaded and is being watched continuously for possible elements not caught yet. The day after the demonstration ABRI people took him to his place, broke the doors down, destroyed many things and took with them all the files, documents, tapes, videos and posters they could find for their court case . . .
>
> Indonesians and foreigners alike are being kept ignorant about the real events in Dili as well as in connection with the demonstration. People don't have a clue what is going on here, and pin their hopes on this Indonesian Commission going to Dili to clean the military from reproach of deliberate brutality. I am certain it is going to be a complete farce, which the donor countries, mainly western ones, however, will use as justification for continuing their aid programs.

João had been singled out by the Indonesian authorities as the 'mastermind' of the demonstration. In fact, he was being made a scapegoat. The appeal that the demonstrators had attempted to deliver to the UN had been written jointly by the heads of the student resistance organisations. Because João was articulate and spoke English well, he was the one who functioned as a spokesperson for the group and liaised with the foreign media. For years after this Victoria couldn't forgive herself for teaching him English, a language skill that had resulted in his imprisonment.

At around Christmas time, Victoria related later, João was taken out of his solitary cell and from the corridor of his upper floor cell block was shown his Timorese co-detainees. By then they had respiratory problems, skin diseases and other malaises. Then, at a meeting in which his interrogator fiddled with a pistol on the table, he was given the 'choice' of signing – or not – a declaration that he was the head of a subversive organisation, and had organised illegal gatherings and an unlicensed demonstration. With a heavy heart he signed, in order to save the other detainees.

My heart went out to Victoria. Her comrade-in-arms, the man she loved, had been suddenly wrenched from her life. As she said, it was like a death. I felt we were kindred spirits and she was clearly in need of support. Although I did not directly experience the Santa Cruz massacre, I felt inextricably bound up with what had happened there. My sadness and outrage at the loss of life and ensuing whitewash galvanised my will to do something more for East Timor – this problem wasn't going to go away. And so my mind was made up: I would move to where I could work more effectively for the East Timorese cause.

Chapter four

IBU KOTA – JAKARTA May 1992–May 1993

MY PARENTS WERE not surprised when I announced that I was moving to the Indonesian *ibu kota* (capital), Jakarta. After all, I had long harboured a wish to deepen my understanding of Indonesia and Indonesians by basing myself in the country for an extended period. Being a tourist – or 'just passing through' – had its limitations when it came to penetrating a culture very different from one's own. But just as important as this desire to know Indonesia better was my wish to join forces with Victoria and those other maverick individuals and organisations that dared to stand by the East Timorese in their brave quest for independence.

I did not find the idea of turning up in Jakarta without a place to live or a job particularly daunting. I knew that I could count on friends like Victoria and the Skephi/Infight crowd to point me in the direction of work and a place to sleep. I had some savings to draw on to tide me over until I found paid employment.

So in early May 1992, having farewelled João in Oxford, I arrived on the doorstep of the offices of Skephi/Infight in

Rawamangun, East Jakarta. There I encountered Emma Baulch, a young Australian activist who had been resident in Jakarta for some time. She spoke Indonesian fluently and gave the impression of being an old hand at the business of NGO politics and the way of life that went with it. She had perfected the art of *nongkrong* – the Indonesian activists' habit of squatting whilst talking politics, usually with a cup of sweet Javanese tea and a clove-scented cigarette close at hand. I was put to work straight away helping Emma translate the defence speech of Fernando de Araujo, who, like João Freitas da Camara, had been arrested in connection with the protests over the Santa Cruz massacre. The two were about to face trial.

The New Order government did not look favourably upon the work of Skephi/Infight, which was supported by small grants from NGOs in Europe and Australia. The documents they published on the role of the Indonesian armed forces in dealing with internal dissent and the protests of workers and environmentalists provoked the ire of the regime. It was not uncommon for the director of the two organisations to receive visits from the military as a warning not to push too far in publicly exposing the foibles of the regime. With a *pemilu* (general election) planned for June, sensitivities were further heightened at this time, so I was warned early on that it might be necessary for Emma and me to lie low if the authorities decided to monitor more closely the comings and goings of the office staff. Since Infight had launched an initiative to document 'irregularities' in the election campaign and at the polling stations, there was a good chance that we would indeed be more thoroughly scrutinised at this time. I took my lead from Emma, and made sure that I came to and went from the office as discreetly as possible, since the presence of foreigners in the organisation was, in the paranoid logic of the Suharto regime, bound to be taken as proof of external interference in Indonesia's 'internal affairs'.

Fernando de Araujo and João Freitas da Camara were sentenced to nine and ten years jail respectively for 'expressing feelings of hostility, hatred or contempt toward the Indonesian Government'. It took some time for the terrible implications of João's sentencing to sink in for Victoria. For months since his arrest she had been beating on the doors of the Indonesian Legal Aid Institute and international human rights organisations in an effort to ensure that João had access to legal counsel and was protected from the brutal excesses we both knew to be the daily bread of political detainees. Unable to visit João herself, and fearing for her own safety given the active role she had played in advocating on his behalf since his arrest, Victoria accepted a job at the university in Kupang, West Timor. Remaining in Jakarta only seemed to highlight her impotence in relation to João. And besides, she was hopeful that by being physically closer to East Timor and 'centre stage' of the struggle, she could more effectively fly the flag for João and the resistance. I knew that she would now rely on me to ensure that João had a friend in the capital.

After a month or so of living out of a suitcase and sleeping wall-to-wall with others in one of the bedrooms at the rear of the Skephi/Infight office, I began to crave a little privacy. And so began the hunt for rental accommodation. It was not easy finding a place that suited my need for privacy and my limited budget (all foreigners, it seemed, were thought to be raking in the dollars). I did much of my work of translating reports and other documents in the evenings, and it wouldn't do to have them falling into the hands of prying landlords. After two weeks of looking, I found a small but clean room in a housing complex owned by a wealthy Sumatran couple. It was conveniently located in a quiet kampung called Setiabudi, a small, incongruous rural oasis which nestled at the foot of the skyscrapers lining Central Jakarta's main thoroughfare, Jalan Sudirman. Unsure of where my work for Skephi and Infight might lead, I deemed it wise to sign my rental agreement in the name of Anna . . . just in case.

By late June my precarious financial situation led me to seek work as an English teacher. Having obtained a diploma of education from Melbourne University in 1988, I soon found myself a job with English and Management Programs International (EMPI), a small in-house training institution run by an Englishman and his Acehnese wife. The pay was good (Rp 35,000, or roughly A$20, per hour), and since I was only required to teach between the hours of five and seven in the evening, there was minimal disruption to my work for Skephi/Infight. One of my students was the Managing Director of Bimantara Artika Citra, one of a group of companies belonging to President Suharto's second son. I was often obliged to wait while Bapak ('Sir') concluded some important business deal or other over the phone before I could begin our lesson. He wore Giorgio Armani suits and his office décor exuded power and affluence. He spoke English with an American accent and it seemed to me that having a private English tutor was just one more status symbol that he was adding to his already vast collection. It was odd but strangely satisfying to straddle two such different worlds: one, the world of privilege and wealth that built a protective cocoon of marble, glass, chrome and air-conditioned comfort between itself and the squalid reality beyond; the other, a world that was engaging with and attempting to transform that harsh reality.

I had by then re-established contact with many of the East Timorese students I had met on my first visit to Jakarta, and was increasingly being sought out by them to assist with procuring funds for a range of humanitarian activities, and with the drafting of statements and advice on matters affecting them. I became the account holder for an organisation called Canvisti (East Timorese Non-Violent Solidarity Committee), which was established to give humanitarian assistance to young East Timorese persecuted following the Santa Cruz massacre. It was potentially dangerous for an East Timorese to hold an account into which funds from abroad were received, so I was approached by Martinho Pereira, Canvisti's director, to help administer an account for the funds. The organisation provided money for school fees and rental payments to those without access to alternative sources of funding.

In early August, red and white flags and banners were erected in the streets of Jakarta to celebrate forty-seven years of Indonesia's independence from Dutch colonial rule. It was an annual ritual, but in 1992 the decorations served a dual purpose. As well as stirring a spirit of national pride in the population in the period leading up to and following the 17 August holiday, the neon billboards and fairylight sculptures of independence heroes also provided an impressive backdrop for the tenth Non-Aligned Movement (NAM) Summit meeting. Jakarta, as that year's host of the meeting, was going all out to enhance its image in the eyes of the roughly one hundred heads of state scheduled to attend the summit from 1 to 6 September. Coats of paint were applied to footbridges, and flowers and grass were planted on sidewalks where till now a strip of dusty earth was thought to be good enough for the throngs of public transport users. Street traders, themselves the victims of efforts to remove the city's substantial informal sector from public view, spoke cynically of a tree being planted for every beggar conveniently 'disappeared' off the streets.

In West Jakarta, residents of Kampung Sawah village were evicted from the five-hectare site near the intersection of the Jakarta–Tangerang toll road and had their homes demolished. The government ordered the area to be cleared to accommodate its plans to turn the village into a green zone in connection with the summit. On 18 August villagers staged angry demonstrations, protesting that the 2000-odd displaced families had not been given adequate time to vacate their homes before the demolition began.

In addition to stage-managing an atmosphere of socioeconomic prosperity and nationalist fervour, the authorities employed some far less subtle methods in order to ensure that only a picture of social harmony and unity was presented to their important summit guests. On 11 August, Major-General Harseno, Commander of Jakarta's Military Command, announced to the local press that demonstrators taking advantage of the worldwide attention focussed on the city in the first week of September would be shot on the spot. These threats were no doubt aimed particularly at the East Timorese community, which was still reeling from the shock of the harsh prison sentences handed down against João, Fernando and nine others. Despite requests by some heads of state that the East Timor issue be included in the summit agenda, it was not discussed.

The government actions made hollow the message displayed on the side of one of the skyscrapers inside which I taught a weekly English class: 'Through NAM We Will Fight Against Poverty.'

I flew to Singapore to have a working visa processed. It was a requirement of the Indonesian Department of Immigration that such a document be applied for from outside the country. With its law and order and absence of squalor, this couldn't be Asia, I thought when I arrived in Singapore. I returned to Jakarta a day or so later via Tanjung Pinang in the Riau Province of Sumatra, choosing this circuitous route home because I was concerned that my activities for the NGOs and the East Timorese might have been noted and that I might not have succeeded in re-entering the country. Throughout the years of Suharto's regime a so-called blacklist of known 'subversives' was kept. It included many people, from academics to activists like myself, who were thought to pose some sort of threat to the unity and stability of the country. Careful research had revealed to me that the small port of Tanjung Pinang was accessible by sea from Singapore and, even better, had no computers. Hence there was little likelihood of the port authorities having access to a blacklist against which to check the names of incoming passengers.

I left Singapore early and arrived in Tanjung Pinang way ahead of the scheduled departure time for my flight. Since I was hungry and the café wasn't open yet, one of the air traffic controllers, a guy from Medan, invited me over the road to his house where his neighbour prepared me a delicious bowl of boiled noodles. I spent the rest of the afternoon chatting with him and the other air traffic controllers (only about three planes landed each day, so they weren't exactly run off their feet!), while watching the planes land from the traffic control tower and generally savouring being back in Indonesia.

Juggling the teaching responsibilities with my other work for

Skephi/Infight was beginning to take its toll, and I was glad to have the opportunity to join my parents in Bali for a brief holiday in mid November. East Timor was never far away, however. On the morning of 21 November, my father and I were with an East Timorese student, João Travolta, when the news reached us of the arrest in Dili the previous day of Xanana Gusmão, the leader of Falintil, the national liberation army.

I had heard of Xanana Gusmão, the legendary and revered leader of the guerrillas. In the late 1970s he had been on the Central Committee of Fretilin, the leftist political party in favour of independence. By the mid eighties, after most of the Central Committee members had been picked off by the Indonesian armed forces, he was one of the committee's few surviving members. In 1984 Xanana left Fretilin and founded the Revolutionary Council of the National Resistance (CRRN), a nationalist organisation focussed on achieving independence for East Timor. In 1987 it changed its name to the National Council of Maubere Resistance, or CNRM.

In the library at Melbourne University I had worked with João on translating letters from Xanana. Each time a letter from the resistance leader reached the outside world – it might have been two years since he had written it – João insisted that it be translated and circulated immediately. Xanana was so highly respected by the Timorese that his words were regarded almost as gospel. His letters and documents assumed a magic aura, and there was a certain possessiveness among those entrusted to carry them. Acting as a courier for the resistance was of course a risky and highly political act. It was only after 1989, when parts of Timor were opened up to international visitors, that information flows between the resistance and the outside world became more steady.

I had seen pictures of Xanana in photographs and on campaign posters. During my first visit to Timor I had been given a roll of film – photos from the bush – and asked to process it 'outside'. Some of the pictures, which we had developed and printed in Jakarta, showed Xanana smiling and joking with his soldiers. He had the air of what I imagined to be a charismatic leader – I hadn't met too many at that point. In 1990 Robert Domm, an Australian lawyer and journalist, had managed to conduct an interview with Xanana in the mountains. In 1991 we had tried to interview him for the Yorkshire Television documentary, but at the last minute the owners of the house in Dili in which he was sheltering got cold feet. The news of Xanana's capture was yet another setback for the independence movement after the events at Santa Cruz just over a year earlier.

It was a rainy day in Kuta, and the tragedy of the capture was written all over João's face. The Coke we had ordered for him at the roadside café went untouched, and he kept muttering to himself and cradling his head in his hands. We found news of Xanana's arrest in the local newspaper, but it was difficult to separate fact from propaganda, and soon João wandered off to make a phone call to Dili from a public phone. He returned frustrated, not having been able to get onto anyone prepared to talk openly on the phone about the circumstances of the arrest, the present whereabouts of Xanana, and whether or not others had been detained.

Back at work in Jakarta, I was summoned to the office of the EMPI director, John Read. He waved a piece of paper before me, shaking his head and tutting like an old schoolmaster. When he handed me the document, I noticed that it was a press release from Pat Walsh that had come through on the office fax in my absence. It related the news of Fernando de Araujo being awarded the Reebok Human Rights Award for 'his work against great odds defending human rights'. Whilst the fax's contents were not particularly incriminating, John was clearly unimpressed. He sat me down and began to tell me the story of a foreign cosmetic company that earlier that year had been renting one room in the EMPI office complex which doubled as John Read's home. The company, whose name I didn't catch, was involved in some kind of pyramid selling outfit involving the cultivation by company members of a cosmetic culture. The company came to grief when it was accused of fraudulent practices by a disgruntled recruit who lost money on his initial investment. The police were called in to investigate and this had resulted in the EMPI offices being raided and the good name of the institution being called into question.

'I don't know what your involvement with these East Timorese rebels is, but we don't want any more trouble here. We'd appreciate you keeping your politics to yourself, understood?' John Read's 'don't-rock-the-boat' attitude and suspicion of anyone associated with East Timor was typical of the vast majority of expatriates resident in Indonesia in the early 1990s. I had no choice but to feign ignorance, and left his office muttering to myself about how the fax had clearly been intended for another recipient. Finally out of his sight, it was all I could do not to whoop with delight at the news of Fernando being granted this award!

I was more than surprised when, a week or so later, I was offered some administrative work in the EMPI offices in addition to my twelve hours of teaching per week. The extra pay was welcome. As my sympathy for the East Timor cause became more widely known, I was being approached by a growing number of young East Timorese students needing assistance with their study fees and rental payments. Having access to the office computer and telephone during the day would be useful in maintaining contact with my Timorese friends and their supporters abroad, as the fax machine was kept under lock and key in John Read's office!

Whilst I was appreciative of the job with EMPI and enjoyed my teaching work, I found the neo-colonial attitudes of most of the expatriate teachers employed by the company difficult to stomach. One of my fellow teachers, a Scotsman named Douglas, I knew to be helping Indonesian call girls find rich Western men. Douglas and my other colleagues revelled in the life made possible by their status as native English speakers and teachers of the language. They earned in one hour what one of my landlords' maids at my home in Setiabudi earned in one month. They spent their time in the air-conditioned office blocks, five-star hotels and shopping plazas that abounded in Jakarta; at home, they employed a handful of household servants, drivers and gardeners; and they spent their weekends frequenting massage parlours and expat bars. Strange that it was *my* extracurricular activities and interests that were met with reproach and suspicion by my employers.

In early 1993, I moved into a house in South Jakarta with one of my EMPI colleagues, an Englishman called Charles. I was outgrowing my tiny room in Setiabudi and craving a place where I could cook for myself and to which I could invite friends. None of my NGO friends earned enough money to be able to share the costs of renting a house, so Charles it was, and I must say that I entered into this new housing situation with some degree of trepidation.

Within a week of moving into the spacious three-bedroom home in Gandaria Selatan, Charles had employed Yati. The idea of employing someone to keep house had never sat well with me, even though I had heard the argument that it provided someone with a job often enough. Yati was from Central Java and, in spite of my misgivings, I liked her immediately. Like many poor rural women, she had left her family in her hometown of Purwokerto and come to the *ibu kota* to seek work. She had left behind three children aged between four and seven and a husband who had neither the skills nor the will to earn a living. She was a hard worker, discreet and, unlike most Indonesians, at ease with her own company.

One of the first people to visit me in my new home was a young man, José Neves, who had escaped from a Dili prison in late 1992. He needed help with negotiating his departure from Indonesia as he had been informed that the house where he was renting a room was being staked out by the military.

José was one of many East Timorese nationalists who came and went from my house in Jakarta between 1993 and 1995. Like the others, he came unannounced. If an appointment *was* made, it was usually from a public phone. Background noises, mostly traffic, often made it difficult to determine the purpose of the proposed meeting whilst the hushed, conspiratorial tones of the caller would leave me intrigued and sufficiently curious to agree to whatever was being suggested. So come and go they would, at all hours of the morning and night, usually refusing all offers of refreshment and light conversation, and launching instead straight into stories of brothers, sisters, uncles, friends who were in some sort of peril and in need of assistance. Sometimes it was a loan of some money to buy school books or a Jakarta–Dili boat ticket they needed, but most often I was sought merely for my sympathy for their cause and for whatever practical help I could offer.

Many a steamy Jakarta night was spent transcribing, translating or editing some ghastly tale of friends beaten or 'disappeared', of little brothers arrested, never to be seen again, of sisters raped and in need of safe passage out of the country. I was shocked to find myself becoming immune to the implicit horror and inhumanity of this litany of crimes. Listening to, documenting, and conveying tales of terror had become my 'job', and eventually my tears just stopped coming.

So why me? Why was I chosen to be their confidante? My status as a white foreigner conferred on me a certain immunity to the dangers they faced as the most maligned and distrusted of Indonesia's colonial subjects. I was one of very few foreigners living in Indonesia who was prepared to put my privileged position and my ability to remain in the country on the line by actively supporting their cause. I had the added good fortune of being a woman and therefore doubly innocuous.

And me? Why did I trust them? Perhaps because they trusted me so implicitly. Along with tremendous bravery and determination, faith in the foreigner appeared to be a distinguishing feature of the East Timorese and their struggle. Was it because they were conscious that their independence depended on and was to an extent the responsibility of the international community? A remnant of their colonial past perhaps? A sign of their lack of trust of one another? Whatever it was, I didn't believe that I was the only foreigner to have succumbed to the seductive power of this trust, of the sensation that came with it – of being granted an important role in a worthy and just cause.

Soon after my move to South Jakarta, I was in touch with staff from the Overseas Service Bureau (OSB), the Melbourne-based volunteer-sending agency for which I had worked in an administrative capacity when I finished university. They asked whether I would consider accepting a part-time contract to facilitate the processing of work permits and visas for Australian volunteers coming to Indonesia to work. I accepted because of the challenge this role of liaison officer presented: I was to liaise between the OSB's national office in Melbourne and the various government departments responsible for granting authorisation to the volunteers to work for a two-year period in a range of organisations across the archipelago.

In May 1993, I purchased a computer and printer to facilitate this work and set up a corner of my bedroom as my office. Around the same time I befriended James Combe, who was working as a volunteer for the Legal Aid Institute, better known by its Indonesian acronym, LBH. James was basically a tech-head with a psychology degree and a social conscience, and it was from him that I came to know of the existence of a communication tool called 'email'. It sounded too good to be true, particularly since, in tandem with a thing called encryption, it was apparently possible to make one's communications one hundred per cent safe. And so began my forays into the world of computers and electronic communication, 'weapons' that were to become indispensable in all areas of my work, but most of all in East Timor's war against silence and disinformation.

Chapter five

FENCE-JUMPING
Mid 1993

IN THE MIDDLE of 1993 I accepted a new challenge in my work for East Timor. It was more difficult and more risky than anything I had undertaken to date. When I first met Florencio in April 1993 I was struck by the calm way he recounted his family's long history of involvement in the clandestine movement and the horrific toll the war had taken on them, including the murder and 'disappearance' of cousins, aunts, uncles and two older siblings. Like many other young people of his age, he was forced to give up his high school studies in Dili because of his involvement in the peaceful demonstrations leading to the Santa Cruz massacre. His studies became untenable when the military began to attempt to arrest him, daily, at the gates of his school. So he fled to Jakarta. What the capital was able to provide in the way of anonymity and relative security it lacked in familiarity. Florencio's first months in Jakarta were ones of isolation, fear, suspicion and great physical hardship. Beyond the few hundred thousand rupiah his family had scraped together for his travel, he had no means of support.

Florencio's softly spoken manner, his intelligence, and the almost permanent smile on his lips belied his experience and made it impossible to refuse to help him. And so when he asked for my assistance in facilitating his exit from Indonesia, I felt compelled to give it my best shot. He explained to me how he and a group of six friends had been on the run from military intelligence operatives for two months. They claimed that the intelligence operatives were acting under orders from Brigadier General Theo Sjafei – the Udayana military commander (the region that took in East Timor) – to arrest them and have them state publicly that they were among the sixty-six youths reported missing since the Santa Cruz massacre. Florencio and his friends were well aware that the aim of this latest operation was to hoodwink the international community into believing that the Indonesian government was serious about following up the identities of the dead and missing. Not by chance, the UN World Conference on Human Rights was in full swing in Vienna, and there were points to be scored by Indonesian authorities if they were able to strike half a dozen names from the list of those unaccounted for in the wake of the Santa Cruz massacre.

Florencio and his friends decided to enter the Swedish and Finnish embassies on 23 June 1993 to seek asylum. During the first couple of weeks of June I spent every spare minute in meetings with the seven youths and conferring with friends in Australia on how to go about the asylum bid. I translated biographies of each of the youths, and statements, so that there would be information to distribute to the press after they went into the embassies.

On 17 June we met for a photo session by the side of the road in the inner city suburb of Kuningan. I knew that there was a good chance that a large group of young East Timorese men would be followed, and it was safer for them and for me if we met in a public place rather than my home. I saw their dark, serious faces as I struggled off the crowded bus, juggling my shopping bags and my English teaching texts. Typically, a number of them were late, so I prepared the camera and passed on the documents I had collected for them, including an English translation of the statement they had prepared.

With every photo I snapped their courage grew, and soon they were pulling Timorese woven shawls from their bags, draping them around one another's necks and adding raised, clenched fists to their poses. Unfamiliar letters and numbers appeared in the camera's light meter, but I pressed on, anxious to finish the job and get home. I searched for anything more than casual interest on the faces of the passing Indonesian office workers. I gave the Timorese youths money for transport, haircuts and respectable clothing. As we parted, Florencio promised to call me at 10 pm the following evening to discuss the next stage of preparations. That was how it worked – I relied on his contacting me from public telephones. Since he, like his colleagues, lived in a shared household, a phone call from a foreign woman would not have gone unnoticed. Mobile phones were not yet a feature of the struggle.

The next day I enjoyed an iced coffee in the air-conditioned cool of the World Trade Centre while I waited for my midday appointment with James, my Australian friend who worked at the Legal Aid Institute. We needed to discuss how we would get seven East Timorese youths into the Bina Mulia Building, which housed the Swedish and Finnish embassies, on Jalan Rasuna Said. We conducted our reconnaissance visit, familiarising ourselves with the layout of the building, the entrance and exit points, and the efficiency or otherwise of the security guards on duty in the glass and marble foyer. Back on Jalan Karet, under the flyover, we squatted on our haunches for lack of a bench, sipping iced tea and discussing strategies. We would enter the building in two groups, James leading the three bound for Sweden via the basement entrance with me leading the remaining four via the foyer on the ground floor.

I was an hour late for my next teaching session but was too exhausted even to apologise. It was adrenalin that kept me upright through the three-hour class.

To my horror, at home that evening I discovered that not a

single one of the photos I had taken the day before had turned out. The roll was completely blank. I decided to keep my appointment with Chris, a friend visiting from Melbourne, anyway. He had agreed to carry the roll of film out to Australia with him the following afternoon and to make the photos available for the international media and human rights groups once the youths were safely inside the embassies. He encouraged me to attempt to organise another photo session for early the following morning.

On my way home to wait for Florencio's 10 pm phone-in I dropped in at a Hero supermarket and armed myself with a new roll of film and a bottle of beer, the latter proving indispensable for my next test of nerves, patience and faith in humanity! For no sooner had I put down my bags at home than Yati informed me of the visit earlier in the evening of the wife of a man named Herman. Herman, she told me, was a house painter who had painted my housemate Charles' bedroom the previous week. In as close to hysterics as a Javanese would allow herself to come, Herman's wife had revealed to Yati how her husband had since disappeared without trace and how, during his period of employment in our house, she had discovered ganja in the pocket of his trousers.

Charles was not home, but had apparently phoned repeatedly in the course of the evening to quiz Yati as to whether I was aware of Herman's wife's visit and therefore the details of the mini-scandal he'd now been caught up in. All I could think of, however, was that the police investigation of a ganja case could lead to our whole house being ransacked and my box full of 'subversive' literature being uncovered. While I was still cursing them all, Florencio phoned, and I told him of the unhappy outcome of the previous day's photo session. He agreed to seek out his friends immediately and to arrange for them to be at my house the following morning at 6:30 am.

Some minutes later, the phone rang again: it was Charles, calling from the home of his bosom buddy, Phil. He informed me that he and Phil were going away for the weekend and would be popping by to collect his things at 6:30 the following morning. Just what I needed – Phil and Charles turning up as I was snapping pictures of seven very East Timorese–looking young men on our front lawn.

To cap things off, on consulting my camera manual, I discovered that the strange light meter reading indicated that the batteries were flat. Where, at 10:30 pm, was I going to find a replacement battery? For a moment it seemed there was no alternative short of abandoning the whole idea of photographs. But no – I had to borrow someone's camera. Finally, after two unsuccessful attempts at late-night scrounging, a good friend in Menteng agreed to lend me one, so off I headed in a taxi.

I was too tense to sleep immediately when I returned home at 12:30 am. The day's only saving grace came when at 3 am Charles dropped by, collected his things and then disappeared for three days.

When there was a knock at the door at 6:30 the next morning I was not pleased to see on my verandah an angry and distraught little lady. Herman's wife. Anticipating the arrival at any moment of my seven friends, I was far from sympathetic when she began to use me as a sounding-board for her whinings about her husband. Before too long, she understood that I was impervious to her tales of woe and I managed to send her on her way. The last two boys didn't arrive until close to 7 am, and Florencio and I were in a taxi to rush the film to Chris by 7:30. In the absence of Charles, and Herman's fretful wife, and with my preparations for the next week's big event complete, the rest of the weekend passed uneventfully and in relative calm.

The following Monday was a public holiday and I decided to take Florencio and Mateus along to meet Herb Feith, a professor of international studies at Monash University and a former lecturer of mine who was visiting from Melbourne. My nervousness and sense of responsibility for what was looming in two days time was growing, and I knew Herb's calm and supportive words would have a soothing effect.

On the way in the taxi, Florencio revealed the results of research he had done into relevant clauses of the Universal Declaration of Human Rights. In line with this, we altered the third paragraph of the statement we had prepared to read: 'We are here today, therefore, not as youths seeking adventure or a free trip out of this country (as no doubt the Indonesian government will attempt to convince you of in the days to come), but as persecuted individuals who fear for our lives. We trust that the government of Sweden will assist us with our bid for political asylum, in accordance with International Law and the Universal Declaration of Human Rights, Article 14, Clause I of which states that "Every human being has the right to seek and be granted refuge in another country for the purposes of avoiding persecution". Article 15, Clause I of the same Declaration states that "Every person has the right to citizenship", and Clause II "No human being may be arbitrarily denied citizenship of a country or be refused their right to alter their citizenship".'

The line I found most moving read: 'This military brutality has robbed us of the right to education, has made us prisoners in our own country and has now forced us to leave our beloved homeland, our families and friends.' Over the years of my involvement in the East Timor struggle it had occurred to me that in many ways, this deliberate uprooting of the youth and the denial of their right to education was an even more insidious aspect of the Indonesian campaign of genocide than the murder and rape. More insidious because it was subtle, its effects enduring, and it robbed almost an entire generation of the opportunity and the means to contribute meaningfully to the life of the *pátria*, that almost mythical sovereign 'homeland', which they knew only through the speeches and exhortations of their leaders.

Herb, Florencio, Mateus and I sipped Javanese tea while I outlined the plans for the asylum bid, the outcomes we hoped for and our fears about what might go wrong. 'I have tried to convince them of the risks and to make them look at other alternatives, but they're as stubborn as mules, these East Timorese,' I told Herb, half-grinning in the direction of Florencio and Mateus. Herb concurred that given their determination, the only thing to do was to be as well prepared as possible, both in terms of possible reactions from embassy officials and of maximising the local and international media potential of the event.

The next morning I briefed my colleagues at Skephi and Infight on the events planned for the following day, passing them copies of the individual testimonies and joint statements. I printed off business cards for each of the seven young men and one each for James and me. These were intended to verify our corporate identity should a security guard or other employee of the Bina Mulia Building question our purpose in being there. 'University and Executive Language Programs' was the name of our fictitious company. During the printing a lengthy power failure set me on edge and I didn't leave the office until 2 pm.

I then took a taxi to the Bina Mulia Building in order to get hold of a business card from one of the many companies housed in the building, thinking that this, too, might prove useful in the event of the security guards taking an interest in our destination. PT Eres Revko, a cosmetic firm and agent for Revlon, was on the ninth floor. Perfect! The receptionist introduced me (Irene Thatcher, training manager for University and Executive Language Programs) to the personnel manager, who was taken in by my English training spiel and, at my request, gave me her card – though she seemed a little suspicious when I asked for another.

Soon it was time to catch the bus to the Hotel Borobodur for the report-writing class I was teaching. By the time I reached my next class, at the Hong Kong Bank, I was feeling positively unwell. My stomach was churning and it was hard to know whether it was due to pure nerves or the fact that I had not eaten since the morning. Two glasses of strong, sweet Javanese tea got me through the two hours of teaching. I fell into bed almost immediately upon reaching home that evening and prepared for a sleepless night.

On Wednesday, the day of the asylum bid, Silvia, my German friend from Bandung, arrived at my house only a little ahead of the seven boys. I shepherded them all into my bedroom to keep them, as far as possible, out of sight of Charles and Yati. Despite the fan, the temperature in my crowded room soon rose by about five degrees. The seven nervous young men smoked and checked their new haircuts and business-look clothing in the mirror. I handed out the individualised business cards and briefed them on the tactic we would use to enter the Bina Mulia Building. Finally we distributed drinks and bowls of rice and chicken. Goodness knows what their next meal would consist of.

As Yati called two taxis, some of the guys began praying, heads bowed, rosary beads guided through sweaty palms. James arrived before we boarded the two waiting Blue Bird taxis, and we farewelled one another with embraces and good wishes.

The air-conditioning in the taxi was a relief after my steamy bedroom, and we made the convoy trip in silence, each of us absorbed in our own private thoughts and fears. My heart was racing despite the fact that we were on schedule. We found a good place to stop, just a couple of blocks before our destination, and we scattered so as not to draw undue attention to our presence. At 1:35 pm we reassembled again and stopped two more taxis. We were closer to our destination than we had first thought, and Silvia was already in place by the curbside. She had left my house half an hour earlier than the rest of us in order to check the security at the Bina Mulia Building. Through the taxi window I passed her my set of the biographies and statements. She would return these to me afterwards, when we met up at the offices of the ABC. She reported that there was no evidence of heightened security, 'but watch out for a guy in plain clothes who's chatting to the security guy on the first floor. Looks a little suss . . .'

We proceeded, the hearts of the four young men in the back of my taxi no doubt thumping harder and faster than my own. I cast one quick glance to check that James and his three friends were close behind us. As we pulled up at the main entrance to the building, I scrambled in my bag for Rp 2000 to pay the driver, took a deep breath and prepared to look as cool and officious as possible. Was it my imagination or were there more men in uniforms loitering around the lobby than normal?

I marched swiftly in the direction of the elevators, my nervous but well-dressed 'staff' following at my heels. I avoided the gaze of the security guard and began stabbing away impatiently at the 'Up' buttons. The wary security guard asked Mateus where we were going and, in a flash, I stepped forward, extracting the PT Eres Revko business card I had ready in the pocket of my jacket and thrusting it at the guard, who – thankfully – retreated with an 'Oh ya, Bu'.

To my relief (and amusement), James and the other three Timorese youths were in the elevator when we got on board. Its interior was like a mirrored chamber of peace. I could see the mixture of terror and excitement in the reflected faces of the boys standing behind me and the silence was at once welcome and excruciating. According to plan, the two groups didn't acknowledge one another, which made the remainder of our journey all the more painful. James and his *companheiros* got off at the seventh floor, heading for the Swedish Embassy. I didn't dare even whisper 'good luck' to them as they disappeared behind the closing doors. We remained in the elevator until the tenth floor. I saw my four friends through the doors of the Finnish Embassy and then jumped back into the elevator to descend.

I exited the Bina Mulia Building undetected and immediately went to the offices of the ABC where Silvia met me with the statements and biographies of the boys. Later, at home, my ears were sensitive to the sound of every car slowing down outside our house. I wondered whether I had been followed.

Nervous about what they might contain, I put off buying the next day's newspapers until the afternoon's teaching session at the Hotel Borobodur. Before my class commenced, I rang the ABC journalist I had given the copies of the statements to the previous day. He filled me in on the latest details and informed me that the ABC news in Australia would broadcast a piece on the asylum bid that evening.

The *Jakarta Post* reported the event on the second page, saying that an 'unidentified white woman accompanied the seven to their destination'. I was gripped by a combination of panic and paranoia, restless and on edge throughout the lesson. On the way to my next class I bought a copy of *Republika*, which carried a picture of a throng of journalists scrambling for photos and interviews at the door of the Swedish Embassy, plus a caption that also made mention of the mysterious white woman.

Silvia was waiting for me at home. I presented the papers to her with a mixture of satisfaction and nervousness that quickly turned to fear and concern when Saleh phoned from Infight to say that the four had left the Finnish Embassy. Silvia took the news worse than I did.

Fortunately nobody was at home to notice the smoke billowing forth from the garage as we burnt all the asylum-related material I had accumulated over the previous weeks. Then we moved on to destroying the boys' statements. As the pieces fell into the rubbish bin, I wondered where the four were, what pressure was brought to bear to make them leave, and what the effect of their leaving would have on the other three, still holed up in the Swedish Embassy. A couple of phone calls later, we learnt that Francisco Lopes da Cruz, Indonesia's faithful puppet and roving ambassador on East Timor, had successfully convinced the four that their request for asylum was doomed to failure and that they would be safe in his care.

As Silvia left, she exhorted me to return to the walls the portraits of President Suharto and Vice-President Sutrisno, the first items to be removed when I had moved into the house. I glumly acceded to her request and then contemplated how fortunate it was that Yati had left that day for a week's break. My suspicions that the fact of a white person accompanying the asylum seekers would be used as evidence of 'foreign interference' were borne out when the papers reported Foreign Minister Ali Alatas' statements to this effect.

The four students in the Finnish Embassy were eventually

released into Haji Princen's care, following government assurances of their safety. It was over a week before the three in the Swedish Embassy abandoned their asylum bid after receiving an Indonesian government assurance that they would not be prosecuted. They too went to stay with Princen. He and the workers at Skephi/Infight advised me to limit my contact with the boys in case the connection with the 'unidentified white woman' was made.

It was on 29 December, while I was in Melbourne for Christmas, that the seven Timorese asylum seekers finally left Indonesia for Portugal. Foreign Minister Ali Alatas said they were allowed to go on humanitarian grounds. I couldn't help but feel partly responsible for what must have been six hellish months of virtual house arrest for my young friends.

Chapter six

A SOPHISTICATED WEAPON
October 1993–July 1994

'PAGI, NONA KIRSTY [Morning, Ms Kirsty]' was the greeting of the uniformed security guard at the entrance to the Australian Embassy. My frequent visits to the embassy for the purpose of processing paperwork in connection with the OSB volunteers' work permits meant that I was quickly known by name to almost all the Indonesian staff there. I would often stop for a chat – about the weather or traffic conditions – on my way in or out, and they soon dispensed with the formality of checking my identity. This particular morning in March 1994, however, I hadn't come to the embassy to have documents photocopied or signed. I had come for a swim in the embassy pool. It was welcome relief from the tedium of chasing letters of approval through the Indonesian bureaucracy and one of the few perks associated with my liaison officer role. Since most of the embassy staff had swimming pools in their residences, I almost invariably had the one at the embassy to myself and was able to enjoy some quiet hours of solitude there, catching up on reading or correspondence which was not easy to focus on with all the comings and goings at home.

I lay back on one of the wooden lounges and contemplated the blue of the sky, which was only vaguely discernible through the smoggy air of Jakarta. The sounds of the traffic on Jalan Rasuna Said was a dull roar, punctuated occasionally by the shrill screech of brakes or the impatient honking of a bus horn. I took from my bag the letter I had received that morning from João Freitas da Camara.

The previous year I had begun to correspond on a regular basis with João, who was serving the second year of his ten-year sentence in the Cipinang high-security prison in East Jakarta. Knowing that some years earlier João had attempted to seek safe passage out of Indonesia through the Vatican Embassy, I had written a carefully worded letter to tell him about the asylum bid at the Swedish and Finnish embassies, saying that while the long months of waiting for a decision to be made must have been harrowing for the seven, in terms of international public opinion the action had succeeded in drawing attention to the situation inside East Timor.

In mid October 1993 I received a letter from João describing how, one night at the end of September, Xanana Gusmão had been moved from Semarang prison in Central Java to Cipinang. João called Xanana 'our new guest', and though Xanana was isolated from the other prisoners, João quickly established contact with him through the 'internal network'. Apparently, after Xanana had been sentenced by the court in Dili to life imprisonment (a sentence which President Suharto later commuted to twenty years) he had asked the authorities to be moved to Jakarta, most likely because he knew there were other Timorese political prisoners in the capital. When they didn't listen to him, he threatened a hunger strike. Instead of moving him to Jakarta they moved him to Semarang. So he had to repeat the threat of hunger strike until he got his way.

Xanana was housed in a leaky cell in a separate block from the other Timorese, but he still managed to let them know he couldn't sleep at night because of the mosquitoes. João used some of the 'consumption money' the prisoners received from outside each month to buy a mosquito net for their leader. But Xanana still needed a pair of blue trousers, size 31, a blue shirt and a sheet.

In November 1993 there was a crackdown on prison visits. The usual practice was that, to avoid suspicion, visitors to Cipinang wishing to see João or Fernando de Araujo would mention the names of two other Timorese prisoners, Marito or Albino, whose 'crimes' were not so fresh and who were therefore considered to be relatively harmless. Still, it had been the case that João and Fernando could go to the *ruang besuk* (visitors' hall) to wait for visitors, who could talk freely with all the prisoners. Now this was stopped. On visiting days – Sundays and Wednesdays – only the prisoner whose name was written down by the visitor was brought to the visitors' hall. And although – according to the prison's internal regulations – all prisoners who had been sentenced by the courts were permitted to attend the prison church or mosque or Buddhist temple (and US diplomats visiting Cipinang were shown these places of worship), Xanana was not allowed to go to church.

Xanana told João that officials from the Strategic Intelligence Agency had warned him not to talk about politics with the other prisoners because it would only harm him and his own situation. 'Kita adalah satu nusa, satu bangsa' (we are one land and one nation), they repeated, 'as if to brainwash him', João wrote. João was confident that they would never convince their new guest. Nevertheless, Xanana was offered ways of keeping his mind off politics: the chief of security promised him a sewing machine and the head of the prison wanted him to clean his house and water the garden outside his office.

João asked me to request support from abroad for Cipinang's new guest and for the five other Timorese prisoners. Xanana wanted books in Portuguese on sociology and politics. The prisoners also needed money for food, toothpaste, soap and medicine. He estimated that Rp 60,000 per prisoner per month should cover their needs. In response to his request I had sent summaries of João's letters to friends and supporters in Australia and to Amnesty International. Help was forthcoming, and after December 1993 I was able to send some money each month to cover the cost of food supplements, medicine and the bribes payable to the guards who smuggled our correspondence in and out. João duly completed, signed and returned the receipts I attached to my letters. All very accountable!

So now I sat by the pool reading João's latest letter, which described how, after five months, some of the restrictions on Xanana's movements had been lifted and it was now possible for him to meet with the other Timorese political prisoners at the prison chapel each Sunday. He confirmed receipt of the Rp 270,000 I had sent that month and also of the Portuguese language books I had picked up for him in Australia at Christmas time. I had also sent João the prospectus of the Jakarta Open University, although I suspected that it was a vain hope that authorisation would be granted for him to continue his studies in law via correspondence. João described how he had been busy translating the news from the BBC radio broadcasts into Portuguese for Xanana's benefit. 'He doesn't have radio and no permission to read Indonesian newspapers or magazines.'

I ripped a page from one of my notebooks and started work on my reply to João, hoping that the security camera lazily panning right and left over the pool enclosure did not have a zoom function! I shared with João the news of my recent acquisition of a computer and modem, explaining the wonders of email and its use in the struggle. I also conveyed greetings from Victoria, Pat Walsh and Geoffrey Robinson (from Amnesty International's International Secretariat in London). He had recently visited Jakarta but had been thwarted in his attempts to visit the East Timorese in Cipinang.

As was our custom, I used only the initials of people's names to protect their identities should any of our correspondence be intercepted or found in raids on João's cell. It didn't do to write lengthy letters as the only way of getting correspondence in and out of the prison was for trusted East Timorese friends to carry them in on visiting days in a shoe or concealed in the lining of a cap. They would then be passed discreetly to the prisoners with other letters passed back when the guards on duty were not paying attention. João had informed me in one of the first letters he sent out that mail received via official channels at the prison office was routinely opened and censored or withheld completely.

In April 1994 I received a letter from Xanana himself. It came in an envelope marked 'Ruby Blade', the pseudonym I had adopted for the purpose of identifying myself in written communications with the political prisoners and supporters of East Timor abroad. He addressed me as 'querida amiga' (dear friend) and wrote in a mixture of English and Portuguese, thanking me with all his 'patriotic fervour' for my solidarity with the cause of the Timorese people. He told me that he had read my letter to João in which I had spoken of the benefits of email. He referred to email as my 'sophisticated weapon' and asked my permission to make use of it in future to communicate with José Ramos-Horta, the head of the independence movement's diplomatic front abroad.

Xanana went on to ask me to enlist the help of various international support organisations – Amnesty International and TAPOL in London, and the Commission for the Rights of the Maubere People (CDPM) in Lisbon – to denounce the degrading treatment he was receiving from a small group of prisoners residing in the same cell block. He described how, from dawn until late at night, they would insult, ridicule and threaten him in an attempt to exert psychological pressure and make daily life unbearable. Xanana's own analysis of the situation was that the prisoners concerned had been put up to their provocations by officers of BIA – the army intelligence organisation, which had direct responsibility for Xanana and for monitoring his movements and activities in the prison. When the provocations had begun two months earlier he had requested a transfer to the block where the other East Timorese prisoners were held. His request had not been granted.

The letter ended with a request that I attempt to get hold of a series of books on painting with acrylics and oils, and some English grammar texts and cassettes.

I was moved by the familiar tone of the letter and the trust he showed, evident in his request that I assist him with addressing the problem of the prisoners' abusive behaviour. I translated and summarised the contents of the letter and sent copies off at once to the organisations listed, emphasising Xanana's request that a source other than a letter written in his own hand be cited in any campaigns or appeals. My hope was that some pressure from abroad might result in his request for a transfer being granted.

A couple of months later, in May 1994, a conference of the Asia Pacific Coalition for East Timor took place in Manila amidst speculation and fears that the government of the Philippines would, at the last minute, ban the meeting out of fear of angering Jakarta. The aim of the conference was to debate the East Timor problem and to provide supporters of independence from around the world with an opportunity to network and share campaign strategies. The Indonesian government was indeed incensed by the idea of such a conference being hosted in Southeast Asia and they made their displeasure known to the then President of the Philippines, Fidel Ramos. Some of the more high-profile East Timor activists amongst the conference participants found themselves blacklisted and unable to enter the Philippines. This attracted a good deal of attention both internationally and regionally – and consequently the issue of East Timor and the conditions there were also thrust under the noses of the public and world leaders. A letter that Xanana managed to send to the conference was read out during the proceedings by one of the participants.

In early June, Xanana wrote to me again and commented on how, 'ironically, the Indonesian government's efforts to block the conference and Fidel Ramos' own hardline position have contributed hugely to drawing the attention of the world, and particularly of the region, to the East Timor issue. I was astonished by the courage and the attitudes of members of the Indonesian solidarity movement. Our struggle is now experiencing a qualitative boost thanks to the reinforcement from our Indonesian brothers and sisters. Now I am paying more attention to consolidating our links with Indonesian youth.' He also described how he had been moved to another cell block, but continued to be insulted and provoked by the other prisoners 'although on a smaller scale'.

In the same letter he told me that on 3 and 4 June he had been questioned by the prison chief with regard to the letter that had been read by José Ramos-Horta at the conference in Manila. More to free the prison authorities from any blame than to escape censure, Xanana had signed a statement denying that he was the author of the letter. He described to me at some length what his position was on the matter of the smuggling and publication of documents relating to the struggle.

Within a few months of being moved to Cipinang, he had made it clear to the prison officials that for the sake of the struggle and in his capacity as leader of the Falintil and the National Council of Maubere Resistance (CNRM), he would take every opportunity to communicate the aspirations of his people to the world. He refused to promise not to smuggle documents out of the prison, stating that he was happy to take full responsibility for his actions and to be 'disciplined' for them. In the case of other individuals being implicated in his political communications, however, he was prepared to sign written denials in order to relieve others of blame. For the prison officials these denials were vitally important as they were subjected to a good deal of pressure from military intelligence each time one of Xanana's illicit communiqués was made public. If they were to save face and retain their jobs, they needed him to make retractions.

Xanana thanked me for the painting books he had requested, which, with the help of Pat Walsh in Melbourne, I had managed to send him. He enthusiastically accepted my offer to act as his English teacher. And so the following day, after my private lesson with the suave Bimantara boss, I dropped by a bookshop and purchased an English grammar text as the basis for my newest pupil's lessons. In his last letter to me, João had alluded to a new and improved system of mail deliveries that made it possible for larger items such as the painting books to enter and leave the prison, so I was confident that the grammar book would also reach Xanana safely.

Emboldened by the apparent efficiency and security of our communication channels, I also slipped small birthday gifts for both João and Xanana into the bundle. Inside Xanana's card I put a photograph of myself taken some months earlier in West Java. It showed me gazing over a dramatically beautiful scene of emerald green rice terraces. Only the back of my head was visible – I didn't yet dare to entrust to the prison post a picture which more clearly identified me! I then passed on the parcel, which I enclosed in an innocent-looking black plastic bag, to a Timorese 'courier' on a back street around the corner from one of the monolithic office buildings I taught in.

Later in June, President Suharto hosted the visit to Jakarta of the Australian Prime Minister, Paul Keating. Keating flew into quite a storm, with student activists protesting daily over the closure by the Indonesian government of three popular magazines that had dared to speak critically of the New Order regime. The riot police dealt with the protesters promptly and decisively. The sight of heavily armed police with riot shields lining the main streets of Jakarta was a dramatic reminder of the violence and repression lying just below the surface of apparent calm and popular satisfaction with the status quo.

On the other side of town at Pondok Indah Mall, the 'Australia Today Indonesia '94' trade and cultural promotion was about to get underway. A series of cultural events was planned as part of the launch. They were to be witnessed by the visiting Australian Deputy Prime Minister, the Australian Ambassador and a host of other Australian and Indonesian dignitaries. The exclusive Pondok Indah Mall complex was home to all the big brand-name shops – Benetton, Gucci, Louis Vuitton – and since shopping was a favourite pastime of Jakarta's rich and trendy, much effort had gone into creating an ambience of comfort and glamour: glass, brass and mirrors were the central features of the decor. For the benefit of the trade promotion guests, the entrance and foyer of the mall were decked out with ribbons sporting the national colours of Australia and Indonesia.

A Sydney-based theatre troupe had been sponsored to travel to Jakarta to participate in the event. Having been tipped off by friends in Sydney that a small protest action was planned by one of the members of the theatre troupe – a group of five pantomime artists dressed in business suits and bowler hats – I arrived at the mall ahead of the scheduled commencement time with a journalist friend from Reuters and his cameraman in tow. In order not to alert the guests' minders to what was about to happen, we attempted to be as inconspicuous as possible by mingling with the throngs of smartly dressed shoppers. When the guests were finally seated, we took up our position on the balustrade of the first-floor balcony, which had a perfect view of the elaborately decorated stage below.

We didn't quite know what to expect, nor which of the five artists would initiate the protest. As the stage area was teeming with security guards and plain-clothes intelligence agents (recognisable as such only thanks to their crew cuts, dark glasses and barely concealed walkie-talkies), my heart pounded with anticipation and nervousness. I tried to detect a trace of fear or tension in the faces of the artists who had begun their routine on stage, but their expressions, thanks to heavy make-up, were deadpan. And so we could only watch and wait. Polite smiles were exchanged between the politicians and their hosts, who sat at the foot of the dais, and then . . . the tallest and lankiest of the performers quickly drew a white silk banner from his shirt pocket. He held it aloft, and we could make out the words: 'Indonesia–Australia – Hands off East Timor!'

Contrary to our expectations, not a single person in the audience made a move in the direction of the stage where the performer stood, turning slowly so that the words on the banner were visible to all. An embarrassed hush fell over the crowd; the dignitaries and Indonesian officials were too stunned to react. The polite smiles of a few minutes earlier were replaced by awkward grimaces. A full six minutes passed before an intelligence operative in a batik shirt made his way onto the dais and took the man I knew to be called Wayne by the forearm and led him to the side of the stage. If it hadn't been for the presence of Australian officialdom, the reaction would no doubt have been swifter and harsher.

My journalist friends quickly descended the steps and moved in the direction of Wayne, who had by then pocketed the silk banner and was standing in the middle of a circle of security guards and Australian Embassy officials. From the first-floor balcony I watched them conduct an interview with Wayne. The pantomime was over, but Wayne's drama was about to commence. I learnt later from my friends in Sydney that he had been escorted back to his hotel where he received a dressing-down from officials of the Australian Embassy. He remained there under virtual house arrest until he was flown back to Australia the following day. This incident highlighted for me the paramount importance Australia and Indonesia attached to their relationship, at the expense of both East Timor and the freedom of expression of Australian citizens.

The next morning, one of the English language dailies carried a small reference to the Pondok Indah Mall 'embarrassment', giving greater attention to the ongoing protests at the closure of the three magazines, a handful of cases of high-level corruption and bank scandals, and the 'good' news, in spite of all of this, that the International Consultative Group on Indonesia (a consortium of donor countries) had approved an eleven per cent increase in aid to Indonesia.

In early July, Xanana wrote to me again. He thanked me for the birthday gift and related in detail how he had been able to receive a visit, the first since his capture, from family members from Dili and his wife and children from Melbourne. The story of the reunion with his children, whom he had not seen since 1975 and who had left East Timor with their mother in 1991, was particularly moving. Somehow the description was all the more poignant for the originality of the English expression:

I am not able to describe to you what I felt at the moment I pressed them against me, the feeling that I was their father and they my children. A huge hiatus in time, circumstances which had compelled us to part and lead very different lives, only now to find them in front of me once more, debating adult affairs. In the retina of my memory I retained the almost faded image of two children, and yet before me I found two young adults, talking with me about what they wanted to be and inviting me to, one day, take care of my grandchildren! . . . We didn't talk so much about ourselves. It was not necessary. There are things that aren't to tell. They are to feel. Sometimes it happens that the world's silence makes a pain less sensitive and the feeling's ecstasy more wonderful!

In the beginning, I felt a little bit dislocated by the fact of having two such grown up children. But I drank their tears and fed on the love they had kept all these years to tell me they are the children I had 'abandoned' a long time ago. I talked to them about the struggle, about my guerrillas' suffering, so that they could get from me, not the reminiscing of a 'resuscitated father', but the sense of the ongoing demands of 'a patria' – the homeland. I couldn't carry you constantly in my thoughts, I told them. I couldn't dedicate a place in my heart to you because my guerrillas also had forgotten everything and had suffered more than myself.

They listened to me silently and I know they knew it wasn't just an attempt to justify my actions. Throughout our meeting, I was assailed by a range of human emotions – pain at not being able to bring them up, have fun with them, scold them and spoil them with gifts . . . as you spoiled me on my birthday. The 'saudades' [feeling of longing] came afterwards when each minute of the hand of our fate was telling us the time was approaching, the time of our separation. And so they left . . . My daughter had dug inside me and took away all of the love she could find in a father who has always tried to be a stone heart, in order to accept the death of his soldiers.

The words of the letter stayed with me for some days. It was difficult to conceive of what it must have felt like for Xanana and his children to rediscover one another given the gap of years. I was touched and at the same time a little humbled to think that Xanana had taken the time to relate such a personal episode to me. The letter ended with instructions to me regarding the translation and publication of an interview he had granted to my journalist friend from Reuters and apologies that João and Fernando had bothered me with a request for help with purchasing a small television set and medication for kidney pains he had been experiencing. I dealt with these requests between English lessons and the daily wrangle with government officials to obtain recommendations for the work permits and visas for Australian volunteers.

A week or so later, I found myself in a taxi heading for the Sari Pan Pacific Hotel. The UN Special Rapporteur on Extrajudicial, Summary or Arbitrary Executions, Mr Waly Bacre Ndiaye, had just completed a visit to East Timor where he was investigating allegations of human rights violations and compiling information concerning the number of people killed and still unaccounted for as a result of the 12 November 1991 massacre. A group of East Timorese youths had approached me to seek my assistance with translating a petition to be presented to the Special Rapporteur. It contained information on human rights violations documented inside East Timor and an appeal for the UN to conduct a full and independent investigation of the Dili massacre. Since a handful of Jakarta-based students had signed the petition, it was important that it not fall into the wrong hands, so I had offered to deliver it myself to Ndiaye in his hotel room at the Sari Pan Pacific. A white woman would be far less conspicuous there than a Timorese youth.

It took three phone calls to the hotel to line up an appointment with the Special Rapporteur – all calls to his room were being screened and, for obvious reasons, I was not too happy about revealing my true identity nor the nature of my business to the hotel staff. On the third attempt I managed to speak to Ndiaye himself, and to intimate that I had an important delivery to make 'on behalf of friends'. He must have understood me as he invited me to come directly to his hotel room and gave me the number.

I dressed myself up to resemble as closely as possible a guest of the five-star hotel and headed off. The lobby was full of men sporting the familiar crew cuts, batik shirts and blank expressions. Not having visited this particular hotel before, I could not say whether they were part of the furniture or there for Ndiaye's benefit, to protect him perhaps, or to ward off 'undesirables'. Within minutes I found myself at the open door of Ndiaye's hotel room. Spilling out into the corridor were a dozen or so men, all in batik shirts and all looking quizzically in my direction. The air was heavy with the smell of clove cigarettes and cheap aftershave.

I clutched my silver handbag and its contents a little closer to my chest, breathed in deeply and stepped confidently through the door before a single member of the batik brigade had a chance to question me. I muttered something imperceptible in rapid-fire English to one of the men when he stepped forward to impede my progress into the suite. He backed off, a little stunned, I think, at my impertinence. I spied Ndiaye putting on a sock in the bedroom and moved into the doorway where I was able to announce, in a whisper, that I was the bearer of the document. Conscious of the risky nature of my mission, he nodded in the direction of the enormous bed. 'Just toss it there. I am about to attend a government reception in my honour, but I thank you for your visit.' He smiled and nodded as I did as he said. I was out of there again before he had time to put on his other sock!

Back at home, I was still congratulating myself on the success of my mission and preparing to send the contents of the petition in an email to TAPOL in London, when there came a knock at the door. From the sound of the TV and the food rubble in the kitchen, I had gathered earlier that Charles was home. So perhaps this was his friend, Phil, dropping by for a beer. Opening the door, I found not freckled Phil but the imposing figure of Virgilio. Virgilio had completed a two and a half year prison sentence in Cipinang three months earlier, having been arrested along with João Freitas da Camara on the streets of Jakarta in 1991. He had been charged with disrupting public order and with posing a threat to national security and integrity.

'Boa noite, Mana.' He grinned as he made his way past me into the living room and then thrust a familiar-looking black plastic bag into my hands.

'Cipinang?' I enquired, and he nodded his reply. From my first meeting with Virgilio, soon after his release, I knew that there was no point inviting him to sit down or to drink a cup of coffee. He was an affable young man, but business-like when it came to tasks linked to the struggle. Before long I was watching him clamber aboard a waiting orange *bajaj* (a popular form of three-wheeled transport), which disappeared in a cloud of thick, black, two-stroke engine smoke.

As I pulled impatiently at the layers of newspaper around the cylindrical parcel I had received, I thought to myself how ironic it was that Virgilio's period in prison seemed only to have galvanised his will to work for the pro-independence cause. So much for rehabilitation! My train of thought was cut short as I succeeded, finally, in reaching the contents of the parcel. There were letters, some documents, rolled up tightly in . . . a painting. For a brief minute I forgot to breathe as my eyes took in the image on the canvas. The emerald rice paddies of West Java, the hazy blue of the sky, the yellow braid down my back, a signature in white in the bottom left-hand corner: 'With love, X, July 94.' For some reason an urge to put the painted surface to my nose came over me. The paint smelt fresh, the canvas a little musty. I felt a tear escape down my cheek and then chided myself inwardly for succumbing – to what? Pride at having had my image rendered so artistically, shame at feeling unworthy of such a gift, happiness at being in possession of something so beautiful? Before there was time to examine my feelings any further, the phone rang. I was glad to hear Charles' door fly open and his voice, cranky with sleep, as he answered. I didn't feel like talking to anyone just then. After all, there was still a pile of unopened letters to examine.

There was a letter from João. I skimmed its contents quickly. Xanana's letter was short and made no reference to the painting. Instead, he drew my attention to a statement that was enclosed and asked me to examine its contents closely, to do whatever I could to assist its author. It was, Xanana told me in his note, the testimony of a fellow inmate, an Australian called John Edwards. Xanana had befriended him, or vice versa, I supposed. Curious to know more, I took up the statement and started reading. It began: 'Maybe if you have the details of my case, you may be able to unravel its mystery. I have been trying to do this for two and a half years, without success.'

The story, as I understood it, was that John Edwards and his Indonesian wife had become shareholders in a company established by two foreigners in 1991. When the company went bankrupt in early 1992, the directors managed to leave the country in a hurry. The company's offices were raided by the police and John and his wife were taken into custody for questioning. The documents seized in the raid revealed that the company had been registered in the name of John's wife, seemingly without her knowledge. The rest of the story was a litany of violations of John and his wife's rights to legal counsel and to access qualified interpreters and translators. John had been forced to sign a statement that he did not understand and was consequently sentenced to two and a half years imprisonment on charges relating to fraud. It was not clear from the statement what the fate of his wife was.

As I processed this information, piecing together the story from the disjointed account of events, people and maltreatment at the hands of the police and prison authorities, a bell began to ring somewhere at the back of my mind. Somehow there was something familiar about this story, the sad chronology of the tale, the injustice of the accusations – and then my mind, still reeling pleasantly with the happy discovery of the painting, made the connection! But how could it be true? I recalled my conversation with John Read six months earlier, the cautionary tale and his appeals to me to stay out of trouble after the press release about Fernando and the human rights award had come in on his EMPI fax. Wasn't it also a case of fraud he had referred to? And didn't it involve a group of foreign directors? Surely it couldn't be one and the same case. The coincidence was just too great! There was only one thing for it – my flatmate Charles had been working with EMPI since early 1991 and so was bound to remember the incident that had so alarmed John Read.

I ran to Charles' room and banged impatiently on the door.

'Charles, sorry to bother you, but do you recall the name of that company which rented an office from EMPI and went bankrupt in early '92?'

Clutching a towel around his midriff, Charles stood in the doorway to his bedroom, a look of slight irritation on his round face. 'Ah, yeah. It was Athena Cosmetics, I think. Something like that anyway.'

I ran back across the tiled corridor to my room and scoured the first page of the statement. There it was – Athena Cosmetics! I felt the need to tell someone, to share this extraordinary coincidence. But there was no way I could let Charles in on the secret of my contacts with Cipinang, nor the mysterious way in which my activities in Jakarta seemed to be connecting me, so conclusively, to the fate of the prison's occupants.

Chapter seven

MUKYA
August 1994

ON A STEAMY, pre-monsoonal morning in August, Yati was sweeping the front yard, stooping slightly, the back of one hand resting in the small of her back. Her ankles creaked as she moved about, scooping up leaves and pebbles into a red plastic dustpan. I picked up the pile of mail waiting on the kitchen table and escaped with it into my bedroom, closing the door on the sound of those creaking ankles. As I shuffled through the envelopes, I searched my mind for a reason for the growing antagonism I was feeling towards my maid, who was in all respects a most diligent worker and loyal companion. Perhaps it was resentment that her presence in the house robbed me of the privacy I was increasingly craving. Perhaps it was concern that as my East Timor involvement intensified, she may find herself implicated in some way. Guilt by association. I was becoming aware of the existence of a range of different political groupings within the resistance movement and was more and more conscious of the need not to align myself with any particular one. Being a foreigner in Jakarta conferred on me a certain power and immunity, but I was also vulnerable from an immigration point of view. I could be deported at any time and for little good reason. And so I needed to be careful not to get offside with any of my East Timorese friends.

Amongst the mail, I came across a gift-wrapped parcel containing a new novel by an Australian author. My grandmother had posted it from Melbourne, and pasted inside the front cover was a gift tag reading 'love and best wishes, Nana and Papa'. My grandfather had signed the 'Papa' in an almost illegible hand, a sad reminder that he was dying. The sight of his pathetic, childlike scrawl on that little card provoked a sudden sense of something akin to homesickness, a thing I had rarely felt in my years away from Australia. It was a comfort to know that I would soon be holidaying in the Moluccan spice islands with my parents. I was tired and in need of a break.

In the meantime, the correspondence from Cipinang continued to flow. Two days before I left for Ambon, the capital of the Moluccas, I received a parcel of mail from Xanana with a series of documents to be forwarded by fax or courier to others, including José Ramos-Horta. Amongst the papers for José was a micro-cassette containing a taped message. I found myself overwhelmed by a desire to listen to the tape, not so much to become privy to the communication between the two, but simply to hear Xanana's voice. The peculiarity of the situation suddenly struck me. Xanana and I had begun to 'speak' to one another in our letters with the intimacy and trust of lifelong friends, but I had never heard the sound of his voice. But I didn't own a micro-cassette player and there was no time to purchase one as I needed to dispatch the correspondence before I left for my holiday. Along with the instructions on how to deal with the letters for José and others, Xanana's letter to me expressed his concern that, for security reasons, it was time to bury 'Ruby Blade' and to invent a new pseudonym for me. He offered me 'Mukya', a word in the Fataluku language of Los Palos, meaning 'fragrant'.

'My dear,' he wrote, 'thanks for the photo of my son of war. Do you believe he is not my son of war? Yes? No?' I had sent Xanana a photograph of a boy aged around ten. It had been taken by my friend Silvia during a recent visit she had paid to Venilale, site of one of the largest orphanages in East Timor. Silvia had been told by the nuns at the orphanage that the boy, Nolasco, was Xanana's son, and so Silvia had photographed him and sent me the picture to pass on to Xanana. I had done so, although I wasn't sure of the veracity of the nuns' story. His response read:

> He is the son of one of my best commanders who headed up a guerrilla company in the eastern part of the island. He had captured more than a hundred weapons from the enemy and was one of the greatest commanders of operations in the history of Falintil. He died in combat . . . because of his son.
>
> You may already have heard that, in the heart of Falintil, there are those who bear amulets. Some of these amulets are 'lulik' which are central to the belief systems and faith of my people. There are many kinds of amulets with different rules attached. A common rule concerned relationships with women. This particular commander received from his own lulik a kind of protection against bullets. It permitted him to get married, but on the condition that his wife did not bear him a son. His first child was a daughter. He was punished with a serious wound. When his wife gave birth to a second child and his soldiers came to know that the baby was a boy, they all cried. They all knew that their commander will die because his substitute had been born. It was the rule, the relentless rule of our beliefs which modern standards classify as 'superstition'.
>
> At that time I was on Matebian mountain. He died near Loré in an ambush he laid on the road between Loré and Los Palos. In recognition of his feats which had contributed hugely to our military resistance, I wrote to Father Locatelli

> at Fatumaka College, asking for help. And so one day, at night, guerrillas from another military unit near Baucau brought the boy to the priest. Since then, he was known as my son as I gave to him my name. His name is Bere Koro Gusmão Nolasco. His father was Koro Asu Nolasco.

Once again, I was moved that Xanana had taken the time to share this story with me. The insights it offered into the ways and beliefs of the armed resistance fascinated me, and I found myself wanting to know more about the world that had shaped Xanana, as a person and as a leader.

He was proving to be a diligent student of English. With each letter he sent me two or more pages of completed grammar exercises, which I duly corrected and returned to him. Since he was wrestling with the use of the subjunctive in English, I wrote him a couple of sample sentences to help with his mastery of this particular grammatical point:

'If *I had* (I don't have) a million dollars, *I would* bribe someone to release all East Timorese political prisoners.'

'If *I were* the Indonesian Minister of Justice (I am not), *I would* allow Xanana's English teacher to visit him twice a week for English lessons.'

It was the language of wishful thinking! The thought of entering the prison under some pretext or another had indeed entered my head. I knew that, in addition to the routine twice-weekly visits, there were Christian prison service groups whose members made goodwill visits to prison inmates during the Christmas and Easter holidays, but I had not heard of any foreigners being allowed to participate in these events.

On the morning of 22 August 1994, I boarded a Merpati jet bound for Ambon. The feeling of excitement and anticipation of a much-needed holiday was tinged with something bordering on sadness and guilt at 'abandoning' Xanana. What if he or João or Fernando needed something urgently in my absence – some money or medicine, an important letter translated or faxed? I comforted myself with the thought that there were the East Timorese students and a growing number of Indonesian activist friends on hand to deal with any pressing needs that might arise, and after all, two weeks was not so long.

Nevertheless, there was no getting away from the fact that I would miss the contact with Xanana. His letters and the daily business of the struggle – the developing links with Indonesian solidarity groups, the liaison with friends and supporters around the world – had become, in just a few short months, an integral part of my life. However, beyond our common concern for the cause of independence, there was something more – a kind of bond or feeling – which seemed to be drawing us closer together with each letter we exchanged. I found myself wondering whether this wasn't merely the result of Xanana's charisma and his tremendous skill at projecting himself through his words. Did he perhaps write to others, too, with the same degree of affection?

The flight eastwards from Bali was enchanting, with views of the rugged, volcanic peaks of the islands of Lombok and Flores. Finally, as the plane penetrated the low-lying cloud, I caught my first glimpse of Ambon, the lush green of the hills surrounding the town rimmed by the milky turquoise of the sea. Within minutes of collecting my luggage from the feeble old baggage carousel in the arrivals hall, the heavens opened and the din of the monsoonal downpour made conversation with my waiting parents difficult. However, the days ahead were to offer us ample opportunity to catch up on one another's news and for me to regale them with tales of life in the cement jungle of Jakarta.

Two days later we found ourselves sipping cinnamon tea on the mossy balcony of the Flamboyan Homestay on the island of Neira and snacking on freshly baked loaves of bread smothered in sweet nutmeg jam. The island was home to 5000 people, four motorised vehicles, a couple of hundred scrawny dogs and the derelict foundations of at least one Portuguese fort, its rusty cannon jutting forlornly out to sea. We climbed the flanks of Gunung Api, a live volcano whose eruptions had threatened to curtail the spice trading activities of the Dutch East India Company in the eighteenth century. A short canoe ride south of Neira lay pretty Lontor island, where we soaked our aching calves in the warm sea and watched our guide spear a rainbow fish for dinner. Some days my mother and I would head for the cool of the towering banyan trees down near the pier and attempt to capture the serene beauty of the place in charcoal sketches. We would turn around to find bands of curious children gathered at our backs and giggling – perhaps at our inexpert attempts at artistic expression, perhaps at their own cheekiness. No doubt they were wondering why we didn't just take out our cameras like other self-respecting tourists.

The sights and smells of this sleepy Moluccan paradise were the perfect balm for my weary mind and body. Literally and metaphorically, Jakarta was another world away. And yet I found that Xanana was never far from my thoughts. I kept a kind of diary for him, recording events and my observations of the island, the beauty of places we visited, the taste and the feel of the sea, an account of my snorkelling excursions into the silent underwater world of the tropical fish. I was not sure whether these entries would be a satisfaction or a torment to Xanana, representing as they did the world of things and experiences denied him in prison. Nevertheless, he had implored me in his last letter not to forget him during my holiday – the diary was my way of proving to him that I hadn't.

In spite of the slow pace of life on the island, the two weeks passed quickly and soon it was time to farewell my parents and make the return trip to Jakarta. I felt rested, my energy restored. I was ready once more to take up the challenge of juggling my official duties with those associated with East Timor.

On the flight home I endured a tedious hour-long conversation with a Balinese business executive who insisted on having my answers to the string of inane questions he fired at me. Where are you from? Are you married? Why not? Do you like Indonesia? Why didn't you spend your holiday in Bali? Relief came only when I feigned sleep and he turned his attention to a blonde woman sitting across the aisle from him.

As my taxi wove and honked its way through the streets of Jakarta to my home, I found I was increasingly anxious for news from Cipinang. Nevertheless, two days passed after my return before I received a phone call from the courier to say that he had mail for me. We agreed to meet at a popular burger joint in the teeming shopping precinct of Blok M. I treated António, the younger brother of my regular courier, to a Coke and hotdog. As he wolfed down his lunch, my eyes devoured the black plastic carry bag hanging over the back of his seat. I knew it contained the mail he had for me. I was anxious not to seem rude, but the truth was that I just wanted to get home and be alone with its contents. After what seemed like an age, António swallowed the last mouthful of his hotdog and we exchanged black plastic bags. My own contained a letter and the monthly allowance for João, and the diary I had prepared for Xanana. I had also arranged some sand, shells and sprigs of dried nutmeg in a box – a sea and spice garden – to present to him as a souvenir of my holiday. I had wrapped everything in layers of newspaper, each one girded with sticky tape, and written 'Aluno de Mukya' (Mukya's student) on the top right-hand corner of the outermost envelope.

Back at home, I took a pair of scissors to the two parcels inside the black plastic bag – I was in no mood to unravel the tangle of sticky tape, which Xanana and João had made even more liberal use of than me. The first parcel contained a fat white envelope. I imagined that its contents must be documents and letters for translation or forwarding. As I fingered the bulk of the paper inside, I smiled to myself, thinking that it was just as well that I had returned reinvigorated from my holiday. My 'boss', it seemed, was going to make me pay for my time off work. But as I rifled through the pages in front of me, I discovered, to my surprise and delight, that they were all addressed to me – all twenty-five of them! The first, dated 22 August, the day of my departure for Ambon, began: 'I am sad, very sad, knowing that tomorrow I will not receive your letters. My thoughts seem to be a bird trying desperately to reach the outside of his cage. If these little birds which have the habit of making nests in my cell knew your home, I would take care of their young, forgive them for leaving their excrement on my clothing, and send them to deliver a letter to you . . . to wish goodbye to my dear Professora.'

I found myself smiling in spite of the melancholy image of the birds and the imprisoned thoughts. I read on: '25 August. I have just received your latest letters, but you are so far away from me! I will keep a diary for you. All the morning I spent imagining you laughing at my English. You are lying on a beach somewhere. My teacher had promised to write to me every day, but she has so many things to tell her lovely parents. What are you telling them, my dear? Hmm? That I am an annoying old man who torments and tires you with work?' A description of the daily comings and goings inside the prison, the ongoing attempts of the other prisoners to provoke and ridicule, followed.

Between the entries of 25 and 26 August came a poem in Portuguese entitled 'Concept'. The first two verses read:

To love life is cruel
Life is nothing
A destiny in a shell
On an endless beach . . .

It is cruel to love nothing
A life lying dormant
In a shell which opens up
In the boundaries of the beach.

I read on, resisting the temptation to turn to the last page of the wad of letters. In search of what? I couldn't quite say.

> Kirsty, sometimes, like right now, a fog of sadness covers my thoughts. I have to be sincere with myself and, above all, with you. You see, my dear Teacher, I need you, I know. But more than this, dare I say it, I love you! But how

many differences are between us, dear. I don't want for anything in the world to make you suffer, now or in the future. At the same time I am happy to think that it is still possible for me to suffer like this for the love of someone. A selfish masochism perhaps, I don't know . . . I fear that I am unable to make you happy as you would like, and as I, too, would like. And all of this makes me so terribly sad!

Today I went to the chapel twice, once in the morning and once in the afternoon. I prayed for you, for me, for us. I miss you, querida, every day more. I don't know if I was wrong to do it, but I begged God to protect our love. I feel you love me, too, is it true? In the past, I thought that I would like to stay in prison for longer even than Mandela. How ambitious I was, eh, my dear? Later I realised that, if the struggle demanded it, I would accept to be free so as to contribute more decisively to the liberation of my homeland. But in more recent times, the idea of remaining in prison until I am old upsets me terribly. I would have only an aged heart to offer you!

Now, do you want to know a funny thing? Don't laugh, please. One of the inmates here is a former soldier and we, the five East Timorese prisoners, have befriended him. Yesterday, although I am not allowed to, I visited João and Fernando's cell block. This friend was there. In the middle of the conversation, he asked to take a look at my left-hand. It turns out he is a fortune-teller!

Don't be amazed, don't laugh, don't be angry with the following, okay?

'Can you really tell fortunes?' I asked him.

'You will have a long life,' he replied.

A little interested, I asked again, 'To what age? Eighty, Ninety perhaps?'

'In short, very old,' was his reply.

'Oh, if I have to endure being senile, then I would prefer to die young,' I protested. 'Now, I don't want to be rich or anything, but can you tell me whether or not I will be happy?' I asked.

Studying my palm again, he answered, 'Yes, in your fifties and sixties.'

(It's a bit late, don't you think, my dear? And, of course, I didn't ask him what his concept of happiness is.) Believe me, my dear, I don't know why, but I took a risk and asked him: 'Will I get married again?'

He read the thumb of my palm and said, 'Yes, you will.'

João, who had been following our conversation, smiled over the dinner he was cooking. Very excited, I yelled a lot of hurrahs which made João goggle his eyes.

'I want to nurse babies, Sir. How many children will I have?' I cried out, hopefully offering my palm to him again.

The long silence, which was only a few seconds, was broken, 'Two or three.' It was what he read. True!

'But by the time I am sixty I will be past it!' I retorted.

'I'm telling you, you will have kids,' he said, smiling.

I went back to my block, smiling at everybody. I know that they thought that I was unusually bright because some of the guards commented on my disposition. I ignored them and whistled a song, the tune of which I didn't know.

I know you are, by now, laughing . . . at me! Your holidays are coming to an end. Have you forgotten me? I send you a hug warmer than the sun of Ambon.

An indescribable feeling welled up inside me like tears. And yet it wasn't anything like depression I was feeling and so there were no tears to shed. I smiled to myself, feeling my cheeks flush red with the blood of pure happiness. Xanana Gusmão in love with *me*? Disbelief, relief and a dull ache of longing competed for space in my brain. Disbelief because my rational mind told me that to fall in love with someone you have never met face to face is foolish, if not impossible. Relief because there was another part of me that glimmered with the certainty that the impossible would become possible. It was the same part of my being that fed my belief in and commitment to East Timor. Longing because – and admitting it to myself caused me to gasp a little – I, too, had fallen in love with Xanana.

There followed some lines in Tetum. With the help of a dictionary, I managed to decipher their meaning: 'Kirsty, do you want to know a big secret? It is a secret about myself, about my past. I want to share it with you but I am afraid that you will be shocked and angry with me and that you will not want to write to me any longer. First of all, before I tell you my secret, you must promise me that you will continue to talk to me. There are things I need to tell you, but I fear so much hurting you . . .'

I switched my pedestal fan onto full. Suddenly I was feeling warm, my palms damp and clammy. The blast from the fan sent the twenty-five pages of correspondence flying across my bed, and as I scrambled to recover them, I heard a door fling open and the deep rumble of Charles' voice emerging from his bedroom across the hall. He had answered the phone, which must have been ringing for some time. Lost in the world of my letters, I hadn't heard a thing. It was John Read calling to enquire about my whereabouts. I was an hour late for my conversational English class at the Hong Kong Bank. Looking at my watch, incredulous, I discovered that it was 6:30 pm already. The bank was an hour's taxi ride away through rush-hour traffic, so there was nothing for it but to invent a sudden and debilitating illness.

It was 11 pm by the time I sat down in front of the computer to compose my reply to Xanana. The night was unusually quiet, the only sound the occasional plaintive honk from the satay seller's horn. The pages of Xanana's letters lay about me on the bed. I had reread them a number of times already, but even so I found myself taking them up again and again to try to understand and interpret the words on the paper.

'Dearest Aluno,' I began. I had to be honest with Xanana, to voice the questions and doubts that had arisen as a result of his declaration of love.

> If I have not expressed my feelings for you until now it is because, like you, I was struck by the madness of it, the impossibility of it. The idea of being in love with you worries, torments and, at the same time, enchants me. Am I right to love you? I ask myself whether it is not rather the idea of me, what I represent – human warmth, solidarity, femininity, all the things lacking in your life right now – that you have fallen in love with. It is true that there are countless differences – age, culture, life experience – which separate us, and whilst it would be excessively romantic to discount them, I must confess to you, dearest Aluno, that I feel there is an inexplicable commonality between us. What can it be? What name should I give it? Perhaps I am merely a vain young woman seeking to justify a feeling born of a selfish wish to be considered worthy of a great man? I don't know! But I do know that it makes me so happy to receive your letters and to feel that, by falling in love, we are defying the logic of prison walls. It makes me want to cry out 'venceremos', 'we will win'. And then your 'fog of sadness' descends on me and I am once again nothing but an unhappy young woman, pathetic in my longing for something unattainable.

Would Xanana feel slighted or offended by my doubts? Would he opt not to share with me the 'big secret' he alluded to in his letter? I closed my letter with a promise that whatever it was that he had to say to me about his past, I would continue to write to him. I slipped Rp 20,000 into the envelope as João had informed me that one of the prison guards was offering his services as express go-between – for a small fee, of course.

Only four days passed before I received Xanana's reply to my letter, but the wait seemed interminable. I found myself cursing the couriers at either end of the correspondence chain who seemed to be oblivious to the urgency of their deliveries – sometimes they waited for twenty-four hours or more before advising me of the arrival of the prison mail. Perhaps they interpreted my impatience to receive letters from Cipinang as proof of my selfless dedication to the struggle and my commitment to the work for Xanana. Indeed, it seemed that in resistance circles I was slowly gaining a reputation as Xanana's 'private secretary'. On the day I received Xanana's reply, a fax arrived from José Ramos-Horta. In it, he requested that I meet with him in Macau at the end of September to discuss a range of issues relating to Xanana's status and my work for him. Being the Indonesian state's public enemy number one because of his vocal defence of the independence cause on the international stage, it was not possible for José to visit Jakarta. I thought it appropriate to seek Xanana's view on my participation in such a meeting, and so did not respond to José right away.

I felt an involuntary smile appear on my lips as I ripped open the parcel containing Xanana's letter. His great skill at conveying his persona only added to my quandary. It became difficult to focus on my work and the business of preparing myself for the trip to Macau – Xanana was enthused by the idea of my meeting with José and had encouraged me to accept the invitation.

My brain or my heart, or both, seemed to be gravitating constantly in the direction of that prison in East Jakarta, which I both hated and loved; hated because its walls stood between me and the person I longed to be with, and loved because that little world of inmates and guards, of daily comings and goings, of freedoms bought and sold for the price of lunch at a roadside stall, was increasingly becoming my world, too. And it seemed to me that there was a perverse kind of magic attending the whole evolution of my relationship with Xanana. Perhaps it was the miracle of seeing love, hope and a sense of purpose flourish in the midst of hostility, oppression and resignation. Whatever it was, it helped me reach the decision to attempt to enter Cipinang prison. I didn't have a clue how such a thing would be achieved, but I did know that I was going to try.

Chapter eight

GETTING IN
September–December 1994

In the meantime, there was work to be done – the visas of five new volunteers to process, two English classes per day to teach and the ongoing tasks of reporting, translating, faxing and emailing for the most demanding of all my bosses, Xanana. Whilst the requests for my assistance now came couched in terms of endearment and with promises of payment in the form of kisses and eternal devotion, the declaration of our feelings for one another altered very little at the work level. Xanana shared with me the plans being devised to stage a demonstration of East Timorese youth to coincide with the forthcoming APEC Summit to be hosted by Jakarta. He pleaded with me to mobilise some funding to support the action, which would require a large number of East Timorese students to travel from various cities across Java to the capital. However, he warned me that there was a need for the utmost care to be taken in the communication of details of the plan. The success of the demonstration and the safety of the demonstrators depended on it. Xanana nominated a student code-named Naga Soru, a member of

Renetil, the youth wing of the National Council of Maubere Resistance, to liaise with me in refining elements of the strategy to be adopted. With a large number of heads of state planning to be at the summit, a unique opportunity existed for the East Timorese to draw their struggle and aspirations to the attention of the world.

The summit was one of the matters to be raised and discussed with José Ramos-Horta in Macau. Xanana outlined the other issues he wished me to talk about with José in a six-page briefing that I had time to study closely only on the flight between Jakarta and Hong Kong. The plane was filled with a mix of sunburnt tourists, perhaps fresh off the beaches of Bali, and executive types in business suits staring earnestly into the screens of their laptops. I felt a little out of place – I was the only envoy of an incarcerated freedom fighter on board. More out of habit than because of any real sense that I was being observed, I glanced furtively over my shoulder every now and again as I scanned the pages of Xanana's letter. The issues he addressed ranged from the practical matter of funds to support the work of the *estafetas*, or couriers, who conveyed letters to and from Xanana and the armed resistance inside East Timor; to scholarships for Renetil members and opportunities for them to begin to reflect on the process of reconstruction of East Timor; to the importance of the intensification of the campaign for Xanana's release and participation in the dialogue with the Indonesian authorities.

In many ways I felt ill-equipped to play the role of emissary for Xanana. I was inexperienced in the ways of clandestine movements and resistance struggles. Nevertheless, I had embraced the work of advancing the cause of the East Timorese because my conscience dictated that it was the correct thing to do, not because my life experience or skills qualified me for the job in any way. So if Xanana trusted me to represent him in a meeting with José Ramos-Horta, I knew that I had no choice but to do so to the best of my ability.

Macau was an enchanting mix of Europe and Asia. Elegantly dressed couples sipped glasses of Portuguese red wine under the awnings of outdoor cafés that, if it weren't for the Chinese characters emblazoned over the door, could have been mistaken for fashionable eating establishments in Lisbon or Rome.

José was a gracious host. We discussed the matters in Xanana's briefing document over two days. I found it a tremendous relief to be able to speak openly with someone about the nature of my work for Xanana and the difficulties associated with the role. With the exception of my parents and a handful of friends in Australia and Europe, very few people knew of my connection with the prison. In spite of having promised Xanana that I would do so, I found myself hesitating to divulge details of the emotional link between us. I feared that José would see our relationship as mere infatuation on my part and hopeless romanticism on Xanana's. What Xanana didn't tell me was that he had confided the full story of our growing feelings for one another in a tape-recorded message he had made for José, which I had given him soon after my arrival in Macau. And so, on the second day of our meeting, José fixed me with a knowing look and, placing a paternal hand on my shoulder, began: 'So, Madam Professora, it seems to me that you have won the heart of your pupil. What can I say except that I wish you both every happiness.' I tried in vain to stop myself blushing.

I had met José on a number of occasions before, at protests, campaign meetings and fundraising dinners in Melbourne, but this was the first time that the subject of our exchanges had shifted from the political struggle to the arena of emotions and feelings. I must have cut a pretty pathetic figure, standing there with my cheeks flushing red and struggling to find the words to respond to José's unexpected felicitations. Finally I managed to untie my tongue: 'Apart from being a capable leader, Xanana is a wonderfully warm human being, José. I can imagine what you must be thinking. How is it possible? Love? In those circumstances and between two people with nothing more than a dream in common. I don't know how to explain it to you . . .'

Sensing my discomfort, José squeezed my shoulder, his eyes smiling at me over the rim of his glasses. 'Don't even try to. The heart has reasons that reason doesn't understand, to quote . . . now who was it? Someone French, I believe.' It seemed that José had a saying or an anecdote for just about every situation. He had collected many of both in the course of twenty years of work as East Timor's roving diplomat. 'I just hope that you appreciate that as the woman in Xanana's life, you are destined to have me nickname you "First". When all this is over and Xanana is sworn in as president of an independent East Timor, you automatically will become – '

There came a loud knock on the door of the living room and José's sister, in whose apartment we were meeting, entered with a tray of coffee and Portuguese custard tarts. I was grateful for the opportunity to change the subject.

I was in fact very keen to discuss with José the problem of the growing costs associated with maintaining our regular communication channels between the prison and the resistance movement abroad and inside East Timor. I explained to him that I felt that I could not justify using the prison support funds from Amnesty International for this purpose. This money had been granted for humanitarian purposes only, in strict accordance with Amnesty's mandate of campaigning for and assisting prisoners of conscience. I had no other money with which to pay the prison guards and the transport and telephone costs of the small group of East Timorese couriers who lived hand-to-mouth on their minimal scholarship payouts. My salary was proving to be insufficient to meet the growing number of unforeseen circumstances – the hospital expenses of a youth with a bullet lodged in his thigh, the cost of a Dili–Jakarta boat ticket for a prison escapee – I was being presented with. José seemed to be grateful for the first-hand account of the problems and activities of the resistance movement within Indonesia, and gave me his undertaking that he would lay his hands on some money to assist with the needs I had outlined.

But he, too, had an important message to convey, and I understood it to be a matter of the utmost confidentiality, since he was reluctant to commit it to either paper or an audiotape. It was a message for Xanana, and it related to plans José was developing to break Xanana out of prison in a commando-style rescue operation. In spite of the serious expression which José wore as he outlined the plan to me, I found it difficult to keep from grinning as I pictured the scenario in my head. I saw men clad in black balaclavas descending on ropes from helicopters, which hovered like toys above Cipinang prison. I saw guards running hither and thither in the prison yard below, stopping once in a while to scratch their heads and gaze, with jaws agape, at the Arnold Schwarzenegger look-alikes dropping from the heavens.

And then, from a nearby cell block, Xanana appeared, suitcase in hand, the high-powered beam from the helicopter lights illuminating his features and causing him to turn away momentarily. Within seconds, one of the swarthy prison invaders was scooping Xanana up into his arms like a baby and hoisting him to freedom on one of the ropes anchored to the helicopter, the roar of its rotor blade drowning out the sound of the gunfire from the dozen or so red-beret soldiers who had suddenly appeared.

'It sounds awfully ambitious and more than a little risky to me,' I found myself blurting out before José had had time to finish. Would Xanana agree to such an outlandish mission? I seriously hoped not – the scene with the red berets training their M-16s on the dangling figure of Xanana kept replaying itself in my mind. Nevertheless, I gave José my guarantee that I would ensure that the details of the plan would be communicated in the safest way possible to Xanana for his consideration.

Back at home in Jakarta, I was playing back the messages on my answering machine – Mum anxious to know whether or not I had arrived home safely, a handful of volunteers with questions about the status of their applications for work permits – when there came a knock at the door. It was António, bearing the mandatory black plastic bag. In addition to the mail from Cipinang, he nursed two small ceramic pots containing bonsai plants. 'A gift from Katuas [the old man],' he announced as he placed them carefully on the tiled floor of the living room.

From Xanana's letters, I knew that the cultivation and care of bonsai plants was one of the activities promoted by the prison authorities as a form of prisoner rehabilitation. As I had never owned a bonsai plant in my life, I was relieved to find that one of the letters inside the black plastic bag contained detailed instructions, including pictures and diagrams, on how to prune, water and feed the diminutive trees, one of which appeared to be a cumquat. I didn't dare quiz António on how Xanana had succeeded in smuggling this live contraband out of Cipinang.

Inside the plastic bag I came across a small bundle the size of a packet of cigarettes. It was an audiocassette, and when I discovered that it was meant for me, I could hardly contain my curiosity. I carried the tape to my bedroom, turning it over and over again in my hands, re-reading the inscription on the front ('My first meeting with my beloved Kirsty'), taking in the smell of the perfume that was now part of each and every personal item of correspondence I received from Xanana. I attached a pair of headphones to my cassette player and inserted the tape. My fingers trembled slightly as I pressed the play button.

'Saturday, 4:22 am.' His voice was deep and husky with sleep. I imagined him speaking into his cassette recorder from a mattress in the corner of his cell. 'You are not awake yet, I know. Don't wake up, don't talk. Today is my day to talk to you.' As Xanana continued, the sound of the call to prayer penetrating the silence of the morning, I closed my eyes. 'While our neighbours are bellowing to their God, here I am whispering to my Kirsty.' The clarity of the recording meant that it was possible to imagine Xanana there in my room, with me, caressing me with the tenderness of his spoken words. What followed was an hour-long conversation, which he had recorded throughout the course of an entire day. Parts of it made me laugh out loud, like the episode during lunch when he recorded the sounds of his slurping a bowl of boiled noodles that João had prepared for him. He pretended that he was sharing the contents of the bowl with me and giggled like a child as he chided me for taking the lion's share of the meatballs. 'Oh, now you don't want to eat. Come now, open up, take just one more mouthful, querida.' There were other more sombre moments. He pondered if he would leave the prison as an old man and implored me to think again about whether or not I was prepared to wait for him. What was most remarkable about the cassette, however, was the sense that a new element had been added to our relationship, that we had succeeded in transporting our communication to a new level – one that enhanced our knowledge of one another and our ability to withstand the pain of our separation.

In the days that followed, I set about making contact with a number of Indonesians whom I knew to be involved in prison service activities. With Christmas rapidly approaching, a rare opportunity to see Xanana in the flesh, to be with him, albeit fleetingly, was about to present itself. At the office of one of the Indonesian NGOs for which I translated the odd human rights report, I introduced myself to Vera Nababan, a young lawyer from West Sumatra who, according to João, was a fairly regular visitor to Cipinang. She and a small group of other Christian NGO activists were members of a prison service organisation and they paid frequent visits to political prisoners – of which Indonesia had many during the Suharto years – across Java.

At first, Vera was a little sceptical about my intentions and shook her head glumly when I suggested to her that I simply sign on to the visitors' list and try my luck at getting inside the prison as a member of her group. It was difficult not to betray my real reasons for wishing so desperately to get inside the prison. I spoke to Vera only of my friendship with João and my admiration for Xanana. She was a little more hopeful after our second meeting. The perfect ruse had suddenly occurred to me one evening as I was waiting at the entrance to Blok M mall for my rendezvous with the courier – I would pose as the niece of John Edwards, Xanana's unfortunate prison buddy. I couldn't wait to share my brilliant idea with Xanana and wrote him a hurriedly scribbled addendum to my other mail right there and then. Vera saw merit in the idea and thought that it might well work.

And so, for the next two months, my planned visit became the subject of a swathe of letters exchanged with Xanana and João. While I didn't want to raise my expectations too high in case some element of the plan went awry, it was hard to contain the excitement I felt at the prospect of turning the dream of a face-to-face meeting with Xanana into reality.

Around this same time, I was more than a little relieved when I received Xanana's response to José Ramos-Horta's 'special project'.

> Regarding José's plan, the problem as far as I am concerned is not so much the inherent danger or any fear I might have of being killed in the process . . . although I have to say that I don't really want to die. I would lose you forever, and I have my doubts that we would meet again in heaven. I am far more likely to finish up in hell. But seriously, the problem is more that the plan does not interest me. Rather than hoodwink the regime, I would prefer to defeat the generals in such a way that they are obliged to acknowledge their defeat and bow their heads in shame. Dear Professora, I ask you to accept this small gift I have made for you as a token of my love and in commemoration of my one year of residence in Cipinang penitentiary.

Wrapped in layers of tissue paper and newsprint was a small green fibreglass candelabra with a place for two candles. Fibreglass modelling must have been another form of rehabilitation, along with bonsai. Around the base of the candelabra was an inscription in yellow acrylic paint that read: 'A candelabra for two. I love you, 30 September 1994.'

That night and the following one, from its position on the monitor of my computer, the candelabra kept me company as I worked until the early hours of the morning, translating a three-page letter from Xanana to the US President, Bill Clinton. In it, he appealed to Clinton to see the parallels between Iraq's invasion of Kuwait and Indonesia's military occupation of East Timor. 'I come to you now to appeal for your support in raising with

President Suharto on the occasion of the forthcoming APEC Summit the need for Jakarta to display greater political goodwill in addressing the East Timor question, acknowledging the essence of the problem and the legal and political status of the territory.' I sent my translation from Portuguese back into the prison where Xanana transcribed its contents in his neat hand, signing it 'Kay Rala Xanana Gusmão, Commander of FALINTIL'.

Then came the tricky part. I had organised to fax the letter to José, who was by now in Washington DC; however, just in case my home phone was being monitored, I decided to fax the letter from a public telecommunications office – if the document were intercepted, there would be no mercy for those responsible. I tried to be as nonchalant as possible as I handed the pages of the letter over to the young man behind the counter of the twenty-four-hour Wartel (telecommunications shop). I was glad to note that he looked a little weary and that his assistant was engrossed in a Brazilian soap opera blaring from a TV set in the back room. Nevertheless, I watched his face as he guided the pages through the machine, just in case his eyes betrayed recognition of the name at the bottom of the letter. Finally, after three failed attempts – was it just the poor quality of Jakarta's phone lines or was somebody, somewhere, trying to abort the operation? – the fax machine spat out its delivery confirmation report and I darted out the door and onto the first south-bound minibus to hurtle past the door of the Wartel.

Our attention was now focussed on the upcoming APEC Summit and the plans for the demonstration which, it had been decided, would take place inside the grounds of the US Embassy on 12 November, the third anniversary of the Dili massacre. The participating youth would not seek asylum but rather would use the relative safety of the embassy compound to make their aspirations known to the world. The proceeds from the sale of a handful of Xanana's paintings, auctioned a month or two earlier in Melbourne, were to be put towards the cost of accommodating and feeding the one hundred or so students expected to participate in the action.

I was responsible for translating the written petition of the demonstrators and for ensuring that the foreign correspondents resident in Jakarta, along with the journalists accompanying the summit delegates, were discreetly informed about the plans in advance so that they could bear witness to what would undoubtedly be a hostile response from the Indonesian authorities. The fairy-lights and tinsel used to beautify the city for the NAM Summit two years earlier were dusted off and strung up along Jalan Thamrin once more. Security was heightened significantly. As the summit commenced and the day of the action grew closer, a handful of East Timorese students from East Java were apprehended by police at Gambir railway station as they alighted from their train. Fortunately, none of them had on their person any documents relating to the demonstration, so they were simply sent home.

On the morning of 12 November I sat, agitated, by the phone, awaiting the call from Virgilio that would signal that the demonstrators were in place and ready to converge on the US Embassy. One hour after the agreed time, Virgilio phoned. I placed a call through to the mobile phone of Jeremy, my journalist friend from Reuters, who was already in place in front of the US Embassy and trying desperately hard to remain inconspicuous – no easy task given the presence of his cameraman, who was laden down with professional-looking gear.

'There's only so much footage we can shoot of the National Monument before the boys in green get a whiff and decide to investigate,' he complained.

'Please,' I implored him, 'just stay put. The party will be getting underway very shortly, I assure you.'

Sure enough, within fifteen minutes the demonstrators were scaling the fence of the embassy. Once safely inside, they began drawing their homemade banners from their rucksacks, holding them aloft for the benefit of the passing traffic – 'Free Xanana' – and fastening others to the gates of the embassy – 'Referendum for East Timor'. Only one young man didn't make it over the fence. He was dragged off by baton-wielding police officers, but not before he granted a dramatic interview to Jeremy. We heard later that forty others had been detained on their way to the embassy.

The images from the embassy action were broadcast that evening all around the world, and Jakarta was suitably embarrassed by the daring of the Timorese demonstrators. Who would know whether Bill Clinton had the will or the opportunity during his stay under the fairy lights of Jakarta to raise Xanana's concerns with Suharto.

The other mission left to be accomplished for the year 1994 was, it seemed, my visit to Cipinang. The prospects were growing gloomier by the day. Vera had consulted with the other members of her group about my participation in the Christmas visit, set for 22 December, and the general feeling was that I was something of a liability. But Vera was a good and kind-hearted woman and, noting my downcast response to this news, quickly added that she would do her best to bring the others on side.

On 15 December Xanana wrote to me to say that he had had an opportunity to speak about the plan with John Edwards. He would be a willing participant in the uncle–niece charade in spite of the hazards this venture presented to him. He had been warned off being seen in Xanana's company previously, and by taking part in the ruse we were plotting he faced the prospect of sanctions. The idea was that John and Xanana would stand together, close to the entrance to the hall where the Christmas Mass would be celebrated, so that my encounter with Xanana would appear to be merely casual, the attention of the guards and other authorities focussed instead upon my reunion with 'Uncle John'. It seemed that nothing could go wrong.

However, two days later, I received a further batch of correspondence from Xanana, to which had been added a hurriedly written note:

> Querida, what bad news I have to tell you! This morning, I was chatting with one of the intelligence agents who has been assigned to keep an eye on me. As he took his leave,

> he mentioned that he would see me again on 22 December. Horrified, I asked him as casually as I could what he meant and he responded that he would come for the Christmas celebrations. Oh, Kirsty, what does this mean for our plans for your visit? If your presence is noted by the intelligence, will they not attempt to follow you afterwards? Querida, I want so much to see you, but will I be able to live with myself if something is to happen to you, if I lose you??!!

I resisted the temptation to cry. I was trying so hard not to focus my thoughts on the joy a face-to-face meeting with Xanana would bring, and yet, as 22 December grew closer, I found that I was unable to think about anything else. I had bought a new blouse for the occasion, and the basket of jams, pickles and fruit I would carry with me to present to Uncle John sat perched on the corner of my desk, alongside the other 'props' required for the success of the mission: a fake ID card, a selection of business cards giving my name as Anna Slade and my address as somewhere in Liverpool, England. I had no idea what sort of documentation I would be required to surrender at the gates of Cipinang, but thought it best to be prepared. Now it seemed that all my meticulous planning was in vain.

I wrote to Xanana to assure him that I did not fear the Intel and that since I was in the process of hunting for alternative accommodation – the contract on the house in Gandaria Selatan was about to expire – it didn't matter anyway whether they came to know of my address. On the evening of 20 December, Vera phoned me to say that she had managed to convince the other members of her group and that I should meet her at her office at 9 am on 22 December.

The traffic was unusually light, and my taxi pulled up at the front gate of Vera's office at 8:45 am. She was nowhere to be seen. Had she had second thoughts, perhaps? I felt a little ridiculous standing there on the curb, clutching my basket of goodies to my chest – a modern-day Red Riding Hood, with an incarcerated

'Uncle' in place of Granny and a swarm of eagle-eyed Intel agents playing the wolf. It had been raining all night, and the air was cool, but I could feel the sweat gathering at the nape of my neck and between my breasts already. I was mopping at my perspiration desperately as Vera drew up in a Blue Bird taxi with two or three other passengers. Unlike me, they looked calm and composed and they greeted me cheerfully as I joined them in the cool interior of the car. From her spot in the front seat, Vera glanced back at me and smiled occasionally as we wended our way eastwards and her friends engaged me in polite conversation.

Soon we were leaving behind the concrete overpasses that intersected at the point where Jakarta Pusat (Central Jakarta) became Jakarta Timur (East Jakarta), and the taxi began to weave a course between the motorbikes and jam-packed city buses along Jalan Raya Bekasi. By the time the walls of the prison came into view, my heart was beating uncontrollably and I could no longer make sense of what Vera's colleagues were saying to me. It was as if my brain and mouth had switched to autopilot to permit my soul to run ahead to the place where I knew Xanana would now be waiting for me.

There seemed to be between fifty and sixty people gathered at the heavy gates of the prison. They were all dressed in their Sunday best and the smell of perfume and aftershave was thick in the humid air as we joined them in the prison's muddy forecourt. There was a small square opening in the heavy metal door, the main entrance to Cipinang. Every now and again it flew noisily open and the face of a guard appeared in the dim cavity to bark orders at the waiting visitors. Handfuls of paper and yellow ID cards were passed back and forth through the hole and then, every ten minutes or so, the heavy gates were unbolted and a group of about twenty waiting visitors was ushered inside.

Everyone but me seemed to be well versed in the ritual. I felt like Dorothy at the gates of Oz. I was painfully conspicuous, the only foreigner among the would-be entrants, whose numbers were dwindling as more and more visitors gained entry to the prison.

Vera handed over my fake ID card with those of the members of her group and a list of our names. The ten minutes that followed were excruciating. It was now 10:30 am, and I imagined Xanana glancing impatiently at his watch as the minutes ticked by and the moment of truth approached.

A portly guard with a heavy moustache and an unsmiling expression had appeared in our midst. 'It's Pak Sinaga, the man in charge of prison security,' whispered Vera. I struck up a lively conversation with one of Vera's friends, hoping to give the impression that my presence there was the most natural thing in the world, and that it was neither here nor there to me whether I was able to celebrate the Christmas season with a bunch of unfortunate prison inmates.

Before Sinaga had a chance to notice or approach me, the metal flap clanked open once more and I felt Vera's hand at my back, propelling me towards the door. I was inside Cipinang. I tried not to smile too ecstatically as I heard the sound of the doors closing shut at our backs. I hooked my arm through Vera's as we were ferried beyond the gloomy entrance hall by a woman guard wearing a Muslim veil and an ankle-length skirt. The interior of the prison was more attractive than I had imagined, with neatly kept gardens lining the pathways that led from one section of the prison to the other. The guard instructed us with a stern jerk of her head to wait to be led to the hall, and then she disappeared.

In order to stop myself from trembling, I had to clench every muscle in my body. With her arm still hooked through mine, Vera must have felt the sudden tautness in my torso and interpreted it as fear or nervousness. 'Jangan kuatir [don't worry],' she whispered out of the corner of her mouth. I returned her smile, shifting my weight awkwardly from one foot to the other. I felt like a child who had just been handed a lolly and who feared having it whisked out of reach at any minute.

I glanced around me, taking in the scene as if I was somehow not part of it, but rather viewing it through the lens of a daydream. I smiled a little private smile as I stared up into the grey-blue sky, remembering the descending helicopters of my Macau fantasy. A prison warden strode past us now and again, answering the cheerful 'Selamat pagi' of the members of our group with a cursory nod of the head. Small groups of inmates dressed in navy blue uniforms sauntered by, some of them slowing down to stare at us with expressions of curiosity and others deliberately averting their gaze, perhaps for fear of being recognised by one of us.

The woman guard appeared before us again and muttered something I didn't catch. Soon she was heading down the pathway that ran parallel to the front wall of the prison and the predominantly female members of our group fell in behind her like a gaggle of obedient geese. Never for a minute letting go of Vera's arm, I allowed my body to be swept along with the movement of the crowd. By now it was only a matter of seconds before I would be standing in front of the man I loved. Just the thought of it caused a swarm of butterflies to start ricocheting off the insides of my stomach. The distance we had to walk was perhaps only fifty metres or so, but the sun was by now high in the sky and the slight exertion sent rivulets of perspiration coursing down my back. We rounded a corner and there was the entrance to what I supposed was the hall. Would he and John be there as planned? Or had the delay in our entry made it untenable for them to maintain their position?

As we entered, I released my grip on Vera's arm, shifting the basket from one clammy palm to another and scanning the scene in front of me. The hall was abuzz with the excited chatter of a hundred or more visitors and inmates. Tinsel decorations in the shape of Christmas trees adorned the walls, lengths of tatty streamers slung between them. As my eyes adjusted to the relative darkness of the interior of the building, I made out the tall figure of John Edwards standing at the edge of one of the long rows of chairs, and as I moved in his direction, the man at his side turned from the guard to whom he was talking to face me.

Xanana wore a pale blue shirt and a smile that beckoned me to him. It took every ounce of energy and willpower in my body to resist the temptation to run forward into his arms. Instead, I wrested my gaze from Xanana's beaming face and turned my attention to Uncle John, a tall, sandy-haired man in his late forties. As John stooped to receive my kiss, I said loudly for the benefit of the guard who stood looking on, 'Merry Christmas, Uncle John. I am so happy to see you again.' He accepted the basket I held out to him and then, as the script demanded, he turned to Xanana and announced, 'Let me introduce Xanana Gusmão, my friend and fellow inmate.' Perhaps he added something else about his friend being famous and 'surely you must have heard of him'.

But I heard nothing. All I was conscious of were Xanana's eyes fixed on mine, the pressure of his hand in my hand. As he bowed his head slightly in a formal gesture of greeting, I heard his voice whisper to the floor 'Querida, bem-vinda [Welcome, darling]'.

'Pleasure to meet you,' I replied, forcing my hand to release its grip on Xanana's.

Next to us appeared João and Fernando. Again, the desire to betray my true feelings, to embrace them both, was overwhelming. Instead, the rules of the game dictated that I offer them only a hand to shake and a polite exchange of greetings. We must have been reasonably successful in keeping up the appearance of cool detachment, because there was no attempt on the part of any of the guards to separate us as we moved to the nearest row of red metal fold-up chairs.

As we sat down, Uncle John on my left and Xanana on my right, a wave of contentment surged up from somewhere inside me. Somehow it didn't matter that I was unable to embrace and kiss Xanana as I wished. To feel his presence beside me was joy enough at that moment. One of the prison guards was moving along the rows of chairs, handing out a photocopied program and song sheet. As Xanana passed one to me, his fingers lingered deliberately over mine in a furtive caress. I returned the pressure, searching for the word or phrase that would adequately express the depth of the happiness that I felt at that moment. I found nothing except a sudden and surprising shyness. 'I don't know what to say,' I murmured out of the corner of my mouth. Actually, there was very little to say. I remembered Xanana's description of his reunion with his children. It was another of those moments that demanded to be given over to feeling. And as for news or the communication of practical matters, there was little to add to the copious words of our correspondence.

The attention of the inmates and visitors alike turned briefly to the front of the hall where Pak Sinaga stood blowing at a big black microphone. 'Tes, tes, satu, dua, tiga.' The microphone let out a shrill squeal, causing a collective giggle to erupt from the crowd. The acoustics were appalling, but I gathered that Sinaga was welcoming us all to the prison. He then proceeded to outline the day's program in a monotone that induced instant lethargy in the audience.

John Edwards called out, 'Get on with it, mate,' and, turning to me with a cheeky smile, added, 'It's the heckler in me. Sorry, Anna. Never was one for officialdom. Wanna lolly?' He peeled back the silver wrapping on a packet of mints and offered it to me.

I accepted, popped a mint into my mouth and passed the packet down the line to Vera, who was sitting on the other side of Xanana. As I lunged to retrieve the mints, I caught a smell of Xanana's familiar perfume, the scent with which he sprinkled his letters to me. I turned my head to him, keeping my eyes focussed on the scene at the front of the hall. A choral group made up of a motley bunch of inmates was assembling around the microphone. 'You have the smell of your letters.' Without taking my eyes off the stage, I knew that Xanana was smiling.

'Yes, querida. And you smell like the women I love. Don't be jealous! They are my Professora and my Private Secretary. And today they have made me fall in love with this beautiful prison. You must get angry with them, querida! They make me want to stay here forever, life imprisonment . . .'

I made a tutting noise with my tongue, flashing a look of amused exasperation in Xanana's direction. His face broke into a broad smile, the playful glint in his eyes flashing as he shot me a wink. I was struck by his teeth. They were large and even and the only feature of Xanana's face with which I was not yet acquainted. In all the photos I had seen of him, he was serious, unsmiling. Apart from his teeth, there was an uncanny familiarity about this man I was meeting today for the first time. It was clichéd and nonsensical, but it was as if we had spent many years already in one another's company and the result was the extraordinary sense of ease, security and well-being I now felt in his presence. I wondered whether Xanana had the same feeling, but there was no opportunity to ask.

I noticed the guards making upward motions with their hands. The strains of the first hymn reverberated through the building and we got to our feet to join the choral group in singing 'Sembah dan puji Dia [Worship and praise Him]'. Apart from Vera and the members of her group, few people appeared to know the hymn, and our efforts were tuneless and half-hearted. Xanana nudged me gently, calling my attention to the figure of Sinaga, who was loitering at the end of our row of chairs. As I glanced over at him, he caught my eye and I looked away again quickly, taking a sudden interest in the words on my song sheet. Had he decided perhaps that I shouldn't be there? 'Oh, God, don't let him throw me out now,' I whispered to Xanana's shoulder.

In reply he merely indicated on his own sheet the point we were up to in the hymn. I exhaled noisily as Sinaga walked on past us.

Half an hour and three hymns later, small white boxes and cups of drinking water were handed out to the guests and inmates. It was lunch, the first meal Xanana and I ate together. It mattered little that the prison fare resembled airline food. In the boxes were sticky green rice cakes, a portion of fried rice and a lady's finger banana wrapped in a paper napkin. The decibel level in the hall rose considerably as the official part of the proceedings gave way to the noisy consumption of lunch and conversation between the prisoners and the visitors.

I was hungry and thirsty, but before I could stab the straw through the thin plastic lid of my water cup, Xanana was offering me his own, a mischievous smile forming on his lips as he leant close, whispering, 'Bebe, querida [Drink, darling]. Uhpp, uhpp.' I remembered the words of his first recorded message and stifled a giggle. I let him hold the cup as I drained its contents through the straw, my eyes flitting constantly between Xanana's face and the group of guards standing in a huddle by the door of the hall. It seemed that they were deep in conversation and that Xanana's intimate gesture had gone unnoticed.

Uncle John then stood, hauled me to my feet and passed my camera down the line of seats to Vera. 'Would you do us the honours, love? Only God knows when dear Anna and my paths will cross again. You, too, old buddy.' He motioned to Xanana to join us. It suddenly occurred to me that it was odd that I was the only one who seemed to have brought a camera with me. Was it possible that the guards had forgotten or were too embarrassed to ask me to leave my old Pentax at the front office? In any case, a photo session provided the perfect cover for the hug and squeeze Xanana and I had been trying hard not to give one another during the hymns. Xanana's hand tightened around my waist as Vera manoeuvred to get the three of us in frame. John was calling out to Vera – to move back, to get the focus right, to make sure she didn't cut our heads off – but all I could hear was the sound of the blood rushing through my veins, my heart pounding like a hammer in my chest. I allowed Xanana to draw me closer against his body as Vera continued to snap away. Uncle John edged in closer, too, resting his head on my shoulder so that Xanana, on my right side, could follow suit without attracting the attention of onlookers. I felt his beard tickling the skin of my cheek as we grinned into the camera lens again and again, wishing that the roll of film and this moment of physical togetherness would never end.

But the final hymn was sung at around 3 pm. 'How about dinner and a movie?' I whispered to Xanana as we took our seats again. He answered me with a desolate smile. Sinaga took the stage once more to conclude the day's proceedings with some words of thanks to the visitors and a request that we dispose of our empty lunch boxes and water containers in the rubbish bins on our way out of the hall. My heart was already aching with the pain of our imminent parting.

As we shuffled out of the row of seats, Xanana took me by the hand and the ridiculous thought that I could perhaps ask permission to stay surfaced in my mind. Uncle John, perhaps noting my sorrow, scooped up my face in his large hands and planted a kiss in the middle of my forehead. 'I'll let you buy me a beer when I get out of here in eight months time, Anna,' he said with a wink and a smile.

'You know I'd trade places with you if I could,' was all I could think to say. It was true. At that moment I would have gladly forfeited my freedom if incarceration meant being able to remain within the walls of the prison. I turned to Xanana, who hadn't released his grip on my hand. I didn't care any more whether the eyes of the guards or the departing guests were upon us. I leant forward and kissed him on the mouth. There was a faint tang of tobacco on his moustache from the cigarette he had smoked after lunch.

His breath was warm on the skin below my ear as he whispered, 'We won, querida.' I felt Vera tugging on my sleeve, urging me to join the throng of visitors who were flooding out the doors of the hall. Xanana made a gesture which said 'Go', gave my hand one last squeeze, and then turned and joined João, Fernando and Uncle John, who were smiling their farewells to me from a few metres away.

Once again I fell in behind the crowd of visitors. I felt buoyant. The victory had indeed been sweet. I could still feel Xanana's breath on my cheek, the tender tone of his voice in my ears. But as we reached the prison's front office, I was aware of feeling suddenly empty. Where the butterflies had been flitting wildly only a few hours before there was now only a hollow cavity. And then, as I passed through the heavy front door of Cipinang prison, I was reminded of Dorothy in Oz once again. Leaving the jail was like stepping back into the monochrome world of Kansas after a brief time in the brilliant technicolour of the Land of Oz. Vera was hailing a taxi. I was smiling to myself, reflecting on the irony of the metaphor, as we clambered on board the cab.

The following day I moved into a new house in Tebet, Central Jakarta, taking Yati and my growing collection of bonsai plants with me. Yati had pleaded with me not to leave her with Charles, so we simply packed up and left while he was out at work.

The new house was comfortable and private, with a rooftop garden offering unspectacular views of the grimy Jakarta skyline. Best of all, however, Tebet's rabbit warren of narrow little streets lay just north of the main arterial road linking the fashionable suburbs of Kebayoran to the snaking concrete flyovers of eastern Jakarta. And here, in the heart of Jakarta Timur, the whitewashed walls of LP Cipinang imposed themselves on the local landscape like a monstrous ocean liner that had run aground. The new proximity to Xanana was more of a psychological bonus than of any practical use, since I knew deep down that I was not likely to be granted further access to the prison. Nevertheless, Xanana and I were now virtually neighbours, and I derived a singular comfort from the fact.

Chapter nine

TUNNEL OF TIME
New Year–September 1995

I WASN'T SURE that I believed in destiny, but it did seem that by allowing myself to fall in love with Xanana I had put my life on a parallel course with his and indeed that of East Timor. I now had a personal stake in the future of the country – independence was more than just a political goal, it was the objective which would allow Xanana and me to realise our private dreams. This thought weighed heavily upon me at times. I had always believed myself to be in control of everything, every event, every circumstance, every decision which had a bearing on my happiness. It was more than a little disconcerting and disempowering to reflect on how, seemingly overnight, the shape of my future seemed to have become dependent instead on the decisions and actions of others, mostly men whom I had never met and was not likely to. Men in suits and ties on the other side of the world, men with stars on their shoulders and guns in their hands.

For the time being at least, Xanana himself was effectively excluded from playing a role in negotiating a settlement of the

East Timor case. José Ramos-Horta had updated me in Macau on the status of the diplomatic struggle. Indonesia continued to insist that Xanana was a mere common criminal, refusing to give serious consideration to the CNRM's peace plan and refusing to countenance East Timorese participation in the UN-sponsored process of tripartite negotiations involving the UN, Portugal and Indonesia. The first of a series of UN-brokered meetings involving East Timorese of differing shades of political opinion was planned for the middle of 1995, but it seemed unlikely that substantive issues would be discussed, since the agenda excluded discussion of the political status of the territory.

Nevertheless, I entered the New Year with a happy heart. The memory of my first face-to-face meeting with Xanana still shed its warm glow on my daily life, making the practical difficulties of juggling my various roles all the more bearable. By now I was receiving an almost daily mail delivery and more and more of my time was spent following up the matters of both a personal and 'professional' nature raised in Xanana's letters.

Early in 1995, Xanana sent me a letter which caused me to reflect further upon the notion of destiny and the different belief systems which underpinned our two worlds. It contained a passage describing the long march which he and the population of the easternmost region of East Timor had made in an attempt to flee the bombing campaigns of 1978–79, and the tales of a visionary which had presaged Xanana's eventual assumption of command of the armed struggle. Halfway to Matebian mountain, where the headquarters of Fretilin's Central Committee were established, Xanana was spotted by the visionary, a man in his forties. 'He is the one who will lead this struggle,' declared the man. The onlookers were incredulous, given that Xanana was, at that point, a junior member of Fretilin's Central Committee. Xanana himself was astonished. Nevertheless, it was undeniable that many of the visionary's predictions came true, sometimes within days, weeks or months, and in some cases, years later.

> He described how it would not be long before the people would succumb to the force of the enemy and, like many of the guerrilla fighters, would be obliged to surrender. The period that followed, he said, would be one of great confusion and, finally I would become responsible for taking the struggle forward . . .
>
> Eight years later, one of those who had listened to the man's prophecies, and who in 1986 was a member of the Fretilin Central Committee, recounted this story to us. Many things had happened, just as the man had foreseen them. Don't forget that this prophet was only able to read and write his own name!
>
> Could this be what we call destiny?
>
> He had said also that it will take a long, long time but that we will win. Not with the policy of weapons, but with the weapon of policy . . . and that multinational forces would supervise the withdrawal of the Indonesian Armed Forces from East Timor!

I had never consulted a fortune-teller in my life. I didn't even read the horoscopes. Whilst the future scenario foreseen by the visionary in Xanana's tale was a positive one that I desperately wanted to believe in, the sceptic in me harboured some doubts. My Western rationalist upbringing caused me to question all phenomena and events that did not have a scientific explanation. The spiritual and the power of unseen forces were not part of my world view. By the same token, my parents had always engendered in their children a high degree of tolerance of the cultures and ways of life of other peoples. My brother and I had been taught to respect the deeply held beliefs of others, and I was intensely curious about the world of amulets, taboos and ancestor spirits which Xanana described so vividly in his letters to me. Whilst the milieu in which Xanana himself had grown up and been educated aspired to a more modern, European philosophy of life, he had clearly been tremendously influenced by the pre-Christian animism and spiritualism of the people he fought alongside in the mountains of East Timor.

In Jakarta in 1995, I had the magic of technology and its tools to put at Xanana's disposal in the service of the freedom struggle. My friend Colin Renwick visited me regularly in Jakarta. He was an English car mechanic turned computer techno-wiz, who helped me hone my skills in the area of secure communications using email and the Internet. Over the years, he trained a handful of East Timorese NGOs and human rights activists in the art of email and encryption, ensuring them a safe line of communication with the world. I was intrigued to learn from Colin that the leader of the Zapatista liberation army in Mexico, the enigmatic Subcomandante Marcos, sent out regular email updates on his struggle from his jungle hide-out in Chiapas, southern Mexico.

In early 1995 Colin sold me a diminutive Toshiba laptop, with the latest software installed, to send to Xanana. Certain that Xanana would never have encountered a computer before in his life, I spent many evenings translating the most basic commands into Portuguese and explaining how to perform essential functions such as saving, copying and encrypting files. To lighten things up a bit, I installed a copy of my favourite game – Wheel of Fortune – on the laptop's hard disk. To my surprise, the laptop was safely delivered into Xanana's hands, thanks to the daring of one of the prison guards and the Rp 50,000 note which I discreetly taped to the outermost layer of newspaper encasing the machine.

A week or so later I received a diskette containing Xanana's first encrypted letter to me. A wave of intense satisfaction and pride came over me as I managed to decrypt the file and the hieroglyphics were replaced with Xanana's words – a full ten pages of them. I was proud of him for having successfully performed the operation in the absence of a tutor, and of myself for having managed to teach him in the most difficult and unorthodox of circumstances. We had discovered a completely foolproof means of communicating with one another. Even if the diskettes passing between us were intercepted, their contents were secure and private thanks to a simple piece of public domain software.

Xanana's first electronic letter to me contained an account of the severe back and kidney pain he had been experiencing for the past month.

'I have problems with my vertebral column, a result of, amongst other things, military exercises in Portuguese times. Do you know that I was the one who introduced the mortal jump over the top of cars in military exercises? Now I am suffering the consequences of trying to be the best at everything. I must also have broken my wrist at some time. Whilst the break has healed, it still causes me pain when I lift things or exert myself, such as when I mop the floor. You see I am an old, broken rheumatic thing. Do you still like me?'

I felt powerless to do anything to help Xanana. The previous November he had received a visit from a medical team from the International Committee of the Red Cross. The doctor had suggested that he have an x-ray to determine whether or not he had kidney stones, but the prison authorities were insistent that the x-ray could only be done at the military hospital. Xanana was understandably reluctant to place himself in the care of military doctors, preferring to seek medical attention at the Cikini Catholic Hospital where Fernando had been treated for a kidney ailment the previous year. But Cikini hospital cost money and the monthly allowance from Amnesty International would not stretch to cover hospital bills, medication and the *uang saku*, or pocket money, payable to each of the prison guards required to keep watch over Xanana while he was in hospital. I decided to get in touch with the Joint Committee for the Defence of East Timorese, a coalition of four NGOs and the Indonesian Legal Aid Institute. They routinely advocated on behalf of East Timorese students and activists who were in need of legal counsel and humanitarian support. The committee's secretary was Ibu Ade Rostina, a spirited Sumatran woman whose conservative dress and big hair belied the courage and political daring she was renowned for. I found her companionable and sympathetic to the problem of Xanana's need for medical attention. Not only did she offer to help me with identifying a source of funding for his hospitalisation, but she also invited me to join her and her Christian prison service group in visiting Cipinang at Easter time. I could hardly wait to write to Xanana to share the good news with him.

The sixth plant in my collection of bonsais arrived in March 1995. The time I had to tend to them – to trim, fertilise and de-bug according to Xanana's instructions – was limited, and I felt bad that one or two of them were losing their carefully manicured shape. I began to regret that the green fingers of my parents and grandparents had failed to rub off on me. I joked with Xanana that one day a row of rambling bonsais would sit on the verandah of the *palhota*, or shack, we were planning to build in the mountains of East Timor, their formless branches and oversized leaves recalling the neglect of their former guardian.

In addition to the bonsais, I also began to receive regular deliveries of other prison produce, such as the huge green guavas growing in the unkempt garden of Cipinang's Tim-Tim (East Timor) block, bunches of Chinese cabbage and small loaves of bread which João baked in a rudimentary oven rigged up to a kerosene burner. I knew well that these gifts were Xanana and João's way of repaying me for my support of them and the independence cause. Xanana often lamented the fact that he was unable to do more to ease the burden of my daily responsibilities, and I knew that stocking my refrigerator with supplies was his way of contributing, of feeling that he was being useful to me.

The mail was by now so regular and so voluminous that it was no longer practical for me to rendezvous with the couriers on street corners or in the parking lots of shopping centres. On many occasions, even the Timorese middle man was removed and one or two of the more trustworthy guards would actually make deliveries direct to my home. At first I was a little reluctant for them to know my address and identity, but it soon became clear that Xanana had worked his charm on them so successfully that their loyalty was virtually guaranteed. Often one guard, whom I knew as 'Ruben', would quiz me on the situation inside East Timor as he sat waiting for me to package up the return mail. He seemed genuinely astonished and concerned to learn that the reality in the territory differed greatly from that presented to him by the local media.

I was bitterly disappointed when I failed to get into the prison at Easter time. Pak Sinaga, perhaps remembering me from my Christmas visit to Uncle John, barred my entry with a resolute 'orang asing tidak bisa' (no foreigners) and refused to budge, in spite of Ibu Ade's polite remonstrations. Back at home, my head swimming with images of the Easter service going ahead in my absence, Ibu Ade at Xanana's side, I recorded a tearful message into my tape recorder and spent the afternoon feeling desperately alone and miserable. The following morning Ruben delivered the blossom of a rose which Xanana had cultivated himself, a wad of saturated tissues tied to its stem to keep it fresh. It was no substitute for the second face-to-face meeting I had wanted so much to take place, but it did help take the edge off the disappointment. Along with the flower came a cassette. It contained a selection of songs which Xanana had managed to record from the small television that João and Fernando had purchased for him. They were mainly ballads and love songs – Elton John's 'Can You Feel the Love Tonight?', Mariah Carey's 'Hero' – and each one was prefaced with some words of dedication to me. 'This is one of my favourite songs. Oh, if only I had the voice, I would sing it to you, querida?!'

Meanwhile, the atrocities in East Timor continued. Amnesty International contracted me to conduct a series of interviews with East Timorese women, principally those who had survived rape or another act of sexual violence. In the process of identifying appropriate interviewees amongst the student population in Jakarta, I came across Adelina. She was an intelligent, outspoken young woman whose eyes flashed as she spoke of her experiences as a member of the clandestine front in Dili, only to suddenly grow dim and downcast as she recalled the torture or rape of a friend or relative. Her forthright manner left an impression on me and, since I knew that she was planning to visit family in Dili in June, I recommended to Xanana that we make use of her as a courier of documents and other items of correspondence destined for the resistance in the town and in the mountains.

It was a strange birthday that April. It rained heavily for a while and then the electricity blacked out for a couple of hours. In the morning I received an enormous chocolate cake, which Xanana had asked someone to order from 'outside'. Then, in the early afternoon, another cake arrived along with a huge guava the size of a football, a plate of still-warm chicken fried in garlic, and a Cipinang-bred *ikan lele*, or freshwater fish, still alive and struggling to free itself from its black plastic bag. Yati put an end to the fish's wriggling with a solid clout and he joined the other prison fare as part of my birthday dinner.

In a letter which accompanied the *ikan lele*, Xanana announced the second component of his birthday present for me: his plan for me to travel to Los Palos in East Timor to meet the Falintil guerrillas. This 'gift', offering as it would exposure to his world, was extremely meaningful and generous. It demonstrated both Xanana's power – to be able to organise such an undertaking from prison – and his love for and trust in me. Given the deteriorating human rights situation in the country, the visit was going to be no easy feat. Nevertheless, I responded to the gift enthusiastically and we set about making the necessary contacts, debating the advantages and disadvantages of different dates for the trip.

Xanana turned forty-nine on 20 June. In spite of the fact that he had succeeded in obtaining permission to have his kidney stones removed in a civilian hospital a month earlier, I knew that he continued to be assailed by concerns that he was getting old and succumbing to ill health. I considered that it might reassure him to know that I, too, was prone to angst over the effects of time's passing. As a present, I had Yati take a photograph of me gazing at the painting Xanana had done of me one year earlier. I wore the same hairstyle as in the painting, and, as in the original photograph, only the back of my head and torso were visible. I had an enlargement of the photograph made and I sent it to him with a note which read: 'My Love, you must do another painting of this photo. And then next year I will take a photo of me looking at the painting of the photo of me looking at the painting of the photo . . . until, one glorious day an image of a woman gazing into a time tunnel, contemplating the landscape of her past, will hang on the wall of a *palhota* in the mountains of East Timor. My hope and my wish for your forty-ninth birthday, my love, is this: that the final painting contains the image of very few Kirstys and that the "me" standing in the present of the foreground does not have white hair!'

We gained a fine addition to our technological arsenal at this time: a mobile telephone. In Jakarta in 1995, mobile phones had yet to become the ubiquitous accessory of modern life they are today, and only a handful of business executives seemed to make use of them. Xanana had become aware of their existence inside the prison when a Singaporean 'neighbour' of his, doing time for allegedly laundering money, had one seized in a raid on his cell. And so Xanana instructed one of the Timorese student leaders to look into acquiring a phone. Unbeknownst to us, the first one smuggled in to Xanana was a black-market phone that used someone else's phone line. When the telecommunications company started tracing the number to which calls were being made – namely, my telephone number – I decided that Xanana needed a more legitimate, above-board mobile account and I set about signing up for one.

The telephone changed the tenor of the resistance's communication dramatically. And as well as enabling instantaneous exchanges on all manner of issues relating to East Timor's situation, we could have discussions about feminism and even lovers' tiffs. I harboured a fear that if we ever did have the opportunity to have a normal life together we might not get on. Perhaps that's why I pushed the limits; when I felt it necessary I challenged Xanana, tried to show him what I thought and who I was. I wanted us to be able to disagree, to be able to deal with conflicts, which were going to be inevitable when we finally had the chance to have a day-to-day life in each other's company.

One day he sent me a letter in which I detected, on an abstract level, a hint of a double standard regarding attitudes towards men's behaviour and women's behaviour. I responded with red comments in the margin of his letter, which I sent back to him. Xanana did not receive my queries happily – he promptly returned the mobile phone to me. It was his way of rejecting me. Overcoming my pride, I resolved to return the phone to him. I knew he would be expecting it back.

The prison 'courier' came earlier than I expected that day, before I had had a chance to pack up the mobile phone, and before I had written a conciliatory letter to Xanana. I sat the courier down with an *air putih* (drinking water) and the latest edition of *Gatra*, a popular magazine. I tried in my letter to be as understanding and sympathetic as possible without compromising my 'principles'. Emotional vulnerability was clearly something Xanana had not had to grapple with before. Later that evening, on the telephone, he greeted me with a cold and emotionless 'Boa noite'. I knew the battle wasn't over yet.

Nevertheless, despite my resolutions about establishing an open and honest relationship, his powerlessness, the paralysis of his life in prison, was not easy for either of us to deal with. It was a tradition that every year, on the anniversary of Indonesia's independence, some prisoners would be granted amnesty and some others would be given sentence reductions. On 29 July 1995 the *Jakarta Post* announced the news of the imminent release of three elderly political prisoners, who had been imprisoned for thirty years for their involvement with the Indonesian Communist Party.

Soon after, Xanana related to me his discussions with the other *napis* (prisoners) regarding possibilities of amnesty or at least remission. He was beginning to think about where we would go, what we would do, if he were to be released on 17 August – right down to those fine details of planning that remain his forte. Our conversation was full of laughter and gaiety, but whilst he didn't deny that to speculate in such a way was fraught with potential for great disappointment, it was difficult for me not to feel a little sadness for Xanana.

The next day I arrived home from work exhausted at 5:30 pm, knowing that he must have been trying to call all day. Because it was Wednesday, visiting day, a pile of mail and gifts was waiting for me – a cake, a letter rolled up in a painting (my mother's birthday present), two small containers of brilliant blue ornamental fish. The roses sharing the fish's water had caused some of the fish to die, and I launched a rapid rescue operation to save the remaining ones.

My body was craving sleep and my head was spinning, but I forced myself to read Xanana's letter. The pretty blue fish were Spanish fighting fish. 'You must take care not to mix the males and the females as they will fight to the death.' The letter also related in detail the plans for my impending journey to West Java with Leman. Leman was one of Xanana's prison colleagues – he had served several years on a criminal charge, on which Xanana was sure he was wrongly convicted – and he was to be released on 17 August. A few weeks earlier Leman had dreamt that he had had *rejeki*, or divine good fortune, conferred upon him. In his dream he had been told to share the *rejeki* with Xanana. Leman was to take receipt of his good fortune after he left prison.

As far as Xanana was concerned, Leman's story was convincing. Leman's powers and the special connection between him and Xanana were further verified when a couple of separate prison officials reported seeing them talking under a red umbrella in the prison grounds, when no such incident had taken place.

Leman's mother had died when he was a small boy, and soon after that he had run away from his home in Tasikmalaya. For some years he had eked out a living in Cirebon, assisting a local Islamic cleric or *kyai* in his work and receiving instruction in his 'art'. The *kyai* were spiritual leaders who wielded considerable social and even political power in their communities. Suharto was known to regularly consult a particularly powerful *kyai* who resided in the Cirebon area.

Xanana asked me to receive the *rejeki* on his behalf and proceeded to organise my trip with Leman to his home village of

Purwawinangun near Tasikmalaya in West Java. He worked out what gifts we would give to Leman's family, and how much money we would need. He warned me of all sorts of tests I might have to undergo, presumably as a means of strengthening my resolve and courage. Leman had spoken to him of a dwarf who lived in those parts. He was a man resembling an ugly, dirty troll, no taller than sixty centimetres but with a nose measuring close to half a metre in length. He ate glass, chickens, the heads of snakes, rats and raw eggs. If he was to approach me or even to attempt to kiss me, it was of the utmost importance that I not recoil and that I show him compassion and understanding. This experience, Xanana advised me, would be a form of preparation for the serpents which Leman had warned him were part of the *rejeki* ritual.

He gave me a list of things to ask to the seven *kyai* we would encounter. At the top of the list of requests was the power to influence Suharto on the question of a resolution of the East Timor problem. We were to attempt to locate the *kyai* known to be associated with Suharto and appeal to him to reason with the old dictator to allow the intervention of the United Nations and the eventual holding of a referendum. The other requests were less ambitious. We were to appeal for protection for Xanana for the period of his imprisonment and for me in the course of my daily work, in particular during my forthcoming visit to the Falintil guerrillas. In addition, I was to present the ongoing problem of funding for our activities and those of the resistance generally. 'And, if they could help out with a little something to guarantee that you get past Sinaga [the prison guard] at Christmas and Easter, that would be nice, too.'

In spite of my natural cynicism, I was prepared to suspend my disbelief and to make the trip. My curiosity and fascination with the whole notion of *rejeki*, the insights it offered into traditional Javanese beliefs and spiritualism, were far more compelling than the vague sense of apprehension I felt. Nevertheless, I did think it wise to ask Xanana to consult with Leman as to whether or not the *rejeki* was likely to be forfeited if in the heart of the beneficiary there lurked a deep, dark scepticism. I didn't want my stubborn rationalism to stand in the way of East Timor's liberation.

Xanana's letter this particular Wednesday, 2 August, contained no 'I love yous', and the sensation that he was organising my life for me was beginning to irritate me. I was tired. He didn't call and my irritation grew. I knew that when he did call, he was bound to have a problem with my having been out all day. I drank some beer, which did nothing to relieve the fog that was gathering in my head.

When he finally called at about 9 pm, I said, 'I didn't get home until 5:30 pm.'

'I called you at 5:30 pm and there was no answer.'

There followed accusations, denials, interference on the line, and then we got cut off. I doubted that he would call back, but a few minutes later he did. He said, 'I thought you must have decided to stay out with amigas.'

'What amigas?' I tried an ironic laugh, but my blood was boiling and I couldn't resist launching an attack. 'Look, if you want me to make this trip to Leman's village, I've got to clock up sixty-five hours of work before 17 August, so don't make an issue out of this.'

'You don't have to go to Leman's village.'

'I want to go there; that's not the point.'

When the bullets had subsided a little, he mentioned with calculated flippancy that he had been called up and interrogated twice in the course of the day. The phone connection was typically bad, and he responded with audible irritation every time I asked him to repeat himself. Three Laksus (special task force personnel) had appeared at his cell. He was questioned by the prison chief and the head of security about a letter he had written to the Beijing Women's Conference and which Adelina had carried to Dili for the purpose of collecting signatures the week before. The authorities had seized a photocopy of the letter. The existence of this evidence meant that the usual denials, verbal and written, were not an option. There was almost satisfaction in his voice as he related the various possible consequences of this. Most significantly, any hopes that the Timorese prisoners would be granted the longed-for amnesty or remission were now dashed.

I wasn't sure whether my tears were brought on by my weariness, or by the sensation that this was all my fault (for having spoken favourably of Adelina, which had led Xanana to entrust her with his letter), or the uncomfortable feeling that Xanana was using this 'misfortune', and the inevitability of my feeling directly or indirectly responsible for it, to punish me for having been out all day. As I sobbed into the mouthpiece, I kept thinking how my crying must be a satisfaction to him. The words of comfort, the kisses, the request for me to stop seemed hollow and insincere, the 'sympathy' mere politeness.

In a burst of anger (with myself as much as with him), I told him that there was no need for him to pretend to be upset by my tears. 'This is what you wanted – for me to feel responsible for this incident and its consequences.' I sobbed on in silence until I had no more energy.

'Não há problemas – I am only worried about the consequences for Adelina if they arrest her.'

'Oh, you're so brave and selfless.' I was unable to put out of my mind the previous day's conversation and our hopes for his early release. The fact that he accepted all of this so easily only accentuated my own weakness and he knew it. It was like a bonus victory for him in this private war of ours, and it was all I could do not to put down the phone on his arrogant selflessness.

But I didn't and it was almost 10:15 by the time we did hang up. I was pleased to have the excuse of the email poll from Green Net in London, which came in at 10:30 pm. In order to minimise the expense involved in sending and receiving emails, Colin had made an arrangement with Green Net whereby a call would be received each evening to my modem and encrypted mail packets would criss-cross in cyberspace.

I listened to Yati heading off to bed, aware that she had probably overheard my sobbing. Then I struggled with the decryption of email files. When Xanana called again at around midnight he

Graduation day at Melbourne University, 1987. My unlikely pairing of Indonesian and Italian studies would serve me well in the days to come.

The late Sister Celeste Carvalho and me at the Baucau convent, East Timor, 1990.

The sisters and novices of the Baucau convent.

In 1991 I worked with an English documentary team travelling to East Timor to film the reality of life in an occupied nation. Here, producer Peter Gordon and cameraman Max Stahl get decked out in Bali tourist garb, our 'disguise'!

I was the researcher/interpreter on the crew, pictured here with Max Stahl.

In 1992 I decided to make the move to Jakarta and join forces with others standing by East Timor. Here I am with Victoria at a PDI (Democratic Party of Indonesia) rally.

At home in Jakarta with some of the seven East Timorese asylum seekers, June 1993. Soon after this photograph was taken, I was to accompany them to the Swedish and Finnish embassies in their risky bid for freedom.

Two of the asylum seekers, Florencio Fernandes at left and Clementino Faria.

My mother, Rosalie, and father, Brian, were so important to me during my years involved in the struggle for independence, and I treasured these brief respites when we met up for holidays. Here we are in the beautiful Moluccas, 1994.

Finally, we meet face to face: Christmas 1994 at Cipinang prison with Xanana on the left and 'Uncle' John Edwards on the right. Xanana's smile was a revelation to me.

Xanana working in the Cipinang vegetable plot: I would receive many gifts of love from its harvest.

With José Ramos-Horta, East Timor's diplomat in exile, in Lisbon, 1995.

The mobile phone became an indispensable tool, both for the cause of independence, and for our relationship.

Xanana completed dozens of paintings during his imprisonment; some were even auctioned in Australia to raise money for the East Timorese campaign.

Of all his paintings, Xanana's 'tunnel of time' gifts to me were the most precious: here are the second-last and last in the series that we both hoped would not be too long-running!

Xanana at the entrance to his Cipinang cell, around 1997.

My friend João Freitas da Camara in Cipinang prison, 1998.

In 1998 Xanana received a visit from his daughter, Zenilda, and son, Nito, at Cipinang prison. 'My daughter had dug inside me and took away all of the love she could find in a father who has always tried to be a stone heart, in order to accept the death of his soldiers.'

On 10 February 1999, Xanana was released into house arrest. Once more he could officially don the mantle as the leader of the independence movement. In the Salemba prison house, our work brokering peace and freedom for East Timor began in earnest – there was little time for a 'normal' life with Xanana's increased responsibilities.

Once agreement had been reached on a direct ballot for the East Timorese people to decide their future, pro-independence campaign rallies such as this one became a feature of life in Dili.

The evening of 30 August 1999, the East Timorese 'popular consultation': our celebrations in the prison house were tinged with sadness and a sense of foreboding, though none of us could have anticipated the violence and destruction about to be unleashed. At left is Natacha Medan, part of our Salemba support team.

The bloodshed lasted for weeks, and it was not until Indonesia was forced to seek the assistance of Interfet – the UN-sanctioned International Force in East Timor – that law and order began to be restored in Dili and the rest of East Timor.

Xanana on his first walkabout in Dili, October 1999.

Crowds gather to listen to Xanana speak on his return to his beloved *pátria*.

A young orphaned girl is comforted by Xanana, Dili, October 1999.

In July 2000, Xanana and I were married in a small and simple ceremony at Dare, the seminary in the hills behind Dili where Xanana had gone to school.

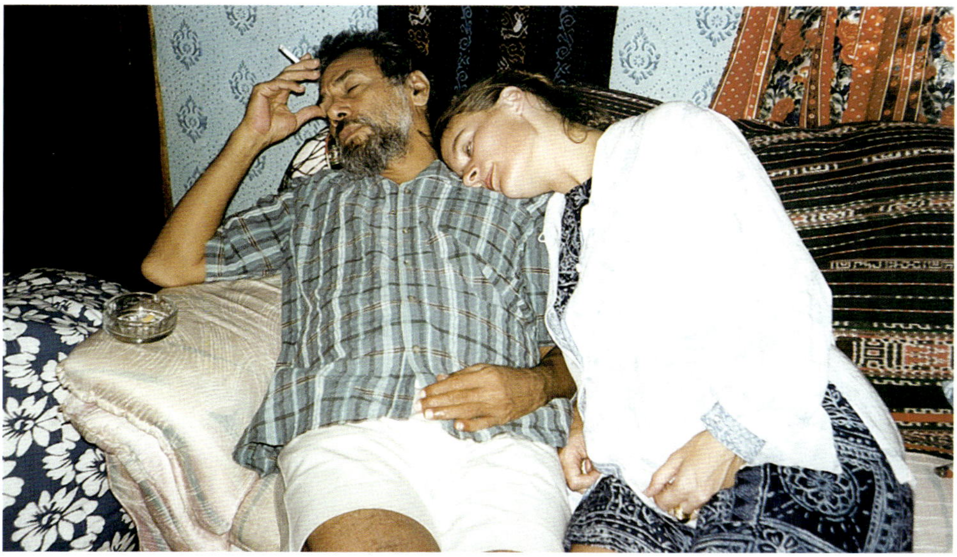

After the wedding, at home in Bemori, Dili: our gruelling workloads didn't allow for much celebration!

The birth of our first son, Alexandre, was a joyful symbol of the new life being built around us, as well as of the difficult love Xanana and I had nurtured through times of adversity.

Alexandre, aged one, in the Australian Army uniform given to him by Interfet Commander Major-General Peter Cosgrove.

In 2001 we decided to move from our house in Bemori, with its infamous open drain – I was getting tired of my fight against the mosquito enemy! Here Australian soldiers join the battle, spraying insecticide around the yard and perimeter.

We found a new home in Balibar, a hillside village ten kilometres south of Dili. The original house was small and poky, but the cool, mosquito-free environment and majestic views were perfect luxury to me.

Presidential elections were scheduled for April 2002, and Xanana was finally convinced to put off his plans for pumpkin farming and accept nomination as a candidate.

The independence celebrations of 20 May 2002 were spectacular and moving. Pictured from left to right here are President of the East Timorese Parliament Francisco Guterres (alias Lu'olo), UN Secretary-General Kofi Annan, Xanana, Indonesian President Megawati Sukarnoputri, President of the World Bank Jim Wolfensohn and me. (Photo: Jenny Grant)

With the family of Juliana dos Santos, nicknamed 'Alola', who was brutally kidnapped by a militia leader.

After working on Juliana's case, I decided to establish the Alola Foundation to draw attention to the plight of women in East Timor. One of the foundation's campaigns promotes breastfeeding to improve the health of mothers and children, as undertaken here in Dili National Hospital.

My new role as first lady of the poorest country in Asia brought tremendous change and challenges. Here I am at the NAM Summit in Kuala Lumpur, February 2003, with the first ladies of Malaysia, Nepal and Pakistan.

Our second son, Kay Olok, was born in Dili in August 2002. (Photo: Martine Perret)

related a conversation he had had with José Ramos-Horta regarding an article in the *Far Eastern Economic Review* entitled 'Who is XG?'. In it the author pointed to Xanana's written denials of his statements as proof of the fraudulence of all his messages and interviews since December 1993. The next afternoon, he told me he had been questioned again, but as ever, he thrived on the adrenalin, the sense of danger, the satisfaction of having provoked the ire of the 'regime'.

Before I departed on the *rejeki* trip I received a letter from Uncle John. He was another of the fortunate prisoners due to be released that August. His letter was both melancholy and prescient. I took heart from his sorely needed words of encouragement.

> By the way, I think I forgot to mention to you that I do have a niece called Anna. Her mother died when she was still not one year old and my other sister and her husband looked after her and took her to the USA. But she didn't like living there and came back to England and got married. She was still in Junior School the last time I saw her over twenty years ago.
>
> Please don't apologise for not writing more often. After all, my daughter has not written to me in five years, and the three boys in Australia, not in ten years. But I know that they love me and I love them, too. So months and years are nothing. I don't yet know the exact date of my release, so I don't know if it will be possible to see you. Believe me, your offer of a beer is a great enticement to a very dry Australian. Even the Simpson Desert or outback of Darwin could not be as bad. At least it's only days to the nearest pub. There's nothing so lonely or drear as a jail with no beer.
>
> So how are you? Eyes red with crying? Body aching all over through not sleeping well? It is called love sickness and no cure has yet been found other than being held in the arms of the one you love. I know that one day you will be cured. Nothing in the whole world has ever been found that will

> stop true love, so just hang in there. Nothing is impossible. When I was a teenager, I used to read a comic called Dan Dare. He would travel to the moon and other planets. My Dad would tell me it was rubbish, but he had to think again when man walked on the moon. Time waits for no man, but many women wait for true happiness for a lifetime. I trust and pray that you will find yours with Xanana.

Uncle John must have managed to negotiate a safe passage for himself out of the country, since I didn't see or hear from him again.

On the morning of 17 August, I packed a bag and headed for Cipinang to wait for Leman's release. We met at the home of one of the wardens who lived on the grimy, narrow street running along the rear wall of the prison. Leman was short, slight and unremarkable-looking – nothing about his looks or demeanour suggested that he was imbued with any special mystical powers, but I had to trust in Xanana's judgement. And so we set off in the train to Cirebon.

He had obviously been out of touch with his family for some years, because there was an emotional reunion with his father on the doorstep of his palm-thatched home on the outskirts of the dusty town of Purwawinangun. The family was very poor. The rooms of the house were separated by lengths of curtain. There were woven palm mats on the floor and no other furniture save a doorless wooden cupboard. Clothes hung from the beams of the roof. Leman's old, withered grandma observed the emotional but tearless reunion from a wooden bench in the corner of the house, seeming not to register Leman's presence. Outside, the earth was red and rich. Women, probably Leman's cousins and sisters-in-law, chased small children with plates of food, exhorting them to eat. In the days I spent with them we ate little more than rice with chilli. But there was not a troll to be found anywhere; the only really frightening spectre was that of the grinding poverty and daily hardship faced by the men and women of Purwawinangun.

And so began the rounds of visiting the *kyai*. At the home of the first *kyai*, a rather severe-looking man in a black velvet *peci* cap, we were served cups of sweet Javanese tea as we waited for two youths to conclude their consultation. From what I could make out, and from the translation and commentary provided by Leman, the two were seeking protection from the weapons of their would-be enemies. Perhaps they were planning a show-down with a rival gang. The *kyai* said a mantra over two glasses of water and then offered them to the youths to drink. Just to be sure, the *kyai* drew two long sharp pins from his chest pocket and showed the boys how to place them in the crook of their arms, the sharp end resting against the forearm. The lace curtains fluttered in the breeze as the two groaned with the exertion of flexing and drawing their wrists up to their shoulders. I gasped slightly, willing myself to look away, but finding myself unable to. To my relief and astonishment, the pins failed to pierce the youths' flesh. The *kyai* nodded his satisfaction with the result and the two boys smiled, rising from their seats to leave. So now it was our turn.

I had no idea what to expect. Leman explained in Javanese the purpose of our visit, his friendship with Xanana and the contents of our list of requests. I half-expected the *kyai* to jump from his seat and call the police to arrest us. But instead he simply listened, head bowed, and uttered a thoughtful 'Ya, ya' at regular intervals. I filled in some of the gaps in Leman's explanatory remarks by providing a bit of East Timor's recent history. After a long silence, he asked Leman to buy a small bottle of bright green *minyak angin*, an analgesic lotion which was commonly sniffed by public transport users prone to motion sickness. He closed his eyes, and said some mantras over the bottle while I wondered whether I was going to be asked to drink it down. To my relief, the bottle was returned to Leman. We were told that the oil, if placed on the temples and clothing, would confer a special protection upon the user. The suggestion was that I apply the oil prior to entering East

Timor later that year and on other occasions when I might be vulnerable to harm.

On 23 August I phoned Xanana from the only functioning public phone in Purwawinangun. He was disappointed to learn, as I had been, that Suharto's *kyai* no longer resided in the area. He sounded relieved to know that I was safe and well, and anxious to know the details of the meetings with the other *kyai*. But I ran out of coins after the first ten minutes.

The visit to the second *kyai* involved a long trek across some picturesque rice paddy fields. I was pink and a little out of breath by the time we reached his home. Leman appeared to know him intimately, as we were welcomed in with open arms. After Leman's introduction, I was invited to sit down on the floor and to raise the sleeve of my left arm. The *kyai*, a man in his early forties with tranquil eyes and skeletal hands, took out a basket of ornate perfume bottles. He rubbed them into my arm at a point between my elbow and shoulder and then took out a Javanese *kris* and gently dragged its jagged blade in a criss-cross motion across the skin there. I felt no pain, and indeed the blade did not break my skin. Then, holding the *kris* some five centimetres from my arm, I heard him mumbling a prayer or mantra in a low droning voice which appeared to belong to someone else. I felt the heat from the *kris* searing into my arm. I couldn't resist: I turned my head to look at my arm, half expecting to see a hot implement like a soldering iron poised at my shoulder. There was nothing there but the *kris*, trembling slightly in the grasp of the *kyai*, whose eyes were shut fast. Good, he hadn't seen me peeking.

On the way home, Leman informed me that this ritual had conferred upon me the power to evade danger and to be forewarned of impending threats to my well-being.

The last *kyai* was Leman's own spiritual advisor, with whom he had completed his apprenticeship so many years earlier. It turned out that he was much in demand; the long line of waiting clients meant that he had little time to attend to our long list of requests. I took away from him a small, clear bottle of white powder which, if scattered at the entrance to Cipinang, would apparently allow me to enter the prison undetected.

I didn't dare ask Leman how and when we could expect to take receipt of the *rejeki*. Perhaps it was something which came to one without one's even knowing it. If I'd shared Xanana's belief in the unseen world, and his trust of Leman, would the outcome have been different? I was relieved to return to Jakarta, taking with me the powder and oil the *kyai* had given me, just in case.

Back in Jakarta, Xanana and I usually spoke several times a day on the telephone. With the acquisition of the laptop computer I'd become his information technology troubleshooter, as well as being his English teacher and private secretary. From the photos Xanana had sent me of his cell, I knew that it was reasonably spacious, and that his living quarters were furnished with a desk, bookshelf and vinyl wardrobe. It was in the nooks and crannies of this furniture that he hid his mobile phone and computer when they were not in use. When they questioned him about such equipment he played dumb – 'I'm from the generation of '74, and then I was in the bush for seventeen years. What would I know about computers or mobile phones?' When they continued the line of questioning he was indignant. He put the key to his cell on the table. 'If you don't believe me, go and search my cell! But if you don't find anything, there will be consequences!' They backed down, the conversation changed tack, and Xanana quietly pocketed his key.

At this time Xanana was putting a lot of energy into planning my forthcoming visit to East Timor to meet the Falintil commanders. We had decided on October. He wrote to each of the guerrilla commanders stationed in the Ponta Leste (eastern point) to advise them of my arrival and to hint at the matters I would raise with them during our meeting.

One night in mid September one of my Timorese friends, Savio, told me of a plan for a new asylum bid involving ten *rapazes* (boys). I was in the middle of packing parcels, money and letters for Colin to take to Timor the following day. I still needed to prepare dinner and bathe when Xanana phoned with a question for Savio. When I replied with an answer which didn't please him, Xanana snapped and hung up. I was hurt by his anger.

Our next few exchanges that evening were brief and businesslike. It was after midnight when he called again and I had the opportunity to tell him that I felt empty, like a hollow shell, thoughtless, wordless, resentful of my role as the transmitter of the ideas and words of others. My whole day had been taken up with the petty problems of the *rapazes*. It was a tiny job really, this passing on of information between various parties, but it felt big and time-consuming enough to prevent me from articulating and recording my own thoughts and responses to the events unfolding around me.

The following day I read a novel Colin had lent me, hoping that the concepts in the book would help give some form to the thoughts and emotions clamouring for attention and expression in my tired brain. The novel was an eclectic blend of sci-fi and cyberpunk – pure, way-out escapism. The phone didn't ring all day and I'd finished the book by early afternoon. At 8:30 pm Xanana called, full of apologies – and we talked about, of all things, computer viruses. After I'd sent the email at 10:30 pm, he called back and we talked until midnight.

A week or so later, the night before the nine-month anniversary of our meeting in Cipinang, Xanana called at the end of a busy day. I announced my intention of going out to buy some dinner because there was no food in the house – Yati was away in her *kampung* (village). A stupid fight broke out over how long my shopping expedition would take.

Minutes later Savio called to say that he had the biographies of the asylum-seekers ready for me to translate. I told him to meet me at the supermarket. I returned home to the ringing phone, which I didn't answer. I knew it was Xanana and there were a few things I needed to get under control before we spoke. He kept trying, every two to three minutes. This angered me because

I felt he was checking up on me. When I eventually picked up the phone I told him that I didn't appreciate the tone of voice he had used prior to hanging up on me. Accusations were answered by counter-accusations.

I started work on translating the biographies, but I didn't get very far before Xanana called again and we exchanged more angry words, which ended in a shouting match. I started crying and, before hanging up, announced, 'Quero matar-me [I want to kill myself].' In preparation for the email poll from Green Net, I turned on the modem. He kept trying to call but I let the modem answer each time. I poured myself a stiff drink and started work on photocopying the latest set of press clippings from Portugal. The phone kept ringing. Finally, at 12:30 am, I answered his call, afraid he was worrying that I was lying in a pool of my own blood. The tears and angry words continued until just before the call to prayer at 4:30 am. Finally we called a truce and made a fragile peace.

At 7 am on 22 September, the day of our nine-month anniversary, Xanana woke me. I tried to go back to sleep after our call but the phone had started ringing and I found myself engrossed in work, stopping only long enough to cook Xanana my favourite blue cheese pasta and prepare some other things for our anniversary lunch. The phone didn't stop, but somehow I managed to get everything ready by 11:20 am, when Ruben arrived. I loaded him up with the pasta, some beer and the other things for our lunch. By 2 pm peace was fully restored and, via telephone, we enjoyed our meal together.

On 25 September the latest batch of five asylum-seekers made it into the British Embassy. Surprisingly, they were out of the country without excessive resistance on the part of the British or Indonesian governments by the end of the month. Still, I was overwhelmed by work and stress and preparations for my trip to East Timor. The *Jakarta Post* headline on the morning of 2 October – 'Suharto still needed after 1998' – was enough to send me back to bed.

That night on the telephone with Xanana I mentioned my preoccupation with getting on top of my work ahead of the visit to East Timor. My comment provoked a small argument, and then tears from Xanana. I listened to his heartbreaking sobs and his anguish at not being able to help me, and regretted the note of complaint in my voice. It seemed my brain was empty of all capacity to respond to anything but practicalities.

As promised, I called Xanana after my emailing session was over at 12:30 am. Although it was our usual practice for him to ring me, which gave him the chance to choose a suitable time, I could, with prior arrangement, call him. This particular night my call went unanswered. He had probably fallen asleep, or the battery of his mobile had died. I noticed strange clicking sounds on the line. Was it just paranoia or were they really on to me at last?

The precariousness of my position and the difficulties associated with our separation were beginning to take their toll. The pressures we were both under were enormous. We had tried to cope with them by using the mobile phone and computer to bridge the distance between us, only to find that, in some ways, these communication tools highlighted our inability to be truly together and Xanana's sense of powerlessness.

For some time, Xanana and I had been discussing my term of usefulness, my 'shelf life'. I had known from day one that I could not continue my work for the resistance in Jakarta indefinitely. Sooner or later, my activities were bound to be brought to the attention of the military intelligence. If the intelligence networks were functioning effectively, they would have known not only of my association with East Timor, but also of my connections with members of the Indonesian solidarity and pro-democracy movements. Perhaps, too, they would have known of my regular visits to the Australian Embassy on OSB business. I had always assumed that these associations with Australian officialdom would afford me a degree of protection, particularly if the intelligence was unclear about the precise nature of my relationship with my home government. They may have feared a bit of a diplomatic outcry if a move was made to arrest me. 'Naughty' foreigners were generally detained for immigration violations. On this front I was squeaky clean. I had a valid visa and work permit. With no other grounds on which to detain me, they would have had no choice but to address the very issues they wanted to keep under wraps – East Timor, human rights, military repression.

My life of subterfuge had become very tiring. It was a lonely life being a friend of East Timor – I had quickly given up trying to talk the non-believers around when an official at the Australian Embassy responded to some small praise I offered the Timorese resistance with an emphatic pronouncement that East Timor's independence was as probable and desirable as Tasmania seceding from mainland Australia. And so when I was encouraged by the OSB to put in an application for the position of Program Officer for Indonesia, I gave the matter serious consideration. The job would require me to be based in Melbourne but involved regular travel to Indonesia. I did have some misgivings, which I shared with Xanana in letters and phone calls. Would I be able to continue to play a useful role as a support person to Xanana from Melbourne? Who would take over from me in administering the Amnesty and other funds entrusted to me? Would I be able to cope with a 9 to 5 job after many years of working flexible hours? After many weeks of debating these and other issues with Xanana, we concluded that this job represented a unique opportunity to move on whilst maintaining my links with Indonesia and the activities of the resistance. So I submitted an application for the job and, within weeks, received confirmation that I had been selected for the position.

Chapter ten

SWAN SONG
October 1995–January 1996

BY MID OCTOBER I was ready, finally, to travel to Timor to take receipt of Xanana's birthday gift. The months of preparation had paid off and it seemed that the guerrilla commanders were ready for my visit. Nevertheless, Xanana had been advised that there were still one or two practical details to finalise – a last-minute assessment of Indonesian troop movements and a decision relating to where and how I would reach the guerrilla encampment from the town of Los Palos. And so I spent close to two weeks in Kupang with Victoria while I waited for the instruction to continue my journey eastwards.

Xanana made daily calls. At first, Victoria refused to believe that it was Xanana phoning her home. It was only when he called João to his cell and put him on the phone to Victoria that her doubts were removed. The wait was long and frustrating but afforded the perfect opportunity to catch up on sleep and on Victoria's news. Nursing gin and tonics and luxuriating in the cool evening breezes which fanned her rooftop, we shared tales of close shaves we had had with the authorities and our employers in the course of our Timor work. The sense of camaraderie was refreshing and affirming.

In late October, when Xanana gave word that it was safe to move, I doused my temples and every item of clothing liberally with the blessed *minyak angin*, and made the journey overland to Dili in a rented car. Whether it was the power of the *minyak angin* or a mere fluke I couldn't say, but the routine passport check in Tibar on the outskirts of Dili was a breeze. I had roused the two police officers on guard at the makeshift checkpoint from their midday slumber, and after sizing me up from behind their dark glasses and giving a cursory flick through my passport, they waved me on.

I hummed all the way to the Villa Harmonia in Becora where I would spend a couple of days with my friends Pedro and Joana Lebre. The couple owned the small guesthouse on the road out of town to the east of Dili. Pedro grumbled to me about the deteriorating security situation since the beginning of the year and its effect on business at the guesthouse. He drew hard on a clove-scented cigarette, leaning forward in his dilapidated rattan easychair, his chin resting in the palm of one hand. 'Things have gone from bloody bad to worse. A bunch of kids burnt down the market in Comoro last month.' Since a number of the larger traders at the market were Indonesian migrants, it was presumably an act of retaliation on the part of Dili's frustrated and disaffected youth. Pedro spoke English with an Australian twang, having spent part of his working life in Darwin and on an Australian gold mine on the island of Wetar.

Joana followed our conversation from the kitchen where she was preparing me a tasty meal of buffalo steaks, fried potatoes and a Portuguese salad. I managed to wash in the two ladles of water remaining at the bottom of the tank in the bathroom. As had been the case in 1991 when Peter Gordon, Max Stahl and I had stayed at the Villa Harmonia, the only other occupants of the guesthouse were an assortment of family members and a pack of hungry dogs which Joana kept shooing from the kitchen with a high-pitched 'Sai, sai'.

Later that afternoon, Pedro introduced me to Zequito, a young friend of his from Los Palos. He was the son of a former guerrilla commander and, with his head of long, tight curls, he resembled a Timorese Bob Marley. On the strength of the smile which never left his face and the trust which Pedro evidently had in him, I confided in Zequito the plans I had to reach the guerrillas in the eastern zone. He offered to accompany me to Los Palos the following day.

The *liurai*, or petty king, of Los Palos was a tall, pale-skinned man with an elegant moustache and the air of a nobleman. He owned one of the few guesthouses in Los Palos and it was here that Zequito left me when we reached the town by bus the following afternoon. I was the first foreigner who had been seen in those parts for some time, and I think that Liurai Quintas was pleased to have the company. He spent the first evening of my stay there hauling photographs of himself out of cupboards, pulling others down off the walls, and telling me the stories behind them. He seemed particularly proud of a mounted and framed photograph which showed him shaking hands with President Suharto in Jakarta. As a means of winning over East Timor's traditional leaders, it seemed that some years earlier the old dictator had summoned the *liurais* from across the territory to the Presidential Palace in Jakarta and given them a pep talk on the need to be good citizens of the Indonesian republic. Liurai Quintas did not comment on his reaction to the meeting with Pak Suharto, but just the same I decided not to trust him with my motives for visiting Los Palos. Zequito kept his distance, turning up at the guesthouse only when there was some news from the bush to convey.

Xanana had given me letters to deliver to the wives of the two principal Falintil commanders in the eastern region. Through the parish priest, Father Palomar, I was able to make contact with them. I didn't need to elaborate on the delicate nature of my 'business' in Los Palos. Father Palomar, like so many members of the East Timorese clergy, supported the cause of the resistance through discreet but dependable offers of assistance, material and moral, to all who were directly or indirectly compromised by their pro-independence stance. He was only too aware of the possible consequences of being seen in the presence of a foreigner and so organised for the two women to meet me in his residence.

Olinda Morais, alias Bi Malik, was the wife of Commander Aluc, with whom I was to meet if all went ahead according to plan. She wore the years of physical hardship and the pain of separation from her husband on her face. Nevertheless, as I handed her the envelope from Xanana, I noticed that her eyes gleamed with satisfaction, a tear threatening to escape down her bony cheeks. She had spent many years in the bush herself, having given birth to her son, Benvindo, in a guerrilla encampment in 1986. The food shortages and absence of medical attention led her and Aluc to decide to place the infant in the care of Aluc's father in Los Palos town. But the child was kidnapped en route by an Indonesian lieutenant-colonel who no doubt wished to use Aluc's boy as a bargaining chip in the effort to force the Falintil to surrender. Olinda had not seen the boy since. Commander Renan's wife, Arminda, had her own sad stories to tell. Both she and Olinda were frequently visited in their homes by officers of the district military command who would question them at length about the whereabouts and activities of their husbands. Not knowing how else to express my sympathy and solidarity with them, I left them both a little money in an envelope.

The following morning, Zequito arrived breathless at the guesthouse. I was in the middle of writing a long letter to Commander Aluc from the creaking, bamboo bed in my room. Zequito informed me that there were military operations underway involving a large number of men from the five ABRI battalions deployed in the area. The specific objective of the operation was to crush the armed resistance and therefore it was deemed too risky for me to make the trek to see the commanders. I tried not to let the disappointment show in my face. But I knew that Xanana would not want our wish for me to experience the way of life of the Falintil to put his soldiers at risk. If I were followed, the present location of the guerrillas would be revealed to the Indonesian armed forces and the response would no doubt be swift and decisive. I felt a little despondent as I added a postscript to the letter to Aluc to say how much I regretted that I would not meet him and his *companheiros*. How would Xanana react to the failed mission? At the same time I was glad to no longer have to run the gauntlet of the swarms of cockroaches that had invaded the guesthouse bathroom.

I returned to Jakarta to find a fax from John Pilger spilling into my study. He was requesting my intervention with the smuggling in of a series of interview questions for Xanana that would form the basis of a feature article on the twentieth anniversary of the Indonesian invasion to be published in a London daily. There were twenty questions in all and I spent every spare minute of each evening for a week translating Xanana's responses.

After three and a half years of residing in Jakarta I had accumulated a large number of books and some items of cheap but attractive rattan furniture that I had grown particularly fond of. In early December I called a shipping firm to help me pack the bulk of my possessions into boxes for transportation to Melbourne. The sight of the folders of East Timor–related documents and the fibreglass figurines Xanana had made me for birthdays and Christmases disappearing into packing crates brought home the irreversibility of my decision. Was I doing the right thing? Apart from my work for East Timor, there were other things about living in Indonesia that I had come to love and would be sad to leave behind. There were the friendships I had formed with Indonesians, ranging from my students and the civil servants I dealt with in my official capacity to the streetside sellers and *ojek*, or motorbike taxi drivers, I interacted with on a daily basis. Even the Jakarta traffic, the noise and pollution and overcrowded city buses, the squalor and colour of the street life, had become my world. I knew that the quiet and order of Melbourne would seem sterile and barren by comparison.

The twentieth anniversary of the Indonesian invasion of East Timor was on 7 December 1995. The brief period of international outrage which followed the bloody massacre at Santa Cruz in 1991 had turned the tide of world public opinion against Indonesia. Nevertheless, there had been little substantive progress made since then in terms of achieving a lasting settlement. This fact was a source of intense sadness and deep frustration to members of the pro-independence movement. Avelino, the softly spoken Secretary of the Timorese Socialist Party, had turned up on my doorstep a month earlier to tell me about the plans being hatched to launch a historic '*aksi*', in which dozens of youths would occupy the Dutch and Russian embassies. They would not seek asylum. His dark eyes glistened and his stutter became even more pronounced as he told me excitedly what it was about this demonstration that would make it historic. For the first time, Indonesian students and activists would stand alongside their East Timorese 'brothers' and publicly condemn the invasion, demanding a referendum. As one Indonesian activist who took part in the *aksi* put it: 'The Indonesian and East Timorese people are two boats with different destinations, but fighting the same band of pirates.'

The action was, in many ways, the culmination of Xanana's efforts over almost two years to cultivate links with the most active members of Indonesia's pro-democracy movement, many of whom were doing time with him in Cipinang. It was becoming increasingly evident that the achievement of a peaceful resolution of the East Timor problem would depend, at least in part, on changes within Indonesia itself. With other political prisoners, with visitors to Cipinang and with the murderers, rapists and robbers who were his fellow inmates, Xanana had shared his vision of an independent East Timor, gaining sympathy and understanding for the struggle and for the principles of justice and international law underpinning it. The Indonesian youth working towards reform in their own country took heart from the bravery and determination of the East Timorese. Friendships and alliances were forged out of a sense of common purpose: to bring Suharto to his knees and to expose the Indonesian armed forces' brutal suppression of the rights of the

East Timorese and Indonesian peoples. Xanana and I had sought and obtained funding for a number of Indonesian activists to attend meetings on East Timor in Australia and Europe. Our investment was repaid with the loyalty and active engagement of Indonesian youth and civil society organisations in our campaign for independence.

I forget now what the reasons were for selecting the Dutch and Russian embassies for the 7 December action. There had been a large number of cases of 'fence-jumping' in the preceding eighteen months – people joked about it one day becoming the national sport of an independent East Timor. Most foreign diplomatic missions had responded by adding a couple of feet of barbed wire reinforcement or steel spikes to their already fortress-like fences. Some posted fully armed ABRI personnel on guard at their gates just to get the message across loud and clear. No doubt a chink in the armour of the Dutch and Russian defences had been detected, and so it was that their embassies were chosen to provide the safe haven for the demonstration.

In the lead-up to the 7 December action I videotaped interviews with several young Timorese who had been forced by the Chief of Intelligence, Zacky Anwar, to speak in a favourable light about the integration of East Timor into Indonesia. They agreed to speak to me on video and retract their earlier pro-integration pronouncements because they planned to go into the Dutch and Russian embassies to make their demands for independence from safety. Against my better judgement, I allowed one or two of them to visit me in my home in the days prior to 7 December.

By now I was something of an expert at assisting with the organisation of such actions. I helped with the translation of the slogans to appear on posters and in the statement to be read to the media and staff of the two embassies. The principal demand was self-determination via a referendum, although the demonstrators would also call for the withdrawal of the military from the territory and the release of all East Timorese political prisoners.

A year or so earlier, Xanana had introduced me to Puto, a

young man with a head of untamed, thick, black hair who had once been his bodyguard and who was to act as spokesman for the East Timorese contingent of protesters. I felt a little protective towards Puto, given his young age and his lack of experience in a big, impersonal city like Jakarta. So I devoted some evenings to preparing him for what to expect inside the Dutch Embassy and briefing him on the importance of resisting the pressure to seek asylum abroad, which would no doubt be the outcome favoured by the embassy officials and the Indonesian government.

In order to capture this historic moment for posterity, I conducted videotaped interviews with some of the members of SMID (Student Solidarity for Democracy in Indonesia), SPRIM (Indonesian–Maubere Peoples' Solidarity Struggle), PPBI (the Centre for Indonesian Workers' Struggle), JAKER (the People's Culture Network) and the STN (National Peasants' Union) who, under the banner of the PRD or Democratic People's Alliance, would participate in the embassy occupations. Smiling into the camera with fists raised, they concluded their comments with a loud 'Viva Timor Leste', which caused me to snap the louvre windows of my study shut with a loud clack. It wouldn't do to arouse the suspicion of my neighbours at this point, so close to the date of my departure from Indonesia.

And so at around 4 am on 7 December, the demonstrators divided themselves into groups and approached the two embassies. Through a tightly coordinated network of couriers and informants, they were able to time their entries to coincide perfectly. Twenty-six East Timorese and twenty-nine Indonesians made it into the Dutch Embassy, the shorter amongst their number clambering onto the shoulders of their friends in order to scale the tall steel fence. Some sustained light injuries in the process, but once inside the atmosphere was one of jubilance and relief. Only about half of the roughly thirty Indonesian youths and seventy East Timorese protesters who had planned to enter the Russian Embassy on Jalan Thamrin actually made it inside, some falling prey to nerves the night before and others to the security guards who pounced and arrested them as they made their dash for the embassy gates.

I felt that it was prudent not to be at home on 7 December – if any of the demonstrators were arrested and talked about my involvement in the action, the first place Intel would go was to my house in Tebet. But I had house guests and, while I was glad of their company at a time of such tension, it made packing up and clearing out on the spur of the moment a little complicated. Colin was in Jakarta, en route to Timor, filling in his time by installing the latest encryption software and a range of other gadgets on my PC. Ed, a student from Sydney who was carrying out research for a PhD, had been staying in my guest room for weeks. He was out interviewing Megawati Sukarnoputri, the head of the Indonesian Democratic Party, when I took the decision to make myself scarce for a day or two. I phoned my friend Margaret, who lived in the house in Menteng where I had first met Victoria and, without divulging the full details of my predicament, asked whether Colin and I could camp out on her living room floor for a day or two. We wondered what Ed would think when he returned that evening to find the house abandoned.

Margaret was organising her annual Christmas party and, feeling guilty for descending upon her with little prior warning, we allowed ourselves to be put to work decorating her Christmas tree. I'd been up at 5 am that morning to meet with Roy, one of the Indonesian activists involved with the demonstration, and to collect a list of names of the people who had succeeded in making it inside the two embassies. I was relieved to see Puto's name there but, knowing that he and the others would be being subjected to intense pressure to abandon their mission and leave the embassies, I felt sick with worry. Colin and I found ourselves looking at each other across tinsel and baubles on either side of the Christmas tree. Perhaps it was the weird juxtaposition of worlds, or perhaps it was our fear that made us laugh.

Thanks to the mobile phone, Xanana was managing to keep abreast of developments from Cipinang. I had given him

Margaret's telephone number so that he could stay in touch during my stay at her home, and he rang every couple of hours to ask me for an update. I didn't dare go anywhere near the embassies myself in broad daylight, so relied for my own information on Roy and the PRD youth. It seemed that the Dutch Embassy officials had invited Princen and the UN representative in Jakarta, Mr Jan Kamp, to meet with the demonstrators to encourage them to leave the compound.

The fridge loaded with Bintang beer, the tree decorated, Margaret's Christmas party rolled around. The house had been beautifully decked out with sprigs of tropical vegetation and scented candles that flickered in the gentle evening breeze. The guests appeared bearing chilled bottles of imported wines and Christmas puddings wrapped in cellophane and ribbons. Laughter and polite conversation filled the night air as the number of guests grew.

That evening the phone kept ringing; it was Puto. How he had tracked me down at Margaret's I couldn't begin to imagine. He'd managed to get access to the phone in someone's office and he rang Margaret's every ten minutes or so to give us a running commentary on the situation inside the Dutch Embassy. In spite of the growing numbers of military at the gates of the embassy and the demonstrators' fears that the security forces would be allowed inside the grounds, the Timorese and their Indonesian friends were keeping their spirits up by sharing jokes and singing songs. Puto giggled like a little boy as he told me how the Dutch Ambassador had berated the youths for smoking in his air-conditioned office. He had said 'Smoke – nee', presumably meaning 'No smoking'. In Tetum, 'ne'e' means 'here'. Despite Puto's humour, I felt a heavy sense of foreboding and dread about what was to come.

It was a pleasure and a relief when Victoria appeared at the party. She was on Christmas leave from her work in Kupang and had decided to pay her old friends in Menteng a surprise visit. From a quiet spot beside the Christmas tree I managed to brief her on what was going on inside the two embassies. Victoria's eyes sparkled when she learned of the bravery of the young Indonesian demonstrators, but grew dim when I shared my concerns for their safety should they be expelled from their safe havens. Victoria suggested we take a taxi ride and drive by the Dutch Embassy. Neither of us was much in the mood for a party anyway. Colin had grown talkative under the influence of the Bintang beer and was engaged in a heated debate with a foreign diplomat over the UN's lack of teeth in enforcing its conventions and treaties. Victoria and I slipped away from the party unnoticed and caught a cab to Jalan Rasuna Said.

Alighting from the taxi in front of the embassy building, we saw men in uniform, lots of them. It was dark and they were waiting at the entrance of the huge glass building. The light from the doors cast ugly shadows on their faces, many of them wearing dark glasses. From time to time, the walkie-talkies on their hips blurted forth static or the barking voices of other uniformed men in another part of the city. There was an air of barely suppressed hysteria and violence and a sense that these men were waiting to pounce on whatever or whoever would emerge through those big heavy doors.

The next morning I returned home. The danger wasn't over but I needed access to my computer and email so that I could feed updates to the media and solidarity groups that were anxious to have the latest news on the action and the fate of its participants. I also had an interview to conduct with three Indonesian women who were candidates for the liaison officer post I would leave in just over three weeks time.

That day ABRI mobilised a group of one hundred or so youths, mainly kids from Flores, Ambon and Kupang, to carry out a pro-integration demonstration against the East Timorese and Indonesians inside the Dutch Embassy. From the front of the embassy compound they taunted and jeered the activisits inside. Later in the day, the pro-integrationists hurled abuse and rocks at the demonstrators. The security guards outside did nothing to stop them, and the Dutch Ambassador himself was struck on the head by a rock lobbed over the fence by a youth wielding a steel pipe. Three other members of the embassy staff were also injured.

Despite this, the action of the pro-independence students was a success. The international media gave the event and the demands of the demonstrators for a referendum in East Timor maximum coverage. The Indonesian media downplayed the involvement of Indonesian youths and the Russian Embassy group of protesters capitulated a little earlier than anticipated to the pressures of their reluctant hosts and the Indonesian military. But the fifty or so protesters in the Dutch Embassy held out for a full three days until they, too, were surrendered to the wolves. Most were taken directly to military headquarters for questioning. Others managed to evade arrest and flee, finding temporary refuge in the anonymity of Jakarta's back streets and overcrowded kampungs. Puto and his Indonesian friend, Bebek, were pursued by intelligence agents on trail bikes. They were chased down an alleyway which ended at a big canal and were forced to swim to the other side to flee their would-be captors.

Puto and Bebek eventually found their way to my home. They were in surprisingly good spirits considering their ordeal and the tension of the preceding days. It was probably the relief and satisfaction of knowing that in spite of the arrest of a handful of their number, their daring protest action had caught the attention of the world. Puto announced proudly that the embassy occupations had been the lead story on the BBC World Service for a number of hours on 7 December. He had tuned in on a short-wave radio he had found in the office of one of the Dutch officials.

Avelino dropped by to pass on his new telephone number. He had not participated in the demonstration. Like me, he remained an observer. And like me, he had deemed it wise to move out of his house while the embassy occupations were going on. Just in case . . . It had never occurred to me that Avelino had a wife and children, and that his involvement in the struggle and the consequences of that involvement were felt by an entire family. How did Avelino's wife feel about having to pack up and move just like that? What were they forced to leave behind? What were her feelings about all this clandestine resistance stuff? They were not things I ever spoke to Avelino or any other East Timorese activists about. Personal needs and matters didn't figure in my relationship with them.

For the Timorese activists, self-sacrifice was taken as a given. It was also an unwritten law of the resistance that the details of a *companheiro*'s life, all those quirks, habits, hobbies and history which form an identity, were deliberately omitted from daily conversation. If asked, I am sure that neither Avelino nor any of his young compatriots, whom I met on a regular basis, were aware of what my job was, how I came to be living in Jakarta or even what my real name was. It was not that they were uninterested. It was just easier to know nothing about a colleague if one found oneself, one day, facing interrogation. Like them, I had my code name, and it was what they used to refer to me amongst themselves and in my company. For some reason, Avelino preferred to refer to me as 'Mutin' or 'Whitie' rather than my more 'official' pseudonym of Mukya.

The weeks that followed were perhaps a fitting climax to my three and a half years in Jakarta. In spite of the danger Puto and Bebek were in, and the risks to me of harbouring them, my home echoed with the excited chatter of the two friends, who took an odd pleasure in recounting the details of their adventure, including the strong bonds of solidarity and mutual support which had kept the group together through the most trying moments. Ed forgave me for having abandoned him and recorded a lengthy interview with the two which he subsequently transcribed, translated and emailed out to interested parties around the world. Victoria helped me answer the phone, which was running hot with calls from journalists and others tracking the fate of those taken in for questioning upon being expelled from the embassies. Indonesian activists and students came and went from the house until the early hours of the morning, comparing and updating lists of East Timorese and Indonesians still unaccounted for, and leaving in their wake plates of half-eaten nasi goreng and ashtrays full of *kretek* butts.

And then, around the middle of December, I received an email which had been forwarded by James, now back in Sydney, from an electronic news digest on East Timor. The item was in the form of an interview with an East Timorese youth called Francisco. He related in the interview how he had been paid by a 'white foreigner' to speak ill of the Intelligence Chief, Zacky Anwar, and to discredit Indonesia's efforts at *pembangunan* (development) in East Timor. The interviewee was asked to identify the white woman concerned. 'A journalist who doubles as an English teacher' was the response. There was no name given but, to my horror, my address was recorded in full. Now I knew that it was only a matter of time – perhaps days – before I would be asked to answer questions about my East Timor work. It seemed that one of the youths I had interviewed on videotape was a spy. Either that or he had been won over with money or torture to betray me.

I told Xanana how I had started to receive strange telephone calls. There was someone claiming to be calling from the telecommunications office; they needed to confirm my address. I refused to give it on the grounds that I had no way of verifying who they really were. Other calls resembled prank calls, with nobody responding when I picked up the phone. But I was in the throes of packing up my life, of handing over my liaison officer job to the successful applicant, and of identifying people who could take over responsibility for paying Xanana's mobile bill, and for disbursing and reporting back on the Amnesty funds in my care. I couldn't allow this setback to paralyse me with fear. I tried as best as I could to carry on as if nothing were amiss. I had a flight booked from Jakarta to Melbourne on 4 January. There were just Christmas and the New Year to get through.

I spent Christmas sipping red wine and nibbling at Cipinang Christmas cake with Dita Sari and Wilson, two Indonesian activist friends who, like me, had been monitoring closely the fate of the 7 December demonstrators. We squatted on the floor on our haunches, as was the Indonesian tradition, not because I was comfortable in this position but because by now the bulk of my household furniture had been either sold or shipped back to Australia.

The following day I discovered that my favourite rattan chest of drawers had been overlooked by the packers when they had come to box up my other possessions for shipping to Melbourne. It was too bulky to carry with me in my luggage when I departed on 4 January, so I decided to send it ahead by air freight. I took Puto with me out to the airport. I had given him strict instructions not to leave my house for any reason in case he was spotted by military intelligence, and after two weeks of virtual house arrest, poor Puto was beginning to feel a little bored and frustrated. So he was glad to have the chance to accompany me. When we returned home later that afternoon, however, Yati greeted us with a look of deep concern on her face. She shifted awkwardly from one foot to the other, avoiding my gaze, as she told me that three men in plain clothes had come looking for me. She had difficulty describing their physical appearance and couldn't say whether or not they were police. But I knew in an instant who they were and what they wanted. I felt surprisingly calm. There was a sense that this moment had been inevitable. I had dreaded it for so long that it was almost a relief to be facing it now, headlong. I knew that I had to avoid being questioned and having my possessions searched – too many other people could be compromised in the process. And it was necessary to ensure Puto's safety. As the 'ringleader' of the 7 December action, there was a definite price on his head.

I phoned Xanana. His mobile was switched off. I needed to find alternative accommodation for my remaining days in Jakarta. I hunted around in my brain for ideas as to where I could go, with whom I could stay. I was all too conscious that if the authorities were on my trail I was a definite liability, and nobody in their right mind would welcome me into their home. My head began to hurt. The tension was taking its toll. I lay down on the bed with the telephone at my side and dialled Xanana's number at ten-minute intervals. There was still no reply. Then an idea came to me. Adrina, who was about to commence work as the new OSB liaison officer, had rented an office in the nearby suburb of Cawang, just over the Ciliwung River. It was actually a small three-bedroom house and, being empty, was possibly the perfect temporary hide-out for me – I wouldn't compromise anyone else by being there. Adrina and I had hit it off since our first meeting. She was a women's activist and we had many friends in the pro-democracy movement in common. I felt that I could confide in her. But the fact was that she had taken a holiday to Lombok and would not return for another few days. There was nothing for it but to try to contact her by phone and get her permission to move into her new office. I felt myself breaking out in a cold sweat. Perhaps it was my frustration at not getting through to Xanana – by now I was desperate to share my predicament with him and to seek his opinion on the best way to deal with it.

After five or six failed attempts, I managed to speak to Adrina. Given that I was certain that my phone was being tapped, I had to be careful about how I spoke about my problem and the solution I was proposing. Gathering from my cryptic form of speech that I was in some kind of trouble, Adrina simply agreed to my suggestion and told me where I could find the key to the house in Cawang. By the time I had finished the call to Adrina, I had difficulty raising myself off the bed. It was as if my limbs had grown lead anchors and were suddenly and painfully heavy. The ache in my head seemed to have taken a hold of my spine as well.

In the living room I found Puto deep in conversation with Jayadi, an art student from Yogya who was a member of JAKER, the People's Culture Network. Jayadi was showing off the 'Free Xanana' T-shirt he had designed and was wearing under a faded denim jacket. I explained the plan to Puto. We would need to pack up my remaining possessions that night and be ready to vacate the house by the following day. To stay on any longer in Tebet would be to tempt fate. The next morning I had organised to be collected by a small group of East Timorese friends with whom I would make my last-ditch attempt to enter Cipinang for that year's Christmas celebrations. After my failure at Easter time, I didn't hold out any great hope of being successful, but this would possibly be my last chance for a long time to come and I couldn't let it pass me by.

I spent my final night in Tebet tossing and turning in bed, fever raging through my body and making sleep impossible. The sound of cars slowing down in front of the house caused my heart to pound like a drum. I kept confusing the thumping of my aching head with the sound of unwanted visitors knocking at the front door, and on more than one occasion actually hauled myself out of bed to peer through the curtains of my bedroom window . . . just to be sure.

By morning I felt weak and drained of all energy. Xanana, oblivious to the events of the previous day, phoned at 6 am and greeted me in a cheerful voice. 'Your phone was switched off. Why didn't you call me yesterday?' I demanded, the tears spilling uncontrollably down my burning cheeks. I explained about the visit of the three men and my plan to get out of the Tebet house that very day. When he learned that I was ill to boot, Xanana recommended that I cancel the plan to visit the prison that morning. Knowing that he would be disappointed if I did so, I refused to consider his suggestion and ended the conversation with a casual 'See you in half an hour'. I put on the same pink blouse I had worn on the occasion of our first meeting one year earlier.

They were all there, all the regulars. Some of the women from the previous Christmas service recognised me and politely enquired after Uncle John. 'Wasn't he released back in August?' asked one of them. I studied my nails, pretending not to hear. I noticed that the small blood vessels at the base of each of my finger nails seemed to have burst. I hid my hands in my armpits, wondering to myself what illness it was that could be causing me to bleed below the surface of my skin.

It was a wet and windy day, and in spite of the humidity the breeze caused me to shiver. Sinaga must have seen my lip quivering and assumed that I was fearful of him, as a smile of pure pleasure spread across his face when he caught my eye. With a last persistent shred of hope, I tossed a pinch of the *kyai*'s white dust at Sinaga's feet, which were planted squarely in front of the big heavy doors. Before he had even opened his mouth, I knew from his composure that I would be barred from entering yet again. 'Tell Xanana that I love him,' I blurted to one of the women standing beside me as I hailed a cab. I spent the journey home to Tebet cursing the *kyai* of Tasikmalaya and whatever the illness was which had taken such a sudden and decisive grip on my body.

We had loaded up the boot and back seat of two taxis within an hour of my return home. I told Yati that I would be back the next day to collect the remainder of my things, including the bonsai plants and my bowl of Spanish fighting fish. I kissed her on both cheeks – a very un-Javanese thing to do. It was tempting to speak to her openly of the danger I was in and just ask her to leave. But I didn't want to alarm her. There was also the problem of my bed and an antique wardrobe that had been promised for sale to a family in a neighbouring kampung. They couldn't pay me for the furniture until early in the New Year when they received their salaries, and whilst I was happy to hand the goods over, Yati had advised me against doing so – 'They will never pay up that way,' she had told me. Xanana's mobile account had become a significant drain on my meagre financial resources and, since I was in need of every rupiah to settle the final electricity and phone bills in the Tebet house, I decided to take Yati's advice and leave her in charge of the house and its contents until the accounts were settled. And so I got into the front seat of the taxi and we set off for Cawang, Jayadi and Puto behind in the second cab.

I was too sick to take in the details of my new surroundings in the house in Jalan Mesjid Bendungan Number 7. With Puto's help I made up the bed in one of the bedrooms and collapsed into it. By now the blood under my fingernails had congealed and turned black. I slept soundly until midnight when I was woken by the sound of the phone ringing. At first I didn't recognise the unfamiliar ring tone through the cloak of fever and sleep hanging over me. I dragged my heavy limbs out of bed. Puto was sound asleep on the couch in the living room. Xanana's voice was soft and serious and I had difficulty hearing him over the sound of the television blaring in his cell. I could tell that he was deeply concerned about me, my safety and my health. I tried to inject a note of gaiety into my voice. 'I'll be just fine. It's only stress, I'm sure.'

It turned out that Xanana, too, was having to take a low profile. He had been questioned by the prison chief in relation to the publication of the John Pilger interview in the London *Guardian* two weeks earlier. Whilst he had signed the obligatory statement of denial, there was the threat of a raid on his cell and he had had to restrict his use of the mobile phone to late at night and turn up the volume on his TV set to disguise the sound of his voice. He apologised for not calling me more regularly over the past twenty-four hours, but he feared losing the phone which, once I reached Australia, was going to be a vital lifeline for him, for us.

Ruben turned up, smiling, at the front door the next morning, having completed the early shift at the prison. He held a restless chicken under one arm and a basket of fruit in the other. From the note that accompanied the fruit basket, scribbled by Xanana at 6 am that morning, I learned that the fruit was for me and that the chicken was to be turned into broth 'for my ailing Professora'. For the time being the ill-fated hen was tethered to the trunk of the papaya tree in the front yard of the office. It turned out that Puto had about as much experience lopping the heads off live chickens as I did. And besides, I had no appetite whatsoever.

I phoned Yati to let her know that I would be coming soon to collect the last of my personal effects and the clothing out of my wardrobe. She told me that within hours of our leaving the house the day before, the men had returned with more questions about my whereabouts. They claimed to be immigration officials. Yati had told them that I had left the country, inviting them into the empty living room to prove her point. They didn't seem convinced, she told me, and had gone on to ask her a series of questions about my work and other activities. 'What was she really doing here? Who were her friends?' – 'She was an English teacher, Pak. She had many friends. Some of them were her students, I think.' Finally, they had left her alone, but only after informing her that they would be back the next day. There was no way now that I could return to the house. I felt nauseous with guilt over having left Yati to deal with the interrogators on her own. Jayadi, who had arrived to keep Puto company, offered to go to the house and collect my belongings.

I felt as if every bone in my body was broken. I now had a rash on my stomach under my breasts. The itch was unbearable and kept me from the sleep my pounding head was craving. Seeing me lying listless and shivering on the couch, Puto offered to fill a Coke bottle with hot water and massage my back with it. The temporary relief from the shooting pain down my spine and legs was welcome. Xanana phoned again and we talked, on and off, until evening. We talked about Yati – he felt that he had come to know her over the months and shared my concern for what might happen to her – and about what I would do if the Intel caught up with me before I could leave the country. Xanana was taking care not to raise his voice and had to hang up a number of times when he heard the footsteps of the guards approaching.

Jayadi arrived just before 9 pm, bringing another taxi-load of my things. The bonsai and fish were not among them. I felt my heart drop into the pit of my stomach as he told me that my neighbours had also been questioned by the 'immigration officials' and, sensing that I was at the centre of some scandal or other which had led me to flee, had helped themselves to my six bonsai pots and the Spanish fighting fish. Yati had been powerless to stop them as she didn't want to contradict the information that she had given to the 'immigration' guys – that I had left the country already.

Later that night, my body aches and itch keeping me awake to brood over my sorry state, I remembered that I had told my neighbours in Tebet the date of my planned departure from Jakarta. If the authorities were really serious about catching me, surely they would have no difficulty getting hold of a passenger list for 4 January. And they would be lying in wait for me at the airport. I struggled out of bed and rang my friend, Juan Federer, of the East Timor International Support Centre in Darwin. I knew that I could rely on Juan to advise me of the safest possible 'back-door' routes out of the country. The other advantage of consulting Juan was that we had already devised a clever code language for phone use, so I would not be giving anything away if my new phone was also being tapped. I realised, regretfully, that this change of plan meant that I would not even be able to farewell my friends in the way I had intended, and the series of funny, quirky presents I had planned to give to Xanana and João as my parting gifts were now impossible.

The following morning Juan called me back and managed to let me know that there was a bi-weekly flight from Ambon to Darwin which would serve my purposes nicely. All I needed to do was to get myself a ticket to Ambon. So I took a bath in the icy waters of the *mandi* (an Indonesian-style bathroom) and headed out in a taxi to purchase my ticket and run a number of urgent errands prior to my departure. I withdrew the remaining Amnesty funds from my bank account account and closed it. I then met up with Ibu Ade and Herbin, her young colleague from the Joint Committee, in a coffee shop on the ground floor of a nearby shopping mall. I handed them the wad of rupiah in a fat, white envelope, conveying instructions on its disbursal and the reporting requirements. Ibu Ade's brow was furrowed, her face serious and worried, as she listened to the story of my flight from the house in Tebet. She offered to send a young lawyer friend by the name of Levi to Ambon to see me safely onto the plane to Darwin. I was not sure whether such accompaniment was necessary, but was grateful for the gesture nonetheless.

That night was New Year's Eve. The house in Cawang was alive with the comings and goings of Puto's friends, but I was not in a festive frame of mind or body, and retreated to my room to pack Xanana's letters and gifts into the few vacant spaces remaining in my suitcase. John Pilger, unaware of the trouble I was in, telephoned repeatedly from London to ask me to request that Xanana retract his denial of having granted the interview. The Indonesians had questioned the authenticity of Xanana's responses, based on the routine written denial he had signed. And now Pilger's professional reputation was on the line. But we were in no position to help him salvage it at that point. If Xanana admitted to giving the interview, he risked losing the basic conditions he relied upon to be able to grant similar interviews in the future.

Xanana, too, called throughout the evening, and I detected in his voice a hint of resentment that the house was full of guests but that he himself could not be with me to welcome in the New Year. I knew, too, that he was frustrated that he couldn't do more to help me and to guarantee my safety and well-being. Though he never said so, perhaps he had a sense that he was responsible for getting me in so deep. By midnight I was fast asleep, the physical activity of the day having taken its toll on my fever-wracked body.

The day of my departure came around quickly. The evening before, Ruben appeared at the door once more with the final black plastic bag from Cipinang to deliver. My eyes filled with tears as I tore open the small plastic box and the familiar scent of Xanana's perfume filled my nostrils. Inside it was a golden ring inset with a large tigereye framed by six tiny diamonds. On either side of the amber-brown tigereye were the initials 'X' and 'K'. I had no idea how Xanana had managed to organise such a beautiful gift from inside Cipinang. The fit was perfect. I was deeply touched and had to spend the next hour behind closed doors in my room to hide the tears which kept welling up every time I glanced down at the ring on my finger. That night, Budiman Sudjatmiko, the Chairman of the Democratic People's Alliance, plus a handful of other pro-democracy activists, joined me in my final bowl of *indomie rebus*, the staple of Indonesian students and others of limited means.

At 4 am on the morning of 3 January 1996, Xanana phoned and we bade one another a tearful farewell. The moment of truth had arrived. Budiman, Wilson, Puto and their friends woke at the crack of dawn to see me off. They stood in a line at the door of the house like a rather motley guard of honour, each one offering me in turn an embrace and some words of thanks and encouragement. I whispered something like motherly advice in Puto's ear as I hugged him goodbye: 'These friends of ours will take good care of you. But stay away from embassies. A luta continua!' Puto, a half-hearted smile playing on his lips, raised his fist in reply as I joined Jayadi in the waiting taxi. It had been raining all night and the road to the airport was under water. We had to raise our feet off the floor of the cab to keep from getting wet. The effort involved helped keep my mind off the fact that our westward journey to Sukarno-Hatta Airport was whisking us further and further away from Cipinang and Xanana, who was no doubt by now commencing another day with a coffee and a cigarette, the morning call to prayer wailing through the mosque's amplifiers.

I heaved a sigh of relief as I boarded the flight to Ambon without incident. Unlike my first views of Ambon one and a half years earlier, the sky was overcast and the sea was a murky grey. My state of mind, too, couldn't have been further removed from that of my visit in 1994, when a relaxed and sun-filled holiday awaited me. This time Ambon was a night in a cheap city hotel, a stopover on a journey that marked an end and a new beginning for me.

The following morning at the airport, a young man lowered the newspaper he was reading and nodded as he caught my eye. My heart skipped a beat. Was he an Intel agent waiting to arrest me at passport control? A smile curled at the corner of his lips and I realised that it was Levi, Ibu Ade's young friend. As I moved safely through Immigration and into the departure hall, I turned and raised a hand in his direction, the only gesture of thanks that the situation allowed. But already he was gone.

As the Merpati jet which carried me to safety penetrated the low-lying bank of monsoonal cloud above Darwin and the city came into view below us, I felt the fever waning in my body and a spark of energy reignite. I was about to arrive back in a foreign land called 'home'.

Chapter eleven

NORMALITY
1996

SATURDAY MORNING in Melbourne. A warm one was predicted, thirty-one degrees or so, according to the previous night's forecast; not a cloud in the sky and no breeze either. I lay and let the sounds of Saturday – the barking of a dog, the chirping of the birds, a lawn-mower firing up – flow in through the window and over me, coaxing me ever so gently back to sleep. I was beginning to succumb when the phone rang. The small sounds of other people going about their business were drowned out by its shrill persistence.

I had no desire to answer it. It was probably for Mum. Nevertheless, I headed slowly and sleep-dazed for the study. Flashing through my mind with the rapidity of an MTV video clip were the nightmare images from outside the Dutch Embassy in Jakarta during the December demonstrations. The phone rang off. It can't be, oh, don't let it be Jakarta, I thought, as I staggered zombie-like back to my bedroom to lie down again. But it was no use. No amount of effort or concentration would return me to the state of peaceful reverie of a few minutes earlier.

I couldn't help it. I was worried about Avelino, and about whether or not the call I failed to answer was from or about him. There had been a concerted effort by the military to round up the 'masterminds' of the December actions in Jakarta, and I knew that Avelino was a prime target.

A light wind blew up from somewhere and a few clouds became visible on the horizon. I wished like hell I'd answered that phone. For God's sake, Saturdays weren't supposed to be spent racked with doubts and fears of what might or might not be happening to friends thousands of miles away. Saturdays were for gardening, for shopping for things I didn't really need, for reading in parks, putting the cares of the 9 to 5 behind me and laughing with mates. Well, perhaps not for everyone.

At thirty years of age, it was odd to be living back at home with my parents. But I had no alternative accommodation lined up upon my return to Melbourne. I remembered my last days in Jakarta with horror: my physical fragility; my insecurity, knowing I was officially being sought by the security apparatus; my fear of being stopped on my way out of the country; my need in spite of all of this to organise my belongings; the unfinished business of my official work and that for East Timor; my feelings of guilt for having caused problems for Yati and others; my inability to say goodbye to friends; my disgust at the rapaciousness of my neighbours in Tebet; and my frustration at being unable to spend my last days and hours in Jakarta in a way that more adequately reflected Xanana's importance to me.

Against this backdrop, there was a sense of unreality about the sudden orderliness of life in Melbourne. On the one hand, the familiarity of the surroundings, the sense of being safe and 'at home', the relative tranquillity and return to routine – three square meals a day (not boiled noodles), eaten at the right time and at the right place – were pleasant and comforting after the turmoil of my final weeks in Jakarta. But the comfort was tinged with a certain anxiety that came from the knowledge that neither familiarity nor safety were things I was accustomed to. Without the challenges, without the habitual adrenalin rushes of the past four years, would I not find this new life a little mundane?

There was little chance to dwell on the answer to this question or to speculate as to the possible consequences of the Indonesian authorities' investigation of my activities in Jakarta. I started work at OSB almost immediately, having made a remarkably speedy recovery from my illness. The OSB doctor concluded that I had contracted a haemorrhagic strain of dengue fever, hence the bleeding I had experienced under the skin of my fingers. I felt fortunate to have had the illness diagnosed only after having recovered fully, since a precise knowledge of what it was that had taken hold of my body would only have served to exacerbate my stress and fear.

It was a busy time at the office, with the briefing of new volunteers underway and an endless round of meetings aimed at familiarising myself with the work of the volunteer program as a whole as well as that part of it for which I was now responsible. In the midst of my intensive orientation, daily faxes arrived from Adrina recounting details of the ongoing investigation of my 'case', which she now found herself at the centre of. An activist herself, Adrina was unfazed by the questions fired at her by men in uniforms claiming to be immigration officials. They asked about the nature of my work for OSB and what else I'd been doing during my time in Jakarta. She denied any knowledge of my East Timor work. 'I don't know what she did in her private time,' she said. 'I'm just taking over her job.'

So desperate were 'immigration' to get hold of any sort of information on me that they even contacted the owners of my house in Tebet. They were a middle-class Javanese couple who, like most sharing their social milieu, avoided comment on, let alone involvement in, the world of domestic politics. They knew little other than that I was an English teacher, and so were unable to oblige with the details of my 'other life' so eagerly sought by the authorities. When the couple learned, however, that I was being investigated for suspected 'subversive' activities, they refused to hand over my bond and the change from the money for the electricity and telephone bills I had left with them. It was with a mixture of sheepishness and annoyance that I phoned them from my parents' home to profess my innocence and appeal for the return of my money. Their response was stripped of all the Javanese politeness and respect they had showed me up until that point – and being, by now, a thousand miles away, I was not in a strong bargaining position.

The relief I felt at having made it safely home was soon replaced by an oppressive sense of guilt. I didn't feel guilty about anything I'd done – I wouldn't have conducted myself any differently if given a chance to do things over. But I felt responsible for the people I'd implicated. Before the difficulties with the authorities blew up, I had attempted to organise employment for Yati with a Singaporean woman I'd met in Jakarta. I appreciated her hard work and companionship and it was the least I could do for her. Now when I contacted Yati and learnt that she hadn't taken up the position, I felt sure that it was because she'd completely lost her faith in me. It was a hard fact to acknowledge when I recalled the trust and affection that had grown between us, her gentle, dignified manner and the laughter we had shared the day we 'ran away' from Charles.

In late January, Adrina phoned to ask me some questions relating to the processing of the volunteers' visas. Towards the end of our conversation she mentioned quite casually that she had been summoned to the office of one of the heads of the Immigration office. There she had been informed by the gruff Sumatran in charge of visa violations by foreign nationals that I had been officially blacklisted. It was not a surprising outcome given the events of the preceding month. Nevertheless, it was difficult to keep my voice from shaking.

'Did they say for how long . . . I mean, did they make it clear over what period the ban would remain in place?' My heart felt like it had dropped into the pit of my stomach.

'They couldn't say, since the addition of your name was recommended by military intelligence. It's not a matter for immigration to decide . . .'

I had anticipated this moment with dread for many years and

now it was before me. What would this development mean for my job, for my work for East Timor and for my prospects of being able to see Xanana again? To my surprise, the thought that caused me the greatest pang of grief and remorse was that of not being able to visit Indonesia again. Since my first trip to the country in the early eighties, hardly a year had gone by that I hadn't travelled to a different part of Indonesia, renewing old friendships and making new ones, filling the holes in my understanding of the complex and diverse nation. During the years when I studied Indonesian language at Melbourne University I had taken on casual waitressing jobs to scrape together money for the airfare to Bali and for the cost of onward travel to the farthest reaches of the archipelago – Lombok, Irian Jaya, Flores and Sumatra. A scrapbook of images and memories of past experiences cascaded through my mind. The thought that this was the end of the road caused me to wince. I was assailed by a profound sense of loss.

The knowledge of my blacklisting magnified my sense of guilt. How would my employers react? OSB had recruited me for a job I now wasn't able to do. And, of course, the opportunity to travel to Indonesia had been a major attraction of the program officer role and one of the main reasons I had accepted the job. Was I now destined to be office-bound?

Although there was nothing surprising about my having been declared official persona non grata by Suharto's regime, part of me remained incredulous. It had something to do with the inexplicable, perhaps naive, feeling I had always had that there was something charmed about my 'connection' with Indonesia and Indonesians, something unseen and mysterious that conferred on the relationship a special magic, an immunity to danger or threats of other kinds. I asked a friend who was about to travel to Bali on holiday whether she would make an enquiry at the immigration counter at Denpasar Airport . . . just to be sure that I was indeed forbidden from entering the country. Pretending that she was asking on behalf of a friend who feared that she had been penalised for overstaying her visa, she gave my name to the official. 'There it was in luminous green letters on the computer screen,' she told me from her hotel later. My friend hadn't managed to get a look at the annotations that appeared alongside my name, although she did think she caught sight of the letters 'BIA' – the military intelligence agency.

I discussed my situation with my colleagues. Simon, my fellow program officer on the Indonesia desk, was sympathetic and shared the angst I felt over my predicament. Whilst he and my other colleagues knew about my work for East Timor, I had never shared with them the details of my involvement. To do so it would have been necessary to divulge the secret of my relationship with Xanana. And I wasn't ready for that. Who would have believed the story of our improbable love affair anyway? It was something belonging to another place, another reality, beyond the comprehension and experience of the world to which I had returned.

I loved OSB. I loved its philosophy of experiential learning, of providing Australians with opportunities to move beyond their comfort zones and to build a greater understanding of the world and our place in it through the experience of living and working as equals with people in the developing world. It was hard, however, to avoid the feeling that I had overstepped the boundaries in my own overseas experience, crossing the threshold of acceptable, rational engagement and getting myself in over my head. Was this how my Timor involvement would be interpreted by those around me?

In spite of the understanding and concern of my colleagues, I felt like a bit of a pariah. Volunteers had been blacklisted before, usually for overstaying their visas or for other minor transgressions. Ironically, during my years as liaison officer in Jakarta, I had assisted a number of them to resolve their differences with the immigration authorities. But there was no getting away from the fact that my case was more serious because it was political.

Xanana phoned me regularly at my parents' home. Jailed businessman and banker Eddy Tansil had escaped mysteriously from Cipinang earlier that month and his case had drawn attention to breaches in the prison's security and the complicity of some of the guards in some of those breaches. Jakarta's dailies were full of the story and speculation as to Tansil's whereabouts. Since he had been a close ally and business partner of one of Suharto's sons, it was presumed that his escape had been orchestrated and financed by a member of the First Family. An investigation was expected, and Xanana feared a raid on his cell. As a precaution, he kept his mobile phone and laptop secreted away during the day, taking them out only at night when the sound of his television turned up loud could be relied upon to conceal his voice and his tapping at the computer keyboard. Nevertheless, I was anxious about the prospect of our losing our precious tools of communication, and it was a great relief to answer the phone late at night and be greeted by Xanana's whispered 'Boa noite, querida'.

I knew that Xanana didn't want to influence my decision as to how I responded to the dilemma of my blacklisting. We debated the options on many occasions, but I knew that ultimately the decision was mine. In the meantime, my parents had convinced me of the need to invest in my future and to look into purchasing a flat. There seemed to be no better way of anchoring me to Melbourne, and to the old/new social sphere of which I was now a part, than through a mortgage. And so I set about doing the rounds of available properties in my lunch breaks and at weekends. By March I had settled on a small, two-bedroom flat in the suburb of Thornbury. The business of dealing with real estate agents and bank managers, and of giving my new home a makeover before moving in, kept my mind off my troubles for a while.

It was not easy re-establishing a circle of friends. Most of my contemporaries were married with children and, I think, viewed my attraction to Indonesia and my work for East Timor as exotic, if not a little off the wall. My attempts at social reintegration were not helped by the fact that I seemed to have completely lost the art of polite conversation. I found it difficult to talk about myself, my feelings, my aspirations and desires. To do so in Jakarta would have been tantamount to suicide. My three and a half years in

Jakarta had been full of work and activities that demanded I perfect the arts of silence and subterfuge. It wasn't a difficult thing for me. I had always been a private person, a listener rather than a talker – an ideal clandestine, perhaps!

My blacklisting had only reinforced my feelings of isolation and the oddball nature of the life I had made for myself. I did my best to take up the thread of family roles and responsibilities that I had temporarily relinquished during the years spent abroad, attending weddings and birthday parties and trying to draw emotional strength from the sense of having returned 'to the fold'. But it was not easy to adapt.

Ironically, my new job as program officer involved briefing volunteers on the difficulties of the process of reintegration into Australian society upon return from an overseas assignment. The intellectual understanding I had of the problems of reinsertion into one's own culture were sound, but somehow did little to mitigate the discomfort of my own faltering attempts at finding my feet.

With the exception of the coup we pulled off at Christmas time in 1994, Xanana and I had never been able to be physically together, so I hadn't anticipated that the separation involved in our new circumstances would be of any significance to either of us. And yet the distance that now stretched between us did affect the way we communicated with one another. First, there was the financial dimension of the problem – the cost of calls to and from Xanana's mobile were exorbitant, and we were not able to chat on endlessly about the people and events, big and small, that featured in our day-to-day lives. Our exchanges became briefer and more focussed. More difficult to accept was the fact that I was no longer able to play such a direct role in his life. Previously Xanana had been able to say to me, 'There is someone in Jakarta I want you to meet,' and we were able to line up the meeting in half an hour. With me in Melbourne, it was harder for him to see me as his eyes and ears in the way he had become accustomed to. For me, too, it was no easy thing to accept that I was no longer quite so available to run errands or respond to 'emergencies' at short notice. The

OSB job was demanding – I no longer set my own routine, and whilst there was a degree of flexibility in my working hours, I was far from being my own boss.

I filled my spare time by maintaining a regular communication with Herbin and other friends in Jakarta. Xanana had taken to sending out encrypted letters on diskette, which he would have Herbin email to me. The emails allowed Xanana to keep me apprised of the details of his life that were necessarily omitted from our telephone conversations for reasons of economy. They came in the form of brief diary entries: '1:10 am – I had just finished reading the final statement of the Second Intra Timorese Meeting and was settling down to a game of Wheel of Fortune on my laptop – Mukya made it into the bonus round and was in the running for the Dream Vacation valued at US$10,000 – when I heard a commotion some distance from my cell. It seems the Ambonese inmates are fighting the Bataks again.'

These emails and my communication with Herbin on the Amnesty support for political prisoners, amongst other things, allowed a certain continuity with the past which was both comforting and counterproductive in terms of my need to find meaning in the world closer to home. I asked myself whether it was realistic to be retaining my grip on my other life in Jakarta. I began to force myself to go out to movies and dinner with friends, to engage in the pastimes of people of a similar social background. Nevertheless, it took a long time to reconcile the pull to Jakarta with my attempt at a normal life in Australia.

I decided to change my name and apply for a new passport. It was a decision I reached after much soul-searching and some detailed research on the processes involved. What's in a name? I thought, as I debated the course of action with myself. In my case, it was the difference between being able to do my job and visit a country I couldn't imagine never seeing again, and not doing these longed-for things.

A field visit to Indonesia was looming in early June, and I was thankful that the process of applying for a new passport was speedy. Since this particular trip was to take me to Kalimantan, Lombok, Bali and only briefly to Jakarta, towards the end of the trip, I was confident that my presence in the country would go unnoticed by all those responsible for investigating my case. After all, I was hardly a household name or face and, in a population of over 200 million, I would be pretty unlucky to run into the handful or so of intelligence agents who were likely to recognise me if they came across me in the street.

In spite of my confidence, I dabbed a drop or two of the *kyai*'s *minyak angin* on my temples as I disembarked from my Qantas plane at Jakarta's Sukarno-Hatta Airport. I breathed in its heady fumes, gritting my teeth as I waited for the immigration official at passport control to hand back my travel documents. I heard him punch something into the computer. I could hardly repress the grin that appeared spontaneously on my lips when, finally, he slapped my passport down on the counter in front of me. Knowing that Xanana was aware of the estimated time of my arrival in the capital and would have his mobile phone switched on, I called him immediately from one of the public phones in the arrivals hall. 'I'm back, I'm here. It worked! See you in half an hour,' I joked. It didn't matter that I wouldn't see him in half an hour. What mattered was that I could, that we had reclaimed the right to occupy space in the same city, in the same country. Instead, I boarded a plane for Samarinda in East Kalimantan and for two weeks I visited volunteers and identified new placements for future volunteers in a range of government and non-government organisations.

On the one hand, it was as if I had never left the land of Pancasila, that this trip was a continuation of the life I had left behind in January. On the other hand, this visit had the feel of a new era or a new beginning.

At the conclusion of the field trip, I spent four days back in Jakarta. It was a strange sensation to be in the city where I never imagined I would set foot again after the 'complications' of the previous six months. There were many people, like Puto, whom I would very much have liked to meet with, but I promised myself that I would not run unnecessary risks. Xanana was not to be dissuaded from his compulsive gift-giving, however. He had Herbin deliver chocolates and a painting to my small guesthouse in Menteng. The painting was the latest in the 'time tunnel' series. It was based on the photo I had taken back in January amongst the summer flowers that filled my parents' back garden in Moonee Ponds. The colours on the canvas were rich and cheering; the smell of the accompanying letters carried Xanana's familiar scent.

I arrived home in Melbourne with the knowledge that my return to Indonesia had been important, and not only from the point of view of my performance of my work-related duties. I now had some happy experiences and memories of Jakarta with which to supplant those of the dreadful days of anxiety, illness and flight six months earlier. It had been like mounting again the horse that had thrown me. I felt like I had taken an important step forward and that the normality of my life back in Australia was something I could now more readily embrace.

Chapter twelve

THRESHOLD
September 1996–July 1997

HOME. HOMELAND. They were concepts that my return to Australia and my ongoing work for East Timor caused me to ponder. I had never had a very strong sense of belonging to the Australian land, and the East Timorese people's notion of *pátria* or homeland, which was the force behind their struggle for self-determination, was both beguiling and fascinating to me. I debated the question with Xanana in a series of written exchanges. He told me that he believed that 'the sentiment of *pátria*' derives from a people's need to seek an identity for themselves, to 'position' themselves in the world and in relation to other peoples. He shared with me his view that love for one's country is born and strengthened only when a threat is posed to the 'position' or identity a people have forged for themselves, and that the absence of such threats, in addition to the effects of globalisation, was the reason why most people in the Western world found the concept of *pátria* an alien one. He explained how he had only really acquired a love of country and a sense of a Timorese identity after the

Indonesian invasion. 'Now you have a second pátria. As for our children, they will have the possibility of choosing.'

Life became increasingly full and busy for me as I took up the thread of my involvement with *Inside Indonesia* magazine once again and became a board member of the East Timor Human Rights Centre, an organisation which reported on human rights violations in the territory and trained East Timorese in monitoring and documentation methodologies. Nevertheless, I did my best to continue to support Xanana in his efforts to stay in touch with the key players in the resistance and solidarity movements abroad, relaying messages back and forth with the invaluable and brave assistance of individuals like Herbin. Failures in the technology that continued to be our lifeline presented challenges not easily grappled with from a distance. On numerous occasions Xanana's mobile connection was cut off, provoking anxiety as to the reasons. More often than not simple late payment of the bills was to blame, but fears of detection by military intelligence and deliberate sabotage were never far from our minds. When Xanana's laptop malfunctioned he had to send it to Herbin for repair. The costs involved in fixing it were very high, and by the time I had managed to raise the necessary funds and get them to Jakarta, Xanana was experiencing intense withdrawal. He had grown accustomed to committing his words to hard and floppy disks and enjoyed badgering me with 'technical support' calls to my office: 'How do I alter the margins of this document?' 'Damn, I've lost the letter I spent three days writing to you! Where can it have gone?' As I whispered my advice down the line in Portuguese, I often wondered what my colleagues would think if they knew to whom I was talking and about what.

The tyranny of distance and the costs associated with bridging it put inevitable strains on our relationship, resulting in an occasional eruption of violent emotion and the odd quarrel. But essentially, by now we had both reached a certain acceptance of our new circumstances.

On the eve of my second field trip to Indonesia, in late

September 1996, I phoned Xanana and was horrified to hear the recording in Indonesian: 'At the request of the customer, the mobile phone you are calling has been disconnected.' There seemed to be no logical explanation. Herbin assured me that the latest bill was paid up. I set off for Jakarta feeling decidedly uneasy and apprehensive.

The feeling that something was missing and amiss intensified as I checked into the room of my guesthouse in Menteng the following evening. I longed to hear Xanana's words of welcome, to celebrate with him the happy sensation of being once again physically close. Each time I dialled his number I encountered the same irritating recorded message.

On the second night in Jakarta, I switched on the TV in my room to distract myself from the absence of contact with Xanana. One of the items on the late news bulletin was the announcement of the 1996 winners of the Nobel Peace Prize: the bishop of the diocese of Dili, Carlos Ximenes Belo, and Indonesia's public enemy number one, José Ramos-Horta. The prize was a diplomatic blow for Indonesia: a body of great repute had raised José's status and profile, conferring international recognition and legitimacy on his work for East Timorese self-determination. Unable to share the good news with Xanana, I phoned Herbin. We chuckled together about how Ali Alatas, Foreign Minister of Indonesia, had appeared, ashen-faced, before reporters to respond to the announcement. He was caught off guard. How could he call into question the Nobel committee's choice of José without appearing to question the credibility of the bishop as a recipient? If he denigrated the choice of José Ramos-Horta, by implication he also, rather blasphemously, called into question the choice of Bishop Belo.

As had happened following the Santa Cruz massacre, the eyes of the world turned to East Timor. It was a small but decisive victory.

Back at home, I attended the Melbourne Cup for the first time in my life and won $40 on a horse called Saintly. This time I was able to share the good news with Xanana as the purchase of a new telephone account had solved our mobile woes. I joked with him that we were on a roll and that my surprise win signalled a change in East Timor's fortunes. It did indeed appear that things were looking up.

In December Kofi Annan was appointed as the new Secretary-General of the United Nations and he immediately announced his intention of working intensively to bring about a rapid solution to the East Timor problem. Annan chose Ambassador Jamsheed Marker to represent him in the ongoing negotiations involving Indonesia and Portugal, and Xanana received his first visit from the amiable Pakistani gentleman in March 1997. He interpreted the visit as proof of the UN's commitment to drawing the East Timorese people themselves into the discussions about their future.

But an equally momentous event was just around the corner.

In July 1997 Xanana wrote to me with an amazing account of his meeting with Nelson Mandela. One afternoon, at 4 pm, he had been on the football field, ready for an important match against another cell block. As the umpire hadn't appeared, he went to find a prison official to take his place. It was while he was looking for one that he was called to the guard post of his block where the head of the prison, the Kepala Kanwil (chief of the District Office of Correctional Institutions) – whom Xanana had once called an idiot – and another official from Deplu (the Ministry of Foreign Affairs) were waiting for him.

They came to his cell and, despite Xanana's attempt to explain how important and decisive the soccer match was, they seated themselves with nods and smiles. They were extremely friendly, enquiring about his health, his activities and the Red Cross. Then the head of the prison asked whether he would like to meet with Nelson Mandela. Xanana was shocked and looked the prison head straight in the eye while the Kepala Kanwil explained that if Xanana would like an audience with the President of South Africa, he would do him a favour and help him out. Xanana, not quite believing what he heard, was silent.

The prison head told Xanana that he was to speak to no one, including the other Timorese prisoners, of the meeting. It was to be their secret. Because of Mandela's advanced age, it was necessary for Xanana to leave the prison and meet Mandela where he was staying. The prison officials appealed to Xanana to understand the risk they faced in allowing the meeting to take place and pleaded with him to behave himself. He assured them that he wouldn't attempt to escape and reminded them that if he wanted to be free and living the good life abroad he could have taken up any one of a number of offers that had been made to him. Perhaps they were incredulous when he told them that if he ever found himself at the main entrance to the prison and the door was open, he would shut it himself.

The prison officials were pleased with his response, which had impressed the foreign affairs chap. But the Kepala Kanwil added that at this stage the meeting was only a possibility – they would do what they could to help him. Xanana let them think he believed them – that they were doing him a great favour and that it wasn't, in fact, Nelson Mandela who had requested the meeting with him. He thanked them and then, because he was about to play a decisive soccer match, asked when the meeting was to take place.

Now, they said. Xanana wasn't happy about this, and because the Kepala Kanwil didn't want him to be cranky when he met Mandela, he gave him permission to participate in the match first. The prison head recommended that he dress neatly and when Xanana commented that this would be noticed by the other prisoners, the Kepala Kanwil suggested that he wrap his good clothes in newspaper and get changed in his office.

Much to his annoyance, Xanana's team lost the game, 2 to 1. They dropped from fourth to fifth place on the competition ladder. His letter to me describing the meeting with Mandela was riveting in its detail and irresistible in its humour.

> After the game, I returned to my cell, took a bath and waited to be called . . . 6:30 pm and still nobody came to call me . . . At ten past seven, I was called by an official from

the office. I got dressed and off I went. Some of my fellow prisoners noticed me passing and one (serving a fifteen-year term) 'insulted me', thinking that I was about to be released. I put on the watch I had bought and carried with me a neck tie which Bintang had given me . . . Almost the entire staff of the prison was out the front. I don't know what was going through their minds . . .

About twenty minutes later we were ordered to depart. When they tried to get me to put on a batik shirt, I refused and told them I was going to put on my tie. They agreed and so off we went.

What looked like a Timor car was waiting outside. Three guys, probably from BIA, Bakin or the police, were my guards. They shook hands with me repeatedly, saying that they trusted me and that they knew nothing untoward was going to happen along the way etc. I tried to put them at ease and the ride to our destination was quite pleasant. We passed alongside the Monas monument, some statues of prancing horses and then a little further on we entered the grounds of the presidential palace.

I was directed to a door and in we went. It was a small compartment, lined with mirrors on each wall. I searched for a door through which to pass, with my reflection staring back at me from every direction. It was only when the door closed that I realised I was in an elevator! The buttons indicated that we were headed for the sixth floor. Getting out of the lift, I was greeted by some officials of the Dept of Foreign Affairs. One of them told me that Chico Lopes [Francisco Lopes da Cruz, a prominent pro-integration figure and Indonesia's roving ambassador for East Timor] was present too, and that I was to dine with the President. I was a little stunned, never having attended before a gala dinner, let alone with a president.

Despite the fact that back at the prison one of my guards had addressed me in English, and so too with one of the

Deplu officials there in the Istana, I was even more stunned when I contemplated how I was going to communicate with Nelson Mandela. The prospect of Chico Lopes acting as my interpreter didn't take my fancy, since I'd already had an experience of this with Clementino Amaral and the National Commission of Human Rights and the Legal Aid Institute.

After about a five-minute wait, I was led down some stairs by a Deplu official, probably from the protocol section. We entered a room which was full of South Africans, and then after passing through another door, I was asked to wait. As I entered, I saw Chico Lopes chatting with the South African president.

I had already prepared to greet him with 'It's a great honour for me to meet Your Excellence'. As I shook his hand this is precisely what I said, and in response I heard him utter 'I'm honoured to see you'. Inside I felt embarrassed, but imagined that such a form of address was more formality than anything. However, for my part it was truly an honour given my situation as a prisoner and his tremendous international political stature.

He guided me to a table whilst explaining that we would eat while talking. I imagined that he would simply indicate my place at the table, however he actually pulled out my chair for me and invited me to sit down prior to taking his own place. I felt . . . so small! And a little horrified by what was happening to me!!! Deep down in my soul, however, I also felt an immeasurable happiness because I knew and I felt that my people were being respected and, at the same time, this was a political lesson for Chico Lopes. Only out of respect for Nelson Mandela did I contain my hatred of the guy.

There were three chairs at the table, however it appeared that either Chico was an uninvited guest or that Mandela had invited him to join us for dinner only at the last minute since there were only two places set at the table.

Mandela said that he hadn't counted on Chico's presence, but that if he wished to eat . . . I knew that Mandela would forgive me my awkwardness in terms of table manners, and besides I was determined not to do anything to embarrass myself. My pride as a Timorese dictated that I avoid giving Chico Lopes the slightest opportunity to call me a 'savage' or 'man of the jungles'.

While we waited to be served, Nelson Mandela began to speak, enquiring as to whether I had been informed that he wished to meet with me. I responded that indeed I had been informed of this at 4 pm that afternoon. As you can imagine, he spoke neither Portuguese, Tetum nor Bahasa Indonesia.

He had told Suharto that it wasn't possible for him to avoid bringing up the problem of East Timor since prior to his departure from Africa various human rights organisations had demanded that he do just this. And he had requested a meeting with me. At first, Suharto didn't accept the request. However, Mandela explained to the dictator that when he himself was in prison he had received visits from various foreign entities (he named them all one by one, but I don't remember now who they were) and also South African government officials. And apparently this had the effect of changing Suharto's mind. He told me that his intervention was in the context of achieving peace, and he spoke of the need for peace . . . and we began our meal.

He spoke of the history of the process of reconciliation in South Africa, the first secret meetings with government officials who demanded that he distance himself from the Communist faction, and then the various compromises reached between the different parties involved. He said that every freedom fighter must remain true to his or her principles, without which he or she ceases to be a freedom fighter, however . . . without abandoning those same principles, one must remain focussed on achieving peace. And peace can only be attained through dialogue.

The conversation was interrupted, because Mandela preferred chicken to fish . . .

He told me that he had known of the East Timor problem for a long time, that he is interested in assisting us to find peace, and that I should consider the possibility of autonomy. He added that Suharto is also interested in the problem, and Suharto 'and you' are good people who have it within our capacity to come to an understanding and to achieve peace.

I had my eyes on him the whole time and gave him my full attention as he spoke, particularly since I needed to concentrate fully in order to understand his words in English . . . When he started talking about autonomy, I began to eat and I let him speak . . . after all, I was hungry by this time. He seemed to note my attitude . . .

He went on, saying that personally 'I support your struggle', but as a mediator, he needed to remain neutral. He said that the Indonesian government is prepared to enter into a dialogue with me and he asked whether or not I myself was open to dialogue with the government.

I apologised for not being able to express myself well in English and he responded that this was not a problem and that he doesn't know Portuguese . . . and then he remembered . . . 'My companion, Graça Machel [wife of Samora Machel, the first President of Mozambique, who was killed in a plane crash in 1986], sends you her greetings, she knows a lot about you and is a great fan of yours. Unfortunately she had to leave for London already because her son is about to undergo an eye operation' . . . and then he explained how Mozambique was a great supporter of the ANC, Samora Machel, Marcelino dos Santos etc. I thanked him and had gained the courage to go on . . .

I told him that I had always been open to dialogue and that we had always shown ourselves to be prepared to talk, however it had always been the Indonesian government which had taken a position of inflexibility.

He then asked whether he could take notes. This assisted me immensely, because it allowed me to think, i.e. to choose my words in English carefully. I regretted so much that Graça Machel couldn't be present as this would have permitted me to express myself more clearly in Portuguese.

I told him that I wasn't sure whether I should be taking the question of autonomy seriously given that Suharto himself had rejected the notion on many occasions.

Chico Lopes then interjected, saying that Suharto hadn't actually rejected autonomy outright, but rather that he was against the general concept of autonomy being granted to all of Indonesia's provinces . . .

I tried to remember the year in which I had proposed dialogue without pre-conditions and the bastard Chico did me the favour of prompting me by saying that it was in 1983 that there had been meetings with Mario Carrascalão, possibly insinuating that already back then I had shown myself open to dialogue with the Indonesian government. Mandela seemed interested and took a lot of notes. He asked me some questions and I explained the process whereby I had proposed a peace plan with UN intervention, but that Benny Murdani had stated that if we didn't surrender he would exterminate us, and that that statement had precipitated the end of the cease-fire.

I mentioned our preparedness to enter into dialogue without pre-conditions, given that if both sides remained inflexible it would be impossible to find a basis for dialogue and then I reminded him of the CNRM Peace Plan.

He referred to the fact that the apartheid regime of South Africa, in the difficult years of their first approach to him, had been most concerned about saving face, and so I told him that the CNRM Peace Plan provided Indonesia with a solution whereby they could avoid losing face . . . Indonesia has always stuck fast to the line that it is us who must accept that East Timor is integrated. I said to him 'Mr President, I'm sure you understand that we can never accept that, under threat of violence, our people must state that they accept integration'. (I should have called him 'your excellency'.) 'I see,' he replied as he noted down what I had said. I informed him that recently the government had arrested (and it was Chico Lopes who helped me with the word 'arrest' in English) over 300 people.

I recalled that 17 July was the anniversary of integration. Mandela asked in what year East Timor had been 'integrated'. Chico Lopes replied without hesitation '1977'. I added quickly that in that year only 10 per cent of the population was under Indonesian control and that 90 per cent were holding out in the bush, dying from bomb attacks, hunger and disease. And that since then over 200,000 had died as a result of the war Indonesia had waged against our people.

Mandela asked whether the same percentage of people continue to resist today and I told him that in 1978 and 1979 large-scale operations were launched against the population and many were taken into custody. I impressed upon him that 17 July had no significance whatsoever in either the political or the legal sense.

I pointed to Chico and told Mandela that he had been the president of a nationalist party and that we acknowledged our mistakes of the past, above all our political immaturity. For reasons of ideological difference, Chico had broken away from the . . . I was searching for the word 'coligaçao' in English, and Chico prompted me with 'coalition'. I continued, saying that Chico Lopes had opted for integration. The bastard interjected with 'no, independence with Indonesia', and I shot a dagger of a look in his direction.

'Now, as Ambassador' – Mandela asked me what I meant by 'ambassador', and so, no longer referring to Chico as 'Mr Lopes' but simply as 'he', I went on to describe his work of travelling the world and defending the position of the Indonesians. Chico tried to correct me by saying 'to handle', and I cut him off, insisting 'to defend the Indonesian government's position'. Mandela continued taking notes and said 'I see . . .'

Chico Lopes looked embarrassed, and he tried to hide this by explaining that the two of us had been colleagues in the seminary and that I was a poet and a painter . . .

When he had finished, I noticed that what he was trying to do was to cut short my conversation with Mandela. I explained to Mandela that it was Chico who travelled the world saying that East Timor was integrated, that all the East Timorese are happy under Indonesian occupation (Chico interrupted with 'I didn't say everybody, I said the majority'), calling us terrorists just as the regime in South Africa used to refer to the ANC. And then I went on 'Mr President, it is a great honour for me to have this opportunity to talk with you, and I am tremendously grateful for the help you have offered, however I must say how very, very sad it makes me to consider that an East Timorese like Chico Lopes (I pointed in his direction) is prepared to deny the blood shed by his own people, to ignore the deaths caused by the war in East Timor . . . This man has chosen to forget the blood of his own brothers and the suffering of our people'. The idiot was embarrassed and all he could utter was 'ya, ya'. I didn't know whether to laugh or to sock him in the face!

Mandela and I then began to exchange a few words in English and I was just getting warmed up when Chico broke in, saying that integration was legitimate because four parties had signed the Balibo Declaration. Without hesitation, I exclaimed that four parties did not necessarily mean that there was majority support for integration. Mandela came to my defence, saying 'no, not necessarily'. Chico then added that it was noted at the UN that UDT had the support of around 50 per cent of the population. I almost shouted at him 'And how can you prove that? Was a referendum ever held?' Mandela had been following our conversation and when he noticed that I was getting heated, he said 'no, no, stop fighting. Please stop fighting!'

I apologised and then he went on to explain that his role wasn't to resolve the conflict, but rather to mediate in a process of dialogue between me and the Indonesian government. And that his sole objective was to see peace returned to the territory.

I told him that I had heard that South Africa intended to become a member of the Non-Aligned Movement. He said yes and that the next NAM conference would be held in South Africa.

I reminded him that Indonesia, co-founder of the movement, had violated the principles of NAM along with international law, universal principles and the norms of decolonisation. I told him that I understood what his intention was in relating the process of reconciliation in South Africa. Whilst the objectives of the struggle of the ANC may be similar to our own, the cases of South Africa and East Timor are in fact totally different. East Timor was a case of the violation of international law. UN resolutions had condemned the invasion and peace in East Timor was an impossible goal in the absence of respect for international law, for universal principles and those of the Non-Aligned Movement.

I found myself searching for the word 'realçar' in English and, as had been the case a few times already, I was forced to turn to Chico Lopes for help. 'Make clear' came Lopes' reply, and so I turned to Mandela and said, 'I want to make clear that, whilst remaining open to any proposals for dialogue, no solution is possible outside the context of the United Nations. I defend the Portuguese position.' Mandela then asked what exactly the Portuguese position was and it was Chico Lopes who responded with 'self-determination'. I added that Portugal is recognised by the UN as the administrative power and therefore whilst I was appreciative of his efforts in attaining peace and of the approaches he had made to the Indonesian government, East Timor continues to be a problem of the international community.

As Mandela was busily taking down notes, the idiot Chico once again attempted to sidetrack the conversation, asking me how old I was and going on to inform Mandela that we used to play basketball together . . .

I went on, 'We want peace. My people have suffered too long already. We have learnt a great deal from what happened in South Africa and I assure you, Mr President, that when peace comes to East Timor there will be no more bloodshed, no more violence, no traitors nor heroes, because what we aspire to is true freedom for our homeland.'

Mandela then said 'I appreciate very much your position' and went on to state that a man without principles is not worthy of respect. He stated that he was pleased to have this opportunity to get better acquainted with aspects of the East Timor struggle. 'You have many friends abroad,' he said, adding that he would transmit the contents of our discussion to Suharto (he kept saying Sukarno or Suharno), including my preparedness to begin talking to the Indonesian government. He gave his commitment that he would do everything in his power to continue to mediate, that he hoped to meet me again and that Suharno [*sic*] is a reasonable man who he doesn't believe will deny him further access to me.

He said that he had already taken his leave of Suharto but that he would report to him on his meeting. As he was

> due to depart from Indonesia the following morning at 7 am, there ended our meeting. I thanked him again for his interest in the problem of East Timor and asked him to present my greetings to Madame Machel. Chico and I then had to help to get him up from his chair due to the rheumatism in his knees!
>
> In the interests of good diplomacy, I exchanged a word or two with Chico, shook his hand. He made some statement to the effect that he hoped we would soon reach a solution, and without hesitating I added, 'Yes, that doesn't offend the spirit of our people.'

Xanana described to me how Mandela and a companion, whom Xanana took to be his secretary, watched and laughed as he and Lopes da Cruz shook hands. He was pleased – it was a diplomatic victory and he wished to convey to Mandela the impression that the Timorese were politically mature.

Characteristically, on the way back to Cipinang he kept the guards amused. They arrived back at the prison at 10:30 pm, and all the night duty staff greeted him as if he was some kind of celebrity. It was the first time that someone wearing a tie had left the prison, only to return a few hours later, he quipped.

Mandela had told Xanana that because he had been pressured by groups outside Indonesia to meet him, if he were asked, he was not planning to divulge all the details of their conversation. Lopes da Cruz had then taken the opportunity to request that Mandela appeal to Suharto to authorise future meetings.

I felt as though I were a fly on the wall reading Xanana's account of how Mandela pointed in the direction of Lopes da Cruz as he related the history of the struggle in South Africa, even though he was speaking to Xanana. Mandela apologised for pointing, saying that he was aware that it was impolite in Indonesian culture. Lopes da Cruz said that it wasn't a problem because the Timorese had been influenced by Portuguese culture. Xanana jumped in to point out 'we are different, we have different cultures'.

The next morning, Xanana related, he was summoned at 8 am by the head of prison security, who wanted to question him about the meeting. Xanana gave a general outline, explaining that Chico Lopes had been present and that he had noted everything Xanana had said with the purpose of reporting it himself to President Suharto. Xanana told the head of prison security that he perceived that Mandela wished to act as a mediator in the conflict and intended to assist in facilitating contact between Xanana and the Indonesian government.

The head of prison security asked whether Xanana was prepared to enter into dialogue with the government and he replied in the affirmative, adding that the resistance had always been open to dialogue. He explained that Mandela's objective was to achieve a peaceful resolution, given that the conflict had dragged on for twenty-two years. Suddenly the head of the prison asked about Portugal. From the unexpectedness of the question, Xanana knew that Chico must have already communicated something about this to them, and now they were seeking confirmation.

Xanana responded with the argument that Timorese in favour of self-determination had stuck to for years: whilst he accepted dialogue with the Indonesian government, he could not deny the fact that East Timor was a case for the UN. Even if he were to come to accept integration, the UN would continue to defend an internationally acceptable solution. He cited the example of Cambodia, where Indonesia had acted as a mediator within the context of UN intervention, and went on to explain that he was unable to act in an individual capacity and neglect the role of Portugal and the UN. The head of the prison nodded his understanding and then changed the subject.

Xanana's meeting with Mandela was clearly not only another turning point for East Timor but also profoundly important to Xanana at a personal level. Mandela's request for the meeting would have sent a strong message to Suharto regarding the international community's perception that Xanana's involvement was a key to the achievement of a political solution – and I sensed from the light-hearted and optimistic tone of his letter that Xanana had derived tremendous satisfaction from this fact. It was hard to resist the temptation to share the letter's contents with my friends. But Xanana warned me that he had given Mandela his assurance that he would not publicly divulge details of their conversation. And so I kept it to myself.

Upon his return to South Africa, Mandela wrote to Suharto calling for Xanana's release. The old dictator responded by granting him three months remission on his sentence.

This focus of international attention on East Timor coincided with the collapse of the Asian 'tiger' economies, including Indonesia's. The economic meltdown exposed how shallow Indonesia's boom had been, built as it was on debt and corrupt and unsustainable practices. Finally the bubble had burst. Optimists with vision might have been able to guess that the region's altered economic fortunes would serve as a catalyst for substantial and long-awaited political change in both Indonesia and East Timor.

Chapter thirteen

THE BEST THING THAT COULD HAPPEN
August 1997–August 1998

DESPITE THE ECONOMIC meltdown, the New Order security apparatus was still on the job. In 1997 I was spotted by intelligence during a visit to Jakarta. Adrina and I had caught up in a large shopping complex not far from her office. I can't remember if we went shopping for office stationery or if we simply met up for a coffee. Later, when I had returned to Australia, Adrina told me that she had been visited by officials who asked her what I'd been doing in Indonesia. She denied I'd been there. They said they'd seen her with me and named the place where we'd met.

Such a sighting was pretty surprising given the size of Jakarta and the density of its population. Two years after my meetings with Leman and the *kyai*, I suppose their *rejeki* was beginning to wear a little thin. I decided to accept the advice of my colleagues and superiors at the OSB and take on responsibility for another country in the region. It was a decision made easier by the sense we had that the calls for reform within Indonesia were gaining momentum and that the New Order regime's days were numbered. It was my great hope that when Suharto did finally go, he would take his blacklist with him.

I became responsible for the OSB's small volunteer program in Malaysia, shortly after taking on the role of program officer for Thailand. The Thai countryside was beautiful, its people and culture engaging. I found the relative detachment – the sense that this was not 'my' country and that my future wasn't bound up with it – pleasantly refreshing. Nevertheless, Xanana did his best to ensure that my commitment to East Timor was not allowed to wane. Prior to my first field trip to Bangkok, he wrote to give me the contact details of a Thai NGO that was actively promoting the cause of East Timorese self-determination amongst the ASEAN member states. I had an interesting meeting with the members of the group, some of whom had managed to visit Xanana in Cipinang in the preceding months.

My main misgiving about my new job in Thailand related to my inability to speak the language. I had grown accustomed in Indonesia to being able to communicate with people from all strata of society, from *pedi*-cab drivers to high officials in the government, and to use the tool of language to 'get inside' their heads. My lack of Thai language skills meant that I could communicate directly only with educated middle-class people who spoke English, and I felt that this stood in the way of my understanding more fully what made ordinary Thais tick.

Not having had a holiday in almost two years, it was a relief to take off for Mexico for a three-week break. Given that my work involved being on the move constantly, my family and friends thought I was mad to opt for such a far-flung destination. Although I wrote to Xanana every day, I was glad to put the problems of East Timor and my work in Asia aside for a while and immerse myself in Central American culture, which was new and different and didn't have the same 'grip' on me that Southeast Asia did. With my two travelling companions, I explored Mexico City, scrambled through the ruins of Aztec temples and climbed the steeply sloping flanks of the pyramids of Teotihuacan. The feeling of being a tourist was invigorating. I returned to Australia via Seattle in the United States. I had lived and attended school there in 1979 when my father was granted a place in an international teaching exchange program. I stayed a week with the gregarious couple who had been our neighbours almost twenty years earlier, taking early morning runs in the woods, enjoying the balmy weather of the late northern hemisphere summer, drinking in the majestic beauty of the Pacific Northwest.

But early one evening, something happened to jolt me out of my holiday reverie and return East Timor to the forefront of my mind. Herbin phoned the home of my American friends to inform me that Avelino and his family had entered the Austrian Embassy in Jakarta to seek asylum, following accusations that he was the mastermind behind an attempt to manufacture bombs in the Central Java town of Semarang. A homemade bomb, supposedly one of many being manufactured to destroy military targets inside East Timor, had accidentally exploded in the home of a youth linked to the clandestine front. Documents seized in the police raid on the house had led the authorities to Avelino. They had also uncovered a letter of Xanana's directed to Nino Konis Santana, the vice-commander of Falintil.

Back in Melbourne, I was horrified – if not surprised – to learn that Xanana had signed a written statement in which he claimed responsibility for the initiative to manufacture the Semarang bombs as a means of relieving Avelino of blame. In doing so, his hope was that Avelino, his children and his heavily pregnant wife would be permitted by the Indonesian authorities to leave the country. For his troubles, Xanana was stripped of the three months remission he had been granted in August and threatened with the prospect of being transferred to the remote island prison of Nusa Kambangan. The thought filled me with fear and dread – I knew about the harsh conditions the island was renowned for, and that Xanana's transfer would deal a mortal blow to our communication.

As we were in the midst of yet another mobile phone crisis – once again delayed payment of the phone bills had caused the connection to be cut off – I was unable to share my concerns with Xanana. He had Herbin send me a fax containing a copy of the statement he had signed. In its margins was scribbled a note:

> Querida, I hope I can count on you to be strong in facing this latest challenge. We will come through it as we have the vast number of other trials. Please don't worry about me. I am trying to negotiate the reconnection of the phone, but the problem is that the last connection was registered in Avelino's name and let's just say that he's presently unavailable to settle the accounts. There are whispers that my cell will be inspected, and so perhaps this little lapse in our communication is for the best. Please try to organise some money to cover the medical bills of João Bosco, who was injured in the Semarang blast. I will write to you again soon. I love you, X.

The matter-of-fact tone of Xanana's note reinforced to me what I had long known: that our separation and the difficulties of sustaining a relationship in our adverse circumstances were, to him, just one more privation in a long list of privations, an additional hardship in the context of twenty years of struggle. He lived by the principle of *a luta continua* (the struggle goes on) and, if I was to survive the incalculable period of his imprisonment that stretched out before us, I knew that I needed to do the same. And so I buried my fears and longing, and filled the hours when I wasn't working at the office or attending meetings on East Timor with carrying out Xanana's requests.

A week after Xanana's note, I received a letter from him carried by one of my colleagues who had just returned from Jakarta. By then, with the advent of email and mobile phone, paper letters were more of a rarity, but it still gave me a special thrill to rip open the envelope containing Xanana's words and feel something of his presence in the fragrance of the pages, the familiarity of his handwriting.

The letter was dated 20 November 1997, the fifth anniversary of his capture in Dili.

> Five years have gone by and, I don't know why, but this year I feel there is something special about this day. Perhaps it was the fact of remembering the anniversary of my capture in the middle of another round of interrogations. Perhaps it is the difficult knowledge that I am unable to share this moment with you. Five long years which seem like a huge chunk of life in which memories abound and memory itself dredges up longing and sadness. It's now four years since I was moved to Cipinang and I believe that it is here that I have reached the apex of all my efforts for the struggle. And at the personal level, too, I feel that we have reached a new phase in our relationship. Love has ceased to be something felt but rather lived, the romanticism of the past having been replaced with a kind of realism, the flowery language of the past giving way to a more pragmatic expression of our feelings for one another. It's as if our love has followed the course of a married couple who, in these modern times, come together only fleetingly in the evenings to share the drudgery of the day and to recharge their batteries in preparation for the following one. And so you see, my love, our lives already carry the seed of the future life that awaits us.
>
> You won't believe it, but I have been chosen by the other prisoners to direct this year's Christmas play and vocal group. It is a shame that you have just taken your holidays as I have a premonition that you would be allowed to attend the Christmas celebrations planned for 23 December. In anticipation of Christmas, I agreed to help make some repairs to the prison chapel. The economic crisis has inflated prices dramatically. Building materials that cost Rp 100,000 before now cost Rp 200,000. Perhaps I shall have to follow Suharto's lead and seek a 'rescue package' from the IMF!

I tried not to allow the thought of a possible Christmas visit to play too much on my mind, nor the promise of that 'future life' of which Xanana spoke in his letter. Instead I tried to stay focussed on my work and on the unfolding events in Jakarta, which carried the hint of promise in themselves.

In early 1998, the price of basic commodities in Indonesia skyrocketed, the value of the Indonesian rupiah was spiralling downwards and Suharto came under increasing domestic and international pressure to salvage the ailing economy. Social unrest and demonstrations were erupting in many Indonesian cities. With phone contact once again re-established, Xanana and I spent many evenings talking until the early hours of the morning, speculating as to where the country was headed, what the prospects were for a peaceful transition to democracy should Suharto resign, and the consequences of all of this for East Timor . . . and for us. There were no answers, of course, but our spirits were buoyed by the feeling we had that change – for better or for worse – was afoot. I wondered whether Avelino was managing to keep abreast of developments from inside the Austrian Embassy. It seemed that the Indonesian authorities had decided not to accept Xanana's declaration of responsibility for the Semarang incident, as the threats of sanctions against him were never acted upon and Avelino's request for political asylum was consistently refused. At the same time, the Austrian government was nervous about the potential for strident criticism from human rights groups if they forcibly expelled the group from their embassy and so the situation was at a stalemate.

At the beginning of 1998 I had the opportunity to convey the news of the effects of the economic downturn on the political landscape in Jakarta directly to the armed resistance inside East Timor. I had my first telephone contact with Nino Konis Santana, who had taken over command of the guerrilla struggle after Ma'Huno was captured in 1993. I was in Darwin teaching a short course in human rights documentation to a group of East Timorese, one of whom had helped smuggle a satellite phone to Konis in his mountain hide-out. A time was set for Konis to call the mobile phone of the friend in whose home I was staying. It so happened that we had organised to see a film that evening, and at the appointed hour we were engrossed in a documentary in the darkened auditorium of a local cinema.

When the phone rang, my heart leapt and I groped my way along the aisle to the exit. I took the call outside the cinema and spoke to Konis as I paced the pavements, which were slick with the drizzle of the afternoon's monsoonal rains. I had written to Konis, and from Jakarta had sent him and the other guerrilla commanders regular batches of Portuguese press clippings about East Timor. But it was exhilarating to actually talk to him.

I tried to imagine the place from which he spoke to me: perhaps he crouched by a bush in a clearing where a good connection to the nearest satellite was guaranteed, or perched on a high rocky plateau on the slopes of Mount Ramelau. Knowing of my contact with Xanana, Konis was keen to speak to him himself. Konis' practice was to turn on his satellite phone for half an hour from 6 pm Dili time. I conveyed this information, with details of the time difference and Konis' telephone number, to Xanana, who subsequently made weekly calls to the bush.

My next and last contact with Konis was on 9 March 1998. On that occasion, I expressed my concerns to him about the security of satellite communications. I told him the story I had heard of how the location of the leader of the Chechnyan resistance had been identified by the Russians through the telephone calls he had made to his girlfriend using a satellite phone. As a result he was killed in an air attack. I advised Konis to take care, particularly with the use of names and references to locations. Konis died tragically of a heart attack two days after our telephone conversation. His death was a blow to the armed resistance, but at a personal level, too, I felt the loss very keenly. Through what had become regular telephone conversations, I had established a rapport with the softly spoken guerrilla commander and derived great personal pleasure from being a sympathetic voice and a source of solidarity and support for his lonely struggle.

In April 1998, a congress of the National Council of Maubere Resistance (CNRM) held in Peniche in Portugal unanimously elected Xanana as president and renamed itself the National Council of Timorese Resistance (CNRT).

After the shooting of six students of Jakarta's Trisakti University in May, rioting broke out across the Indonesian capital. Youth, students and others in favour of reform organised huge demonstrations in cities across Java, calling for Suharto's resignation. Understandably, many people felt a mixture of fear and concern coupled with great uncertainty and nervousness about what was going to happen. There had not been a change of leadership in Indonesia for more than thirty years. Would Suharto's resignation result in a revolution of some kind?

I was temporarily 'recalled' to the Indonesia desk at work to help my colleagues formulate a strategy to deal with the predictions of Suharto's downfall and the country's uncertain political future. In the absence of a precedent, it was difficult to calculate what the consequences of a change of government would be for foreigners resident in the country. We could only keep our finger on the pulse to monitor developments, and this meant working into the evenings; scouring the local and international media for the latest news; making phone calls to volunteers and their employers across the country; allaying the fears of family members in Australia; and assessing and reformulating the evacuation plan we had established. The outbreak of violence and looting in the capital, and the volatility of the situation in a number of other major centres, meant that some of the volunteers in Jakarta opted to come home permanently. Others on assignment in the farther-flung parts of the country only came to know of the problems in Jakarta and the pressure on Suharto to resign from the newspapers and television.

By the time the moment of truth arrived, I was almost too exhausted to celebrate. We had received a tip-off on 21 May that Suharto was going to announce his resignation and we had radios at the ready on our desks, tuned in to Radio Australia. Someone went out to buy champagne in anticipation of the announcement. So we sat around the radio and there were great whoops of joy and popping champagne corks when the old dictator finally stood down. We were euphoric. It was the best thing that could have happened.

I couldn't wait to share the moment with Xanana. As I dialled his number and waited for him to answer, I found myself humming 'Ding dong the witch is dead, the wicked old witch . . .' Xanana was alone in his cell, the sound of the television audible in the background. Despite being unable to celebrate the moment in the company of his fellow inmates, his voice betrayed the elation he felt at learning of the resignation.

To many people, Habibie, Suharto's successor, was an unknown quantity. He was even regarded as a bit of a clown. He seemed to be very impulsive; he made statements and decisions without too much apparent reflection or coordination with anyone else. He always referred to himself as a protégé of Suharto, so there was a fear that his presidency would herald little substantial reform of the kind being demanded by the students and others. Nevertheless, *reformasi* did bring with it some relief from the oppression and rot of Suharto's reign: some corrupt officials were sacked; the intelligence services cooled down a bit; and, at least in theory, it was possible to present opposing and critical political views publicly without facing censure. New political parties were formed and the press was allowed greater freedom.

By the middle of 1998 even the Indonesian-appointed former and serving governors of East Timor had joined presidents and foreign ministers from around the world in publicly declaring their support for Xanana's direct involvement in the brokering of a solution for East Timor. In August 1998, Jakarta and Portugal reached agreement to undertake, under the auspices of the UN Secretary-General, negotiations on a special status for East Timor, based on a wide-ranging autonomy. The East Timorese resistance made it clear that they accepted autonomy within Indonesia only as a step on the road to self-determination.

In early August, I took two weeks leave and escaped the

Melbourne winter. I travelled to Lisbon, where Expo '98 was being hosted. The Timorese had been provided with a pavilion of their own in which to showcase their struggle and cultural identity. This gave them yet another opportunity to bring their cause into the hearts and minds of the thousands of visitors to Expo '98 from all over Europe and the world. I stayed with my friends, Roque Rodrigues, CNRT's representative in Portugal, and his wife, Paula Pinto. Perhaps because we were the non-Timorese partners of men who had devoted their life to their country, Paula and I hit it off right away. Paula and Roque's existence revolved around Timor's cause, so my stay with them was far from relaxing. Like me, they often forgot to eat and spent their days running between meetings and jobs associated with East Timor, taking calls on their home phone at all hours from a host of individuals connected with the struggle. And now this included Xanana Gusmão himself. Xanana phoned me most evenings to fill me in on the latest news from Jakarta and to debate CNRT business with Roque.

Anxious to put the greater freedoms associated with *reformasi* to the test, I had decided to return to Melbourne via Jakarta. One evening, Xanana phoned me in Lisbon, his voice brimming with excitement, to say that he had had a conversation with the head of the prison and obtained his agreement that I be allowed to visit Cipinang every day for seven days during my stay. Xanana had confided in the prison chief about our relationship. It seemed that where the *rejeki* had failed, *reformasi* was succeeding in working the magic required to bring Xanana and me into face-to-face contact for only the second time.

I arrived at Sukarno-Hatta Airport at 5:30 pm on 15 August 1998. Xanana had instructed his younger brother, Manuel, to meet me. Manuel worked for customs and therefore had special access rights within the airport. However, there was no sign of him as I queued up at the immigration counter. As ever, it was a relief to get through the passport check without incident. Manuel had appeared by the time the last suitcase came off the baggage carousel. He dropped me off at the Wisma Bumi guesthouse in

Menteng, where my friend Juan Federer, from Darwin, was waiting for me.

Juan had just concluded some delicate negotiations with the Jakarta chief of BHP, Mr Peter Cockcroft, who had agreed to have a face-to-face meeting with Xanana to discuss the future of the Timor Gap oil treaty. It was a forward-thinking move on the part of Cockcroft, given that the prospects for an independent East Timor were now brighter than ever. Nevertheless, it was also a risky one, as it foreshadowed developments that were not yet officially condoned by either the Australian or the Indonesian government. That evening I spoke with Xanana on the telephone before heading to bed, knowing full well that despite my exhaustion, I was bound not to sleep a wink.

I was finally soundly asleep and dreaming when Xanana's call woke me at 7 am the next morning. I whispered to him that in my dream he had left the prison to spend a day on the outside with me. He reminded me of his theory that the contrary of our dreams usually happens in reality. I dressed and had breakfast, trying hard to contain my nerves and the adrenalin that was churning up a whirlpool in my stomach. Juan went ahead to collect Cockcroft and accompany him to the prison. Not long after, Manuel picked me up as planned in his bright red jeep.

I spent the half-hour journey to east Jakarta trying to put the thought of my last – ill-fated – visit to the prison out of my mind. We drew up in front of the prison at around 9:15, and it was about 9:30 by the time the necessary negotiations for my entry (I had forgotten to carry my passport, a hurdle that was finally surmounted) were completed. There was no longer hostility and suspicion evident in the attitudes of the prison officials, and I wondered whether their boss had let them in on Xanana's and my secret. Even the look of the prison seemed different from the image I carried in my memory. The building was less imposing, more welcoming, and I found myself wondering whether it had been given a fresh coat of paint.

Pak Rahmat, one of the uniformed prison security guards, led us to the visiting room, a pavilion-like structure located directly opposite the main entrance and open to the air along two sides. Four years earlier it was here that I had paused with the throng of other visitors before we proceeded to the hall where Christmas had been celebrated. Juan and Peter Cockcroft were already seated at one of the wooden benches inside the pavilion and I acknowledged them with a nod of my head. I noticed that the tall Australian bore an uncanny resemblance to 'Uncle John'. Budiman Sudjatmiko – who in January 1996 had been a member of the guard of honour that farewelled me prior to my departure for Ambon – was now one of Xanana's fellow political prisoners. He had been sentenced to thirteen years imprisonment a year or so before for alleged 'subversive' activities, including speaking ill of Suharto. He greeted me warmly and introduced me to his girlfriend, with whom we shared the sorry tale of my hasty departure from Indonesia.

Then Xanana appeared, the two guards who had accompanied him from his cell striding off purposefully in the direction of the prison office. There were people milling all around, but as we caught one another's eyes, we became oblivious to the presence of anyone else. Standing at a distance, he beckoned me, more with his eyes than with his hands, into his arms.

Those around us who had long known of our relationship – Juan and a handful of the imprisoned Indonesian activists – whooped and applauded, making my cheeks flush a deep shade of tomato red. It felt odd to be able to express our true feelings for one another given the elaborate subterfuge we had resorted to with the help of 'Uncle John' in December 1994.

Xanana introduced me to his closest friends amongst the other inmates and visitors as 'isteri saya' (my wife). I knew that my face beamed, happiness radiating from every pore in my body.

'I understand you two have other things on your mind,' Juan said, 'but perhaps Mr Cockcroft may have a little of your time?'

Xanana focussed his eyes on Peter Cockcroft's face, listening attentively as they commenced their discussions about petroleum resources in the Timor Sea. All the while, however, he kept my hand clutched in his own. Xanana gave Cockcroft his assurance that a future independent East Timor would respect the rights of the petroleum giants such as BHP to continue to work in the Timor Sea. Cockcroft, for his part, reminded Xanana of the necessity to begin to train East Timorese in technical areas pertaining to the petroleum industry and the importance of exploring the potential of on-shore reserves. Before Cockcroft and Juan left the prison, we took a series of photographs together, the intimate poses we assumed reflecting the friendly feelings we had towards this man of foresight who had paid his visit on a day of great personal significance to the two of us.

As midday approached, the meeting room became more crowded, and finally I withdrew to the next table to allow Xanana to greet the waiting throngs of Timorese youth and members of Indonesian solidarity groups. Among them were old friends, including Ibu Ade and Levi, the discreet but watchful guardian angel who had seen me safely onto the plane in Ambon in January 1996.

The crowds dispersed towards the end of the visiting period at around 1 pm, but Xanana's request that I be permitted to remain inside for the afternoon session was granted and we moved into the adjoining glassed-in room, which afforded us a little more privacy. It wasn't as if we had to sit down and catch up on one another's news; it was just wonderful to be able to spend time in one another's company. Mainly it was a morale boost, food for the soul that was going to help us keep going through whatever was to come. All we knew was that we were on the threshold of something. Lunch, dutifully prepared by João, was Chinese noodles and syrupy Portuguese pudding, which Xanana insisted on serving up to me as he had during our first face-to-face meeting.

Later that afternoon there was not the slightest hint of sadness in our parting kiss at the doors that would lead me back out to the 'free world', given the promise of at least six more meetings in the coming days. Nevertheless, it would have seemed like the most natural thing for me to have taken Xanana by the hand and taken him back to my hotel, and the fact that this was not possible cut like a knife, deep into my desperately happy heart. Back at the hotel, I was unable to hold back my emotions and cried silent tears of happiness on Juan's shoulder.

I didn't anticipate being able to visit Xanana the next day – 17 August, Independence Day. So I walked to the Hotel Indonesia for a swim. I returned in the early afternoon and was about to lie down for a sleep when the phone rang. It was Xanana to tell me that if I wanted to, I could visit there and then. I showered quickly, and dressed. I wore the red and white dress with the elastic bodice that Xanana had given me for Christmas in 1996, deeming the colour scheme – Indonesia's national colours – appropriate for this particular day.

When I arrived there was a demonstration going on in front of the prison involving around 400 East Timorese and Indonesian activists demanding the release of all political prisoners. A group of about twenty-five young people was occupying not only the pavement but also part of the road. An equivalent number of armed and uniformed police were stationed at either side of the prison entrance, with a further half dozen looking on from the median strip of Jalan Bekasi. I quickly put out of my mind the thought that, as much out of boredom than any real interest in my identity, one of the crew-cut mob might decide to question my presence there. I asked the taxi driver to let me off as close as possible to the prison entrance. Forcing myself to avoid eye contact with any of the protesters, I made a beeline for the front door, which was crowded by a small group of waiting visitors. I knew that in all likelihood there would be friends amongst their number and that the temptation to stop and chat would be strong.

To my enormous relief, Pak Rahmat appeared at the door and beckoned for me to follow him. I thanked him in my best Indonesian grovelling fashion and, after the routine body search, bag check and passport inspection, I passed through the dark and cavernous vestibule and entered the meeting space. Xanana was there waiting on the path, looking relaxed in an outfit less formal than the previous day. He was wearing black corduroy pants and the Aussie wildlife T-shirt I had given him as a birthday present in 1994.

We had just poured ourselves a cup of coffee from the thermos in the glassed-in room when the two commanders invited us to move to another more private building to the east of the main door. They delighted in making a big deal of the fact that they understood our desire for greater privacy. The hall we settled in was one used occasionally for family visits and at other times it functioned as a workshop for fibreglass modelling classes and other 'rehabilitation' activities. It resembled a barn that had fallen into disrepair, but the greater intimacy it allowed made it a palace in our eyes.

Xanana extracted a container of green jelly with fruit from a black plastic bag. No sooner had we served ourselves a large helping each than the head of the prison appeared before us, hat in hand and an apologetic look on his face. He came seeking Xanana's intervention to break up the crowd of demonstrators still gathered outside. He explained that their presence on the footpath was delaying the entry of the waiting visitors who, along with their family or friends inside, were becoming agitated. The prison chief pointed out that it had been announced earlier in the day that – unlike Independence Day in previous years – no releases from Cipinang were to be made, therefore there was no point in the protesters being there. In addition, any dissatisfaction with the decisions of the Ministry of Justice would be better directed to the minister himself. 'If I had a say in the matter, I would not hesitate in releasing all of you political prisoners today,' he said.

It was decided that one of the young East Timorese leaders of the protest should be called. Five minutes later a serious-looking youth named Mariano and another of his colleagues who wore an image of Xanana on his T-shirt were seating themselves at the table opposite us. Mariano explained that the demonstration was actually organised by the PRD (People's Democratic Party) and that the East Timorese were present in solidarity with their demands. Therefore it would be more appropriate for someone from the PRD to be summoned to the negotiating table, so to speak. Fajar was brought in and by now the room, which had until then been a quiet haven, was filling up with prison officials and the odd inmate curious to be in on what was happening. Xanana explained at length to Fajar the dilemma of the prison chief, and suggested that a more appropriate target for their *aksi* (demonstration) might be the Department of Foreign Affairs or the Ministry of Justice.

Earlier that afternoon, just prior to my arrival, Xanana and Budiman had addressed the protesters from the balcony of the prison office. It was the first time such a thing had been authorised. It showed how the prison officials both trusted him and recognised the authority he had, not only over the Timorese but over the Indonesian activists as well. Xanana told me that for the address he had worn a T-shirt featuring the Portuguese flag. Finally, once the negotiations were concluded, we were left alone once more . . . that is, until the unofficial prison photographer appeared and snapped four portraits of the two of us, and another one with João.

At around 7 pm, just as the light was fading, the two commanders, respecting the unwritten protocol of intimacy, called us from outside the room and announced that our time was up. Xanana led me to the door beyond which lay freedom for him and solitude for me.

The next morning was taken up with phone calls to and from a number of Indonesian activist friends, and with wrapping the Portuguese souvenirs I had brought from Lisbon as a gift for the prison chief. Manuel arrived to pick me up at around 1 pm and we headed through the thick lunchtime traffic for Cipinang. Xanana was still in his cell when we arrived, so we waited for him for a short time in the glass room. There was fried duck and tiny loaves of battered bread for lunch. Xanana had had the duck killed earlier that day.

We were granted permission to go upstairs to the office of the prison chief, Bapak Subari, and we presented him with the *azulejos*, the blue and white tiles for which Portugal is famous. 'Perhaps I would once have been arrested for having such a gift in my home,' Subari said, laughing, when he noticed that the tiles were inscribed with the word Portugal. A little embarrassed laughter followed. 'Let's hope that Portugal . . .' Bapak Subari didn't finish the sentence. We returned to the glassed-in room but soon found our privacy invaded by a religious singing group, perhaps gearing up for the holiday season. We did our best to ignore them and the curious glances they shot in our direction. Five o'clock came around all too quickly and Manuel reappeared to take me home. Xanana sent him off to enquire whether it might be possible for us to be granted an extra half hour, and while he did I showed Xanana my snapshots of the visit to Portugal.

The following day was Wednesday, one of the two days routinely set aside for regular visits to the prison. Xanana had advised me only to visit in the afternoon in order to avoid the crowds. I spent the morning enjoying the sun filtering through the trees on the balcony of the Wisma Bumi guesthouse, contemplating the reason for the presence of two men with red berets on the street directly opposite the hotel. Indonesia's new openness and reforms had not succeeded in putting me completely at ease when it came to dealings with members of the armed forces.

I then went to the Austrian Embassy on leafy Jalan Diponegoro to try to visit Avelino. I was informed by one of the political counsellors that it wasn't possible to speak with him, so I left the books and letter I had for him.

I felt a slightly skewed sense of fairness and logic in being fed for days on end by the inmates of a prison, so I resolved to do some shopping before the afternoon's visit. I was just about to leave for Sarinah Department Store when Juan phoned me to say that news of Peter Cockcroft's visit to the prison had been leaked. He explained that Cockcroft required a written statement denying any pre-arrangement of the meeting from Xanana. I told him that provided Xanana phoned me prior to my departure for the prison,

I could ask him to prepare the statement and pass it to me during my visit that very afternoon. Just as I was having lunch in the guesthouse restaurant, Paula phoned to make arrangements for the phone hook-up that would enable Xanana to speak to the participants in the Fretilin Conference that was underway in Lisbon. I promised to check with him and get back to her with an idea of the time that best suited Xanana. It seemed that we were not destined to simply be at leisure together.

When Xanana phoned shortly afterwards, I broke the bad news of the leak to him. I had prepared the text of the statement of denial and dictated it to him over the phone so that he could transcribe it in his own hand. At 3 pm I set off for Sarinah, where I bought food for a late afternoon snack and some small gifts for João and the other prisoners. It was almost 4 pm by the time my taxi drew up in front of the prison. We nibbled on the kebabs I had bought as we discussed the Fretilin Conference call and the other messages, advice and news I had to convey. Xanana passed me the signed statement in a book in order not to attract the attention of the guards.

The next morning I breakfasted on my favourite Jakarta speciality, *bubur ayam* (rice porridge with chicken), with Herbin. He dutifully supplied me with a report on the use of the Amnesty International funds which, in spite of the fact that he now had a new job with the ICRC, he continued to administer. Herbin's wife was about to give birth to their first child and I was delighted when he asked me whether Xanana and I would consider being the baby's godparents.

It was 2:30 pm by the time I had waited in line at the door of the prison along with the dozen or so other visitors, passed through the routine body search and passport check and was receiving Xanana's greeting kiss. Today João had prepared a beautiful Portuguese-style *cozido* or stew with duck and potato. We shared our lunch with Manuel and washed it down with glasses of Australian red wine – I didn't ask where it had come from, nor how it had made its way inside the prison – which had been made to resemble raspberry cordial through the addition of a handful of ice blocks.

The day of 22 August brought the last of my visits. Sensing my melancholy state of mind, Xanana assured me that he would try to extract a promise from the prison chief that I would be permitted to enter again at Christmas time. I told him that there would be no better Christmas gift. In the last hour, as night was falling and the early evening mosquitoes began their dive-bombing, I shared with Xanana the insecurity I had begun to feel about my ability to support him adequately given the new phase of the struggle it seemed we were about to embark upon. I felt that I had so much to learn, that my life experience had not prepared me sufficiently for the challenges that lay ahead of us, particularly if Xanana was to be released from prison and granted a role in the negotiations on his country's future.

Our conversation was punctuated by the sound of our hands slapping at the mosquitoes that dared to land on our bare flesh. He answered my doubts with a reassuring smile, saying that he believed deep down that our shared experiences of the past four years and the lessons we had learnt together – about human nature, about Indonesian society, through our struggle and the love we had for one another – represented a solid foundation for a formidable partnership. His words helped lighten the heavy load my heart bore at the moment of our parting.

My father's sudden death the following month left a gaping hole in the part of my being that had gained so much strength from the seven days spent in Xanana's company. For weeks afterwards, my grief consumed me. More than ever, I craved the comfort of Xanana's physical presence in my life. And not just for a day, or even a week.

Chapter fourteen

ROLLERCOASTER September 1998–September 1999

IT SEEMED THAT sooner or later I was to be granted my wish. Foreign governments and a number of high-profile individuals were stepping up demands for Xanana's unconditional release. It was as if the world, which had previously been cowed by the forbidding and unyielding presence of Suharto, had seen in Habibie's presidency a window of opportunity for East Timor – for it spent the next few months slowly but persistently prising that window open for the benefit of the East Timorese, who were fed up with violence, hatred and suffering, and with having their hopes raised and then dashed just as quickly.

I visited Jakarta again in December, on the way back from a field trip to Thailand, and again was able to see Xanana every day for seven days. It was more food for my soul and a salve for the grief and sadness I felt at losing my father. This time, however, we didn't just while away the hours chatting about prison life over João's culinary offerings. Xanana was certain that, as an intermediary step on the road to his full release from prison, he would be granted house arrest. Where and how this would come about was, at this point, anyone's guess. But in the hope that an agreement would be reached sooner rather than later, Xanana had written to the Australian Ambassador to Jakarta, proposing that he be granted a safe haven within the Australian Embassy from which to conduct negotiations on East Timor's future. 'Access to communications and other facilities would permit me to respond more adequately to the demands of this important juncture in the history of our struggle, thus enhancing my ability to participate in the dialogue process which is a key demand of the Timorese people and numerous governments around the world, including your own,' wrote Xanana.

While waiting for a response from the Australian government, Paula and I prepared a proposal and budget for the establishment of a support office to Xanana in Jakarta. After numerous drafts of the document, which we handballed electronically back and forth between Melbourne and Lisbon over many weeks, the proposal was finally submitted to the Portuguese government. If and when Indonesia took the step of releasing Xanana into house arrest, we would be ready with a structure and funds to assist him in what would no doubt be a protracted and complex process of negotiations. No word came from the Australian government. Perhaps they considered Xanana's proposal too outlandish to warrant a response. We would just have to wait and see whether another opportunity flew in through the now open window.

Throughout January 1999 the pace of change quickened, and it was a challenge just to keep abreast of developments. Around the middle of the month, Alexander Downer called for an act of self-determination, at the same time stating that Australia continued to be strongly opposed to independence. I reassured myself with the thought that, provided that an act of self-determination could be realised, it mattered little what the Australian government's feelings about independence were. That was for the East Timorese to decide, and in my mind there was no question what they would choose.

Given the unrelenting load of my official work commitments, my work for East Timor was generally relegated to the hours between 9 pm and 1 am. One evening in mid January, I thought I would go mad if I spent another evening in front of the computer, filling my head with media reports, commentary and analysis on the evolving political situation in Indonesia as it related to East Timor. My friend Sarah invited me out to see her boyfriend playing in a band at the Commercial Hotel in Northcote, a kilometre or so up the road from my flat. I gratefully accepted and, after leaving a few messages on Xanana's voice mail, headed off to let the sounds of Crawfish Dave wash over my tired brain.

I returned home just after midnight to find five messages on my answering machine from Xanana. He was clearly irritated and curious about my reasons for being out so late, and asked in one of the messages whether I was going through a 'crisis'. When he called again at close to 1 am, it was my turn to get irritated, and I barked at him down the line that just because I had decided to spend an evening doing something other than thinking or writing or communicating with someone about East Timor, it did not imply that I was going through a crisis. The conversation ended badly.

The next day I deliberately left the phone at home when I visited Ballarat to attend an organ recital with my mother and some friends. Back at my flat that evening, Xanana called and glumly requested that I contact Herbin and ask him to pass on three million rupiah to a former bodyguard of his who was in need of an operation to remove a bullet. When I expressed concern at our dwindling finances, he interpreted this as reluctance to pay for the operation and coldly wished me goodnight.

We had made peace when, two days later, Xanana phoned to say that it appeared the Portuguese were prepared to fund the support office proposal. Even better than this piece of news, though, was the information João had heard on the radio – that the Indonesian government was planning to release Xanana and allow him to take part in negotiations from Dili. Personally, I had my doubts about this rumour, particularly since I had read only the day before that Alatas had confirmed that Xanana would only be released in the context of a final solution being reached by the governments of Portugal and Indonesia. 'However, we are not and have never used Xanana as a bargaining chip,' Minister Alatas added.

On 18 January 1999, the *Australian* newspaper carried a front-page article saying that the Indonesians were to release Xanana into house arrest. That evening, we chatted until after midnight about what this would mean, both for him and for me. Until we knew precisely where Xanana would be moved to and under what conditions, if any, it was difficult to make plans.

'Of course I'll give up my job and be there in a shot,' I said, stifling a yawn.

'If you do that, we'll never be able to pay these damned phone bills,' replied Xanana. I could hear him clanking metal pots around. He was probably making himself a cup of coffee to stave off the sleepiness that had suddenly crept up on us both.

'If they let you out of beautiful Cipinang, I never want to see another mobile phone in my life.'

'Me neither. Funny, though, I've grown rather attached to these compact little gadgets. We'll have to preserve them as relics for our private museum. Along with the tapes, the truckloads of letters, the bribes and the fanciful dreams that all belong to these unforgettable Cipinang years.' A tone of nostalgia had crept into Xanana's voice.

'Hang on now. You almost sound as though you are going to miss the place,' I protested.

'Perhaps not miss exactly. But I can't deny that these seven years have opened my eyes to a lot of things. A lot of things about Indonesia, a lot of things about myself and my struggle – the political one and the one I have been waging within myself. Against my own inadequacies, against other people's unrealistic expectations of what I am capable of.'

Deep down I sensed that Xanana was about to be cast headlong into a new battle which would require him to draw upon all the lessons he had learned. Both from his 'university of life' – the years of armed resistance in the mountains of East Timor – and from his 'closed university' – his seven years of imprisonment in Cipinang penitentiary.

'So you see, it was all part of the plan. Everything in your life so far has been preparation for this moment. You know that I don't have much time for the concept of fate,' I smothered another yawn, 'but I must say that it does seem to be yours that you continue to lead this struggle for just a little while longer. And you know very well that you only have to ask and your faithful, overworked and underpaid private secretary will be there, ready to serve with all her patriotic fervour, ready to answer the call of duty, ready to obey the orders of the . . .'

There was an eruption of laughter at the other end of the line as I mimicked the strident nationalism and military discipline that featured in almost every item of correspondence that flowed between Xanana and the Falintil commanders. Then I remembered that I had a meeting at 8 am the following day and we signed off for the night.

I was somewhere over the Simpson Desert when Habibie made his historic announcement on 27 January 1999 that if the East Timorese people rejected Indonesia's autonomy proposal, the Indonesian government would be prepared to 'let East Timor go'. En route from Melbourne to Darwin, where I was to attend the annual general meeting of Timor Aid in my capacity as a member of its board, that something momentous had happened in the past five hours was evident from the look in Juan's eyes. He had braved a tropical downpour to collect me at the airport, and his eyes twinkled as he filled me in on the news. 'It seems now that Xanana's release into house arrest is also only a matter of days away.'

My bag seemed to take forever to come off the baggage carousel. I couldn't wait to call Xanana to get his reaction to this latest extraordinary development – he was cautiously optimistic. Indonesia's armed forces had made it immediately clear that Habibie's decision was a personal initiative and one they did not endorse.

'But surely there's no turning back now?'

'No, querida, but independence will not come on a silver platter. The process is bound to be fraught.'

There was no talk yet of dates for Xanana's move from Cipinang. Nevertheless, he had started packing his things away into boxes.

'God, I can't believe how much stuff I have accumulated in seven years – you should see the junk!' In spite of his cautious optimism, his voice betrayed the joy he felt at anticipating the new space – political and physical – being prepared for him.

Back in Melbourne I tendered my resignation. Nobody was surprised. The newspapers were full of the good news about East Timor and my colleagues just assumed that I would now move on to where I could participate more actively in the next and decisive phase of the struggle. Nevertheless, I was uncertain about what this new journey would mean for me. Where would I be? Where would Timor be in one year's time? I felt a pang of sadness at packing up my life in Melbourne, leaving a job that had given me much satisfaction, the support and friendship of my colleagues, the comfort of my flat, and the normality I had reluctantly eased into. Hardest of all, though, was the decision to leave my mother, who still felt the loss of my father keenly and who, with my help and that of my brother and his family, was slowly putting back the pieces of her life.

On 10 February 1999 a large prison van carrying Xanana and his boxes emerged through the heavy gates of Cipinang. Photographers and journalists clamoured at the side of the slow-moving vehicle, snapping and lunging at the figure of Xanana, who beamed at them, fist raised, from inside. I saw the images on the evening news.

Independence leader Xanana Gusmão, it said, was today moved from the Cipinang high security prison to a house in a suburb of Jakarta. Whilst he was formally still in detention, Indonesia had agreed to move Gusmão following heightened pressure from world leaders who insisted that he be granted a central role in negotiations on the future of the former Portuguese colony. Last month Indonesian President Habibie announced that his government would relinquish control of East Timor if its people voted to reject the autonomy plan being devised for the territory. The report concluded that Gusmão's move to the prison house in Salemba was intended to enhance his ability to broker a peaceful solution to the twenty-four-year-old conflict.

The SBS news showed Xanana being let out of a vehicle at the gates of a white house and shaking hands with a long row of uniformed officials who lined the path to the front door. My heart pounded with regret that I couldn't jump on a plane there and then to share in the historic moment. I had had to give a month's notice at work, and the earliest I could leave Melbourne was early March. Paula had already flown to Jakarta to start establishing the support office. She arrived in Indonesia a day or two ahead of Xanana's release from Cipinang into the prison house in Salemba.

I took my mind off what I was missing out on by busying myself for my departure – packing up the belongings in my flat, handing over my job, attending farewell lunches, dinners and morning teas – following closely each step of Xanana's move and the setting up of the support office by phone. With the help of Pak Johnny, one of Xanana's friends, Paula had managed to find an appropriate house-cum-office only two streets away from the prison house. Pak Johnny, whose company supplied food to Cipinang and who had been contracted to refurbish the Salemba house in anticipation of Xanana's arrival, was a good-hearted man in whom Xanana saw a useful ally. When Xanana appealed to him for his assistance with setting up a house for Paula and me, he set to work straight away. By the time I arrived in Jakarta on 4 March 1999, the rental agreement had been drawn up and signed, basic office and household furniture purchased and telephone lines connected. We were in business.

The house into which Xanana moved had been the residence of one of the chiefs of the Salemba Detention Centre, located just around the corner on Jalan Percetakan Negara, along which hurtled crowded microlets (small public minibuses) and the ubiquitous *bajaj* belching black smoke. It was a fairly typical middle-class Indonesian home. The addition of bars to the windows and a layer of barbed wire around its outer walls was, I suppose, aimed at reminding its new tenant that he was not a free man. Nevertheless, the prison trappings were a little half-hearted and perhaps better suited to keeping intruders out than the occupant in – this was probably just as well, given the fears I secretly harboured that a disgruntled member of the armed forces might decide that eliminating Xanana would be the surest way of foiling East Timor's bid for freedom. The large garage just inside the high metal fence had been converted into a guard post. Here stood a large wooden table across the front of which was painted *Tamu harap lapor* (Visitors must report). At any one time five or six uniformed guards sat on a bench behind this table and assiduously recorded the names and purpose of each and every visitor to the house. The table was strewn with grease-stained brown paper packages containing remnants of the last meal consumed, a chessboard, crossword puzzles and newspapers, which were the guards' antidote to the monotony of the job. When these pastimes lost their appeal, there were always the neighbours and roadside sellers to gossip with.

Beyond the tiled verandah of Xanana's new residence was the living and dining room, which had been decked out with a set of the rather garishly ornate Franco Cozzo–esque furniture that was common in the homes of Indonesia's upper middle classes. A couple of the sofa seats seemed to belong to the same family of lounges that had been supplied to our house around the corner, which was not surprising given the hand Pak Johnny had had in fitting out both properties. Xanana's small Cipinang TV had pride of place in one corner of the living room. His other scant possessions, including a framed and signed collage-photo, a parting gift from his fellow political prisoners in Cipinang, were scattered about on walls and table tops. Above the dining table a portrait of the Virgin Mary painted in shades of almost fluorescent pink and blue had been hung.

Beyond the dining area was a dimly lit passage leading to a cramped kitchen, a tiny bedroom the size of a large pantry and an equally small bathroom in which water constantly dripped. And beyond the passage lay a bare, cement-floored courtyard, its only greenery some tufts of grass growing through the cracks in the concrete and two or three rather dishevelled looking bonsai plants that had made the journey from Cipinang with Xanana. Off the living room was a bare but reasonably spacious office with a glass-topped desk and a vinyl-covered swivel chair. A door led from the office into Xanana's bedroom, which was musty and sparsely furnished but reasonably comfortable.

Paula had accompanied me to the prison house, knowing that I was impatient to see Xanana on the day of my arrival. It was a five-minute walk along a pleasant, relatively quiet residential street and then down two narrower alleys alongside which an open drain gurgled. An assortment of 'five feet' sellers (named for the two feet of the seller and the three feet of his cart) and their steaming carts of noodle soup, fried rice and satay ambled by, their various calls, bells and honks identifying them and their wares to householders along the way. The familiarity of it all gave me a rush of satisfaction.

Xanana received me in the office on the day of my arrival. He had just finished meeting with American academic Ben Anderson and *Tempo* editor Goenawan Mohammad, and had changed out of the formal pants and shirt he kept for 'business' into the shorts and faded T-shirt that were his Cipinang 'uniform'. I was still marvelling at how easy it had been to make it past the guards on the post – they had even thrust my passport back at me when I dutifully presented it – and hardly noticed Xanana appear at my side.

'Ahhh, Mukya, you're here. We've been expecting you.' He held a cup of cold coffee in one hand. With his free hand he tousled my hair playfully and then drew me against him in a kind of half embrace.

I planted a kiss on his lips, enjoying the familiar tickle of his moustache, the whiff of tobacco in his beard. 'Nice place you've got here. Can I take a look around?'

By the time my self-guided tour of Jalan Percetakan Negara number 47 had concluded, so had the time available for re-acquaintance and intimacy.

'Terribly sorry to interrupt,' said Paula in Portuguese, removing her pen from between her teeth and replacing it with a cigarette. 'I've just had confirmation of tomorrow's meeting with Madeleine Albright.' She nodded at her mobile phone.

'Hmmm,' Xanana raised his eyebrows and joined Paula in lighting up a cigarette. And then, through a cloud of tobacco smoke, we began discussing the necessary preparations for the meeting – talking points (she would need to be briefed on the deteriorating security situation in East Timor, the actions of the paramilitary groups), clothing (the tan suit and a matching tie), gifts (a vase fashioned from the marble of East Timor, a silver filigree Timor house).

Then João appeared. He had been released on parole in late 1998 and yet had preferred to remain in Cipinang with Xanana until his release. It was the sort of extraordinary act of loyalty and self-abnegation I had come to know João for. Now he had joined Xanana at his prison house in order to continue to be of service to his leader and his struggle. His poky little bedroom at the rear of the house was even more confined and prison-like than his cell in Cipinang. But at least he could come and go from this place as he pleased. We greeted one another with a hug.

He held a docile tabby cat in his arms. 'This is Rumbiak,' he announced. The little cat purred into his armpit. He was named after a former cell-mate of João's and the cat's previous owner, Jacob Rumbiak, a political prisoner from West Papua whom I'd met during my visit to Cipinang in August 1998, virtually on the eve of his release from prison. I had also known a lot of other Rumbiaks over my years of work on the West Papua campaign, including another political prisoner with whom I corresponded for many years in the eighties and nineties. So I came to develop a special attachment to the little feline Rumbiak who, it turned out, knew a number of clever tricks.

Xanana thrust a roll of gift wrap into João's hands and we spent the early evening packaging up gifts and preparing ourselves for the next day's meeting with the US Secretary of State. I had now boarded the rollercoaster that was to send me careering on a breathtaking course of highs and lows for the next seven months.

Back at Jalan Percetakan Negara IX A number 14, I unpacked my belongings and ironed a dress for the next day while Paula whipped up a bowl of tuna pasta for our dinner. In spite of being tired after the long day of travel and the excitement of the reunion with Xanana, we talked long into the night about conditions inside East Timor and the staffing of our small support office. João had agreed to help us out with administrative tasks and the running of the occasional errand. In addition, our little team was soon to be joined by Natacha Meden, who had years of experience working as José Ramos-Horta's media liaison officer in Lisbon. She was French but spoke Portuguese and was presently taking a crash course in Bahasa Indonesia in Yogyakarta. Lucia Lobato was a law graduate – a year or so earlier I had helped find funds for her to complete her legal studies in Surabaya. She was to join us as a researcher and translator, and to keep the lines of communication open with our contacts in East Timor.

In addition, we had the services of five youths from Los Palos who, upon Xanana's release from Cipinang, had taken it upon themselves to guarantee the security of their *maun bo'ot* (big brother). Cesar, Leonel, Mario, António and Tito, all of whom had either abandoned their tertiary studies in Java to work for East Timor or had had their scholarships cut off, rented a small 'pad' just around the corner from the prison house. From this strategic vantage point they kept an eye on the flow of human traffic into and out of the place, visiting Xanana regularly to report on suspicious happenings . . . and to catch a spot of telly in the evenings.

By eight the next morning we were back at the prison house. Again I found the guards there surprisingly cooperative. Whilst we had no official status in relation to Xanana, the Indonesian government could not deny that he required support to arrive at the solution he had been released to broker. And so our presence there in Salemba was tolerated, our frequent comings and goings to and from the house facilitated. None of the subterfuge, altered identities or cat-and-mouse games of the past were necessary any longer. And it was just as well since the unrelenting pace of our work left little energy for indulging in paranoia or fears of deportation.

The morning of the meeting, tall, burly men with wires in their ears were swarming all over the prison house. We found Xanana in his study, sewing a button on a white shirt. Seeing the question in our eyes, he explained, 'They're the security chaps. Checking the place for bombs, I suppose.' Paula left us alone for a bit and went and chatted to the Americans. I helped Xanana with his tie and made him a cup of coffee. He was a little edgy, his thoughts already focussed on what he was to say to Madeleine Albright.

An hour or so later, Paula reappeared, sighing deeply. 'They've decided it's too risky for Albright to visit you here. The meeting's to be held in the Ministry of Foreign Affairs instead.'

This unanticipated turn of events sent everyone into a flap. A security cavalcade complete with police cars and flashing lights needed to be assembled in a hurry, and a vehicle organised to carry our sizeable delegation. Finally we were ready, and we set off in a flurry of whirring sirens in the direction of Jalan Pejambon. We made it through the waiting throngs of journalists and photographers who crowded the steps leading into the Ministry of Foreign Affairs building. Inside on the carpeted landing at the top of the stairs there were more waiting.

Poor Cesar had to keep shifting the weight of the heavy gift-wrapped marble vase from one hand to the other. Finally it and the Timor house were taken from him by an officious-looking American woman who was running to and fro sweating and taking calls on her mobile phone while she summoned one of her colleagues to do a security check on the gifts. Off came the wrappers. I could feel João wincing behind me – all the previous evening's hard work in vain.

It was incongruous that the Americans, among Indonesia's greatest allies, were so security-conscious. By contrast, Xanana, who was still seen as public enemy number one in certain circles in Indonesia, had only a handful of unarmed prison guards and the boys from Los Palos to protect him.

Indonesian Foreign Minister Ali Alatas can't have been surprised when he came across our party in the corridor of his office. Nevertheless, he did do a double-take as he caught sight of Xanana standing there in his suit and looking more like a statesman than a common criminal. Then, to everyone's shocked delight, he grinned broadly and moved forward to shake Xanana's hand. One of the Salemba prison guards, a young man by the name of Seno who had long been an admirer of Xanana, quickly drew out his Pentax camera and snapped the bizarre moment, the most unequivocal proof that times had changed. Xanana, eager to impress on Alatas that he, too, had the heart of a diplomat, smiled graciously and patted the minister on the shoulder as if they were golf partners, not longstanding political enemies.

Finally we were ushered into a large, opulently furnished and decorated saloon. Madam Albright seemed a little taken aback but not displeased when Xanana greeted her with a kiss on both cheeks. The meeting commenced. I hung back against the back wall with João and Cesar and so was unable to hear what the conversation revolved around. An American aide was perched on a chair by Albright's side, his neck craning to catch Xanana's soft voice, pen poised above a notebook into which he scribbled earnestly. His posture and movements were mirrored by Paula.

Back at the prison house, Xanana told me how he had stressed to Albright the need for pressure to be brought to bear on the Indonesian government to rein in the pro-integration militias sowing discord and violence across East Timor. He talked, too, about the commitment of the CNRT and Falintil to dialogue, reconciliation and the peaceful resolution of differences with the pro-integration East Timorese. I could see that Xanana was relieved that the meeting had gone well, that he seemed to have left a positive impression on Albright.

We discussed the schedule ahead. The next day the launch of an Indonesian activist's book on Xanana was to take place in the prison house, followed by meetings with Amnesty International Holland, the former Indonesian Ambassador to Australia, interviews with the BBC and Voice of America and, in the evening, a phone call to Portuguese opposition leader Durão Barroso. Somewhere in the midst of all that, a meeting between Xanana and a delegation of a dozen or so East Timorese youths needed to be squeezed.

Paula presented the list of requests for meetings for the next four days: the ambassadors of South Africa, Norway and Britain; a Brazilian solidarity group; the Indonesian National Commission for Women's Rights; an official from the British Foreign and Commonwealth Office; and interviews with Radio Netherlands, the National Radio of Angola, and Timorese Community Radio in Melbourne.

Looking up from her notebook, Paula added, 'The President of Mozambique has also requested to speak to you by phone. Oh, and Mari Alkatiri [Head of the External Delegation of the Fretilin party] . . .' Xanana exhaled loudly. The tide of adrenalin and excitement was beginning to ebb and he looked suddenly tired and listless. I gave his shoulders a rub and then João appeared to call us to the table. He had prepared a simple lunch that we gratefully tucked into, not having had time for breakfast that morning.

And so commenced the exhausting round of meetings that were to become our daily bread. In addition to the meetings scheduled through our office, there was a fairly constant stream of unanticipated visitors and drop-ins, which necessitated that we abandon whatever we were doing and dash breathlessly around the corner, notebooks in hand, in order to be able to keep a written record of the concerns and commitments of the visitors, and to do any follow-up required. Paula, Natacha and I took turns at interpreting for Xanana, who felt more at ease speaking to his many visitors in Portuguese.

Our English lessons had dropped off over the past year or so, given the new set of demands placed on Xanana's time. Though he had lost some of his confidence and fluency, his halting English did nothing to detract from his skill at articulating the aspirations of his people, the complexity of the situation inside the country, and his analysis of the problems needing to be surmounted in order to guarantee that the will of the people could be gauged in an atmosphere free of violence and fear. We were all astounded by the ease with which he approached the task of debating and exchanging views with everyone from government ministers to representatives of foreign NGOs, unions and the UN. Back at the office we typed up the notes of these meetings and stored them on the small but efficient computer network Colin had set up for us.

Out of the meeting with the Timorese youth came the news that Indonesian intelligence operatives were scheming to mobilise a handful of pro-integration Timorese, backed up by dozens of young men from Flores, to demonstrate against Xanana outside the prison house. A group of East Timorese factory workers from Tangerang and Bogor had been offered an incentive of one million rupiah each for their participation in the demonstration. Most, however, refused to be bought and instead hurried to report the plan to Xanana, who quickly prepared a public statement denouncing the underhanded tactics of the intelligence and at the same time condemning 'the generalised climate of violence engendered by the distribution of arms to the newly appointed war-lords of East Timor'. Xanana was referring to the increasing number of attacks by pro-autonomy militias on civilian populations inside East Timor, the most recent incident near Maubara causing hundreds of people to flee to the mountains. On the eve of the planned demonstration we worked until after midnight, translating Xanana's statement into English, Bahasa Indonesia and Tetum, and then emailing and faxing it off to embassies and news services across Jakarta.

The following morning, the Los Palos boys stood on guard outside the prison house in anticipation of what was to come. Their eyes were like hawks' as they scanned the street, each one proudly sporting a photo of Xanana on his chest as a makeshift uniform. I think they were a little disappointed when only a handful of young men bearing a banner inscribed with the words *Gerakan Pemuda-Pemudi Pendukung Otonomi Timor Timur* (East Timorese Pro-Autonomy Youth Movement) straggled down the street, yelled some almost inaudible slogans at the gates of the house and then disappeared again.

Later that afternoon, Cesar turned up carrying the black plastic folder which was used to courier written communications back and forth between the prison house and the office. I was working on an English translation of a written message Xanana had prepared to read over the radio in East Timor later that day and was agonising over the correct choice of words to best render the meaning of the Portuguese verb *acompanhar*. 'Accompany'? 'Closely follow'? Nice smells were emanating from the kitchen where Paula was preparing a curry for lunch and, after slapping the folder down on my desk, Cesar sidled up to her and offered to help drain the rice. 'You must be hungry, Cesar,' laughed Paula, thrusting a steaming pot into Cesar's arms. Cesar laughed, an embarrassed grin spreading across his handsome young face.

Cesar was the son of the *liurai* of Los Palos in whose guesthouse I had stayed as I waited to visit the Falintil commanders in 1995. It turned out that I had been wrong in assuming that the *liurai*'s collection of photos of Suharto was evidence of his pro-Indonesian political stance. Nowadays the elderly man's house served as the local headquarters of the CNRT, from which the activities of the pro-independence cadres were coordinated. I stopped to eat lunch with Paula and Cesar before continuing to labour over the translation; the first document had now been joined by a second, an appeal for unity and reconciliation, 'to be translated into English and Bahasa Indonesia and returned to me for signature this afternoon'. So said the yellow sticky note attached to the three-page document. Well, that put paid to the hope I was entertaining of spending a couple of hours after lunch in the swimming pool of the nearby Sentral Hotel. I hadn't had a single morning or afternoon off since my arrival in Jakarta.

Each day we received information pointing to a deterioration of the situation in East Timor. We synthesised and translated the reports that we and Xanana received on a regular basis from our contacts inside East Timor, sending out almost daily updates to diplomatic missions and the press as a means of countering Indonesian claims that the violence and murders were the result of deep divisions amongst the Timorese themselves.

The assault by militias on the church in Liquiça on 6 April 1999 highlighted what Xanana had been saying to visitors for over a month – that the Indonesian military and the militias they had created would stop at nothing to enforce their reign of terror on the population, that the climate of fear and generalised violence was the result of orchestrated provocations by one side only. Even the church, hitherto a sanctuary, was no longer safe as a place for the terrified and traumatised people to hide. Fifty-seven people were thought to have been killed in the attack, countless others wounded.

On receiving the appalling news, Xanana summoned us all to the prison house. He was shocked and outraged. There was a fire burning in his eyes in spite of the tiredness also evident in his features and posture. He twirled an unlit cigarette between his fingers as he spoke. He told us that he had just got off the phone from one of the relatives of the dead, a woman who had cried down the line that the people were no longer prepared to bear this suffering – that as their leader, he needed to take action to defend the people from the barbarous attacks they were being subjected to.

'*Um dia não vamos ouvir-te* [One day we will no longer listen to you],' she had said.

'It seems that my appeals for restraint and for reconciliation are being interpreted as a sign that I am out of touch with the reality of the people. A sign that I am content to see defenceless people slaughtered.' He ran his fingers through his hair, focussing his eyes on a spot on the far wall of the office and keeping them there as he continued to speak. 'It seems that our political good faith and our commitment to peace have been perceived as our weakest point. I can't afford to lose the trust of the people. It's time to act.'

There and then Xanana prepared the draft of a press statement entitled 'Falintil resumes their mission in defence of the people of East Timor'. In it he stated that he was compelled to authorise Falintil guerrillas to undertake all necessary action in defence of the population of East Timor and against the unprovoked and murderous attacks of armed civilian groups and ABRI. 'In response to the numerous appeals from the people of East Timor, I also authorise the population to undertake a general popular insurrection against the armed militia groups who have been killing the population with impunity under the indifferent gaze of the international community.'

We set to work immediately on the translation and dispatch of the statement, which we knew was likely to provoke a storm. It did. The Indonesian authorities were incensed by what they referred to variously as Xanana's 'call to arms' or 'war cry'. The international community – in the person of the representatives of foreign diplomatic missions – clamoured to meet with Xanana, to seek clarification of his statement and to express concern at his adoption of a seemingly bellicose position.

'We are merely worried that your statement may be used against you,' said the governments of the US and Australia, appealing to Xanana to remain consistent with his previous position of encouraging restraint.

He explained to the diplomats that he had authorised the people to act against their attackers 'not in the spirit of wanton violence and callous disregard for human life, which motivates the Indonesian Armed Forces, but in pure self-defence'. A few days later he issued a further statement, in which he renewed his appeal for peace, dialogue and reconciliation and reiterated his support for the establishment by Indonesia's Human Rights Commission of a Peace and Stability Commission inside the territory. He also condemned once again the actions of the TNI (as the Indonesian armed forces were now known) and the militias, which, he stated, were aimed at blocking the New York negotiations.

I spent my birthday, 19 April, tapping away furiously at my computer keyboard, churning out yet another report and stopping long enough only to receive the celebratory kisses of Pak Johnny and his family, the office staff and the five Los Palos boys. The contents of the report gave little cause for celebration, really. This time it was the tale of the Aitarak militia's burning down of the headquarters of the *Suara Timor Timur* newspaper and a CNRT office, and their campaign of house-to-house visits aimed at intimidating people into voting for autonomy. For the first time in five years my birthday came and went in the absence of a birthday cake and the quaint, quirky little gifts and poems that I had grown accustomed to receiving from Xanana. 'By foregoing your party this year you will get to spend your next birthday in a free East Timor,' Xanana had cajoled earlier in the day, before he urged me back to the office so that he could attend to the long line of waiting journalists and East Timorese visitors.

I wasn't the only one feeling a peculiar nostalgia for the bad old days. Some of Xanana's compatriots came to resent our support office; they felt that by keeping a schedule of visits, we were controlling and limiting the access they had to their leader, their *maun bo'ot*. For many it was difficult to understand and accept that there were new pressures on Xanana and that it wasn't possible to command his undivided attention, or to spend long hours in his presence exchanging stories of the past and airing anxieties about the future. It seemed to many East Timorese uncanny and unfair that the man they held in such high regard had been more available to talk to and hear them when he was an inmate in a high-security prison than now.

In New York, agreement had been reached on a direct ballot for the East Timorese people to decide their future. Xanana spent the next few months in consultations with Tamrat Samuel, Francesc Vendrell and Ian Martin of the UN, nutting out details such as who would be eligible to vote in the 'popular consultation' (Indonesia objected to the term 'referendum'), how the question on the ballot paper should be framed, what symbols would be used to represent the two options presented, and the presence and mandate of UN Civilian Police and election observers. The reconciliation process moved ahead in fits and starts, the efforts Xanana made at drawing in the less hardline members of the pro-autonomy factions frequently running aground when they fell under the spell of the rupiah once again. The Peace and Stability Commission, which – it was hoped – would serve to facilitate agreement between the pro-independence and pro-autonomy sides regarding the need for mutual respect and a commitment to non-violence, turned out to be ineffective. In the end it was impossible for members of the CNRT to be represented on the commission, as most of them were obliged to go into hiding when the militias published their infamous hit lists.

In meetings with international personnel, Xanana stressed the need for an immediate international presence and disarmament of the militias. It was becoming increasingly clear that TNI lacked the will and the ability to rein them in, although their propaganda machine was working overtime in Jakarta to convince foreign governments that Indonesia was serious about promoting reconciliation and that the violence was being instigated by the Timorese. General Wiranto was reported to have said that disarmament of the militias presented 'practical difficulties', and that it could only be contemplated if Falintil was simultaneously disarmed. Xanana patiently explained to the hordes of diplomats, officials and delegations from all over the world that Falintil – a proud army of national liberation which had fought the Indonesian military for twenty-four years – did not accept being painted as either the equal or the enemy of the militias. The militias, he explained, had been in existence only since October 1998 and were nothing more than bands of murderous thugs acting under the orders of the Indonesian armed forces.

Everyone was nervous about the fact that according to the terms of the New York agreement signed by Portugal and Indonesia on 5 May 1999, Indonesia was to be responsible for guaranteeing security leading up to and following the popular consultation, which was scheduled to take place in August 1999. In response to Xanana's appeals that the deployment of a peace-keeping force be considered, most foreign governments were noncommittal, insisting instead that 'the reconciliation process goes to the heart of the matter' and that 'there has to be some peace to keep' if international peace-keepers were to be effective. It was rather curious reasoning. Back in February, Alexander Downer had stated to Xanana that 'armed troops are a risky business'. Had nobody considered that to be an East Timorese and entrust your physical safety to the very institution which had been killing, maiming and terrorising you for twenty-four years was also a fairly risky business? As far as I could see, at the true heart of the matter was Indonesia's refusal to countenance the presence of foreign peace-keepers on their 'sovereign territory' – and the fact that in spite of *reformasi*, in spite of the sudden groundswell of support for the principle of self-determination for East Timor, the world just wasn't quite ready to put itself at odds with Indonesia.

Apart from the occasional Saturday night when we could relax together with a bottle of wine and mull over our future – as yet so uncertain and so dependent on the outcome of the work we were doing – Xanana and I had little time for private moments. Often even those rare quiet evenings were interrupted by visits or phone calls from East Timorese needing to consult with Xanana immediately, or the guards announcing the arrival of an official from Salemba Prison or the Office of Correctional Institutions. I was fully prepared to accept the absence of personal space, knowing well that we needed to make it successfully beyond the present phase of confidence-building and intensive consultations and negotiations in order to attain better, easier times. Strangely, it was perhaps easier to accept the almost total physical separation of the

Cipinang years than this situation, which enabled daily contact and an unusual quasi-domesticity. It was as if the promise of the intimacy and privacy we had never enjoyed, the opportunity to come to know one another better, was ever-present but always dangling, tantalisingly, just out of reach. The stresses of the work, the unrelenting and unpredictable pace of developments, the pain associated with watching the litany of horrors, atrocities and suffering unfold in East Timor as the day of truth edged closer, all took their toll.

One afternoon, my frustration at not being able to spend at least an hour or two per week of 'down time' with Xanana came to a head. Paula had phoned Xanana to ask for instructions on how to deal with the problem of the hundreds of East Timorese scattered across Indonesia who wished to participate in the consultation. Polling stations were to be set up in only the major Indonesian centres, which meant that those on the outer islands who didn't have the means to travel to Java or Bali were destined to forfeit their right to vote. A decision was taken to commit some of the funds we had received for Xanana's work to the costs of transport for these scattered pockets of East Timorese. In the weeks that followed, a group of East Timorese students was formed to coordinate the work of gathering data on the location and numbers of eligible voters and sending them the necessary funds. Avelino, who had been 'released' from the Austrian Embassy only in April, was part of the group that oversaw this task.

Their conversation over, I took the phone from Paula and enquired of Xanana whether it was possible for us to spend a little time alone together later that evening. I took the phone into my bedroom and closed the door behind me. I don't remember what I said, whether or not a hint of complaint or criticism of him had crept into my voice, but all of a sudden there was an eruption of emotion and anger at the other end of the line.

'I thought we agreed that we both need to be patient, that I would call you when the right moment presents itself,' he shouted. 'You know as well as I do that – '

'It just seems somehow that there is never a right moment,' I interrupted him.

'I don't know what . . . I can't . . .' His words were drowned out by the sound of something breaking, of books being sent flying across the room, presumably the office, of the prison house.

'Don't, never mind!' I implored, shouting now myself to be heard over the thunder of Xanana's outburst. 'Don't, don't,' I repeated as I heard the sound of a bottle shattering and of other objects hurtling across the room. The phone still connected and gripped tightly in my fist, I flung open the door of my bedroom and ran to Paula, who stood before me with her mouth open, a look of concern furrowing her brow. 'He's upset, he's breaking things,' I cried, motioning towards the mobile phone I now held at arm's length as if expecting it, too, to shatter in my hands. Paula gave my cheek a quick, almost maternal caress and then pushed me towards the front door, saying 'Go over there. Go now. Run!'

My legs propelled me down the street as if they had a mind of their own. Loud noises coming from the phone were still audible, but by now I had dropped it to my side and was concentrating on getting to where Xanana was. A group of women standing by a satay seller's cart on the street corner looked quizzically after me as I tore past them. Only athletes and deranged *orang asing* (foreigners) ran anywhere in Indonesia. There were giggles and sniggers as I shot past a handful of children playing ball against a wall. As I entered Xanana's street I could see the guards milling about on the road at the front of the prison house. As I got closer and the sound of the shouting and crashing inside reached my ears, I noticed that the guards were looking with anticipation in my direction. When I was still twenty metres or so away, they flung open the gates and I saw in their eyes something that said, 'You'd better do something about this.' In the living room, Cesar and Leonel were standing awkwardly a short distance from the door leading to the office, shooting looks of terror in its direction. Seeing my face streaked with tears and sweat, they concluded that this was a personal matter and slunk away to the verandah.

The office had been turned upside down. A bottle of red wine had shattered against one whitewashed wall, its contents extending up the side of it like a wave of rich, red blood. Books and papers were strewn about the floor, a coffee thermos lay overturned in the corner, a thick, black pool of liquid next to it. Xanana stood leaning heavily against the wall behind his desk, his chest heaving, his eyes avoiding my gaze. I couldn't decide whether I should feel hurt, offended or slighted by Xanana's harsh words to me. Or whether just to give into the overwhelming desire welling up in me to embrace him. Xanana lowered himself into the vinyl swivel chair and as I moved towards him I let out a small sob. He looked up at me and, seeing the look of pain and deep concern in my eyes, the tears streaming silently down my cheeks, he extended a hand. I dropped to my knees at the foot of his chair and he drew my head against his stomach, his own tears making his body shudder slightly. I cried, he cried, we cried together, giving vent to the pain and frustration we had been carrying inside us all those months, and as we held one another in that tangle of arms and emotions, I realised that there was more to this outburst than a mere lovers' tiff.

'I'm sorry, querida,' Xanana whispered into my hair. 'I just couldn't take it any more. The stress, the tension, the desperation. The sadness of this whole situation. The world offering us aid and technical assistance and lectures on peace and reconciliation when what we need is their intervention to save the lives of our people. In who else's presence can I scream out the anguish of my soul if not in yours, querida?'

I tightened my grip around his waist. 'It's okay, it's okay,' was all I could think to say. I wanted to say 'Everything will be okay', but I wasn't sure that it would be.

We had just begun to regain our composure and were collecting up shards of glass from the floor – Rumbiak the cat slinking and purring between our legs – when there was a knock at the door. Our least favourite of the prison guards stepped into the room and muttered something under his breath. Xanana understood and withdrew an envelope from the drawer of his desk. He had come to collect the weekly *uang rokok* or bribe he exacted from Xanana in return for his team's gracious facilitation of our unimpeded entry into the prison house. It seemed that even our moments of crisis were not our own.

The release afforded by the evening's outpouring of grief and emotion was a welcome relief. Nevertheless, I was happy that my mother was due to arrive in Jakarta any day and that I would have her comfort and caring to get me through the next days and weeks. She was keen to be with us at the time of the vote, a moment she knew her daughter, not to mention the entire East Timorese people, had worked towards for so very long. Moreover, I knew that she wanted to be where I was on the difficult first anniversary of my father's death.

On 27 August, my mother Rosalie and I turned up at the prison house with the black plastic folder stuffed full of letters requiring Xanana's signature. There was a bit of a commotion in the living room, with a mobile phone being passed back and forth between Cesar, Leonel and Tito, who were speaking to whoever was at the other end in high-pitched voices. I noticed that Cesar wore a vacant expression, and when I paused at the door to Xanana's office to ask what was up, he merely stared at me blankly and asked whether *maun bo'ot* was free to speak to him. He filed into the office behind Rosalie and me. With a deadpan face, he told Xanana that he had just received the news from his sister that his father had been surrounded in his home in Los Palos and murdered by militias. His elder brother had been forced to flee the family home, but his fate was unclear. As I translated the terrible news for Rosalie, she gasped and moved instinctively forward to put a hand around Cesar's shoulders. I joined her in her gesture of comfort, taking Cesar's hand in my own. Rosalie's eyes filled up with tears as Xanana uttered some words of consolation and reassurance from where he sat behind his desk. In contrast to our emotion, Cesar stood stiff and expressionless, not allowing himself to give in to his own feelings. He was clearly in shock. It was not until much later that day that he was able to register the horror of what had happened and allow himself to cry. Liurai Quintas had died for beliefs that I could never have guessed at when we met in his *losmen* four years earlier, and I felt sorry for the doubts I had had about him then.

The day of the popular consultation, 30 August 1999, rolled around. In Jakarta, the sun came up on another day of traffic jams and surging crowds of city dwellers. At the support office we started the day much like any other – a quick scan of the newspapers, a sip of coffee made from our favourite packet of Indonesian cappuccino while the email downloaded – but most of us, in our mind's eye, already hovered somewhere over Timor's parched brown hills, the sun of the long dry season having scorched the landscape bare and brittle. All over the country, men and women, young and old, were trekking across fields and along dusty mountain passes, decked out in their Sunday best and chatting happily along the way, the storms, intimidation and uncertainty of the previous months seeming to have vanished into the violent blue of the sky. We followed developments throughout the day. Xanana and João left the prison house to vote at UN headquarters in central Jakarta, accompanied by the familiar security ruckus and media fanfare. When they returned to the prison house that afternoon, reports of the massive turnout at the polling booths inside East Timor continued to reach us. There was the feeling of a holiday in the air. My mother filmed me with her video camera as I gave João an affectionate squeeze and asked him how it felt to vote for the future of his country at the place where, seven years earlier, he had protested and been arrested.

In spite – or perhaps because – of the months of intimidation and violence that had preceded the popular consultation, the East Timorese people refused to forfeit the opportunity they had paid for so dearly. They appeared to have heeded Xanana's appeal of that day: that they abandon their fears and 'draw upon their last reserves of courage and determination'. Our celebrations that night in the prison house in Salemba were tinged with sadness and a sense of foreboding. Whilst none of us, not even Xanana, could have anticipated the extent of the violence and destruction about to be unleashed, we knew the Timorese would pay a price for their choice and that peace would only be attained when the Indonesian military was replaced by an international peace-keeping force.

None of us was surprised when the announcement of the results of the ballot was made: 78.5 per cent of the people had voted in favour of independence. But it seemed that the Indonesian military and their militias had actually come to believe in the warped logic of their own violence and lies, and they gave vent to the dismay they felt at their defeat by launching a bloody campaign of revenge. Churches were looted and gutted. Others became the sites of some of the most brutal massacres of that post-ballot period. All rules, all norms, all principles were sacrificed to the lust for revenge, it seemed. Those who were previously considered to be beyond politics and the self-seeking ways of mortals found themselves, suddenly, victims of both.

I will never forget the hopeless impotence I felt, one afternoon in early September 1999, receiving a phone call from a senior member of the CNRT who implored me tearfully to do something to help as he fled into the hills above Dili. Below him, his home and city were on fire. For months afterwards I found that I could not see my mobile phone as an instrument of pleasure and leisure. Each time it rang I could think of nothing else but the desperate helplessness and inadequacy I felt at that moment of tragedy and extreme human suffering in the lives of others.

On the evening of 5 September, Xanana received the British Ambassador, Robin Christopher, at the prison house. He was a kindly man with sparkling blue eyes and a spontaneity and warmth that were not to be taken for granted in members of the diplomatic corps. As they sat together Xanana received a phone call on Paula's mobile from a group of three priests in the southern coastal town of Suai, who said that they were inside the church with members of their congregation. They were surrounded by the local Laksaur militias, who were armed to the teeth and threatening to attack. They knew they were about to die, but before they died they wanted to speak to him, their leader. They wanted to assure him that they were not afraid to die because they would take with them the knowledge and the comfort that they had died as free men. The atmosphere in the prison house was so heavy with tension and sorrow, I don't recall now how Xanana responded to the callers. What was there to say? They were indeed all killed in the early hours of the following morning.

There was a brief interval during which time the ambassador made an appeal to Xanana to remain a man of peace now that independence had been won. 'Just as importantly,' said the ambassador, 'you must stay alive at all costs.' And then, fixing Xanana with a serious look, he added, 'You are all your people have and you owe it to them.'

Then Xanana received another call from Taur Matan Ruak, the Deputy Commander of the Falintil. He was speaking from the cantonment in the hills of Uaimori, where the Falintil forces had remained throughout the campaign for the referendum. He reported that hundreds of people were arriving at the cantonment site, pleading with them to come and fight, to protect them from being raped and murdered at the hands of the militias. Xanana pleaded with him to order the men to remain where they were and not to give the Indonesian military grounds to claim that the bloodshed and destruction were the result of a civil war. But Ruak shouted that he could not hold them. And hung up. I watched Xanana drop his head into his hands as he choked back tears of rage and frustration. My heart ached for him. For his guest's sake, he kept a lid on his emotions.

In a bid to win back the confidence of the international community, which was shocked and appalled by the extent of the destruction and loss of life in Timor, the Indonesian government announced that Xanana was to be granted his freedom. The nightmare being lived by the people of East Timor made it impossible to feel anything other than a vague sense of satisfaction at the news.

On the morning of 7 September 1999, I made my way through

the cool of the morning to the prison house to help Xanana pack his bags in readiness for his departure later that day. It was exactly one year ago that my father had died. A day associated with sorrow and loss would from now on also be synonymous for me with freedom and new hope.

Chapter fifteen

BLACK SEPTEMBER
September 1999

IN LEGAL TERMS, Xanana was now a free man. For all practical purposes, however, he was still a long way from being able to savour the taste and true meaning of freedom. On the same night that Ambassador Robin Christopher had visited the prison house, we had received news that the Indonesian government was planning to release Xanana and put him on a plane to Dili. Remembering the ambassador's plea, Xanana decided to reject the plan of an immediate return to East Timor and consider a temporary safe haven somewhere in Jakarta. It was Paula's idea that we contact Robin Christopher, who had shared those terrible moments with us only hours earlier. With him she discussed his government's willingness to provide the space from which Xanana could safely continue to work to help bring the situation in East Timor under control – at least until such time as he could move elsewhere, preferably back to Timor itself.

The British government was amenable to the idea and, under Robin Christopher's supervision, arrangements were made for

Xanana and his Los Palos bodyguards to be housed in the British Embassy compound in central Jakarta. A large auditorium functioning as the embassy's Trade Reception Centre was cleared; partitions were erected, six beds were acquired, and the makeshift residence and office were ready. Over the entrance to the room, an awning had been erected. I sensed that the embassy authorities feared that someone with ill feeling towards East Timor's bid for freedom might take a pot-shot at Xanana from one of the many surrounding high-rise buildings. It was not what I had pictured for Xanana when he finally walked free from prison. Nevertheless, we were grateful for the warmth of the welcome from our hosts and the political courage of their decision to offer us this sanctuary.

Inside a building adjacent to the large room we came to refer to as Xanana's 'bunker' was a staff recreation room and pub called 'The Goose and Durian'. After a hastily organised press conference, it was here that we spent some hours on Xanana's first evening in the embassy. Someone had switched on the TV and pulled a few beers, which were handed around amidst laughter and some toasts to freedom. Xanana looked relaxed and at ease for the first time in months, but not too far in the back of all of our minds was the knowledge that terrible things were still happening in East Timor. Indeed, our mobile phones didn't give us a moment's peace that evening. Dili continued to burn as the militias torched everything in their path, from private homes to public property. There were further reports of killings and of CNRT leaders and their families fleeing into the hills above Dili. East Timorese in Indonesia were also falling victim to attacks from pro-integration groups.

The following day, Lucia, Paula, Natacha and I were obliged to abandon our office in Jalan Percekatan Negara IX A. A series of violent demonstrations against foreign targets was staged in Jakarta as international pressure on Indonesia to allow the intervention of a multinational force was stepped up; for the first time since our arrival in the capital we were at risk. It was a fairly familiar scenario.

In the past, when Indonesia's sovereignty was perceived to be threatened by foreign 'neo-colonial' forces, hardline nationalist groups within the country would come out in force and, with a nudge from the Indonesian military, vociferously and sometimes violently protest against the foreign *ikut campur*, or interference in Indonesia's internal business.

And so, amidst rumours of a military coup against Habibie, we packed our home and office into boxes, ready for transportation to the Mandarin Hotel where we would set up a temporary base. The hotel was conveniently located across the road from the British Embassy on the other side of the busy Hotel Indonesia roundabout. The dynamic and tireless head of the Portuguese Interests Section, Dr Ana Gomes, offered to cover the costs. Colin and one of his Indonesian activist friends, Bimo, helped us dismantle our computer network and equipment and reassemble them in the plush elegance of our new accommodation. My mother, Rosalie, set to work packing my clothing, books and other odd items into suitcases, and the contents of the kitchen cupboards and refrigerator into boxes. Nobody talked. We were all focussed on the task of getting out of the house as quickly as possible in case the rumoured turmoil became a reality. Even if the military decided to tolerate Habibie a little longer, there was still the threat of an attack from the same pro-integration groups that were terrorising East Timorese students and activists across Java.

Colin, who had taken a short break from stuffing monitors and cables into boxes, caught sight of Rosalie taking to the fridge with a soapy sponge. 'Jesus, Rosalie,' he called across the room, a mixture of pique and good humour in his voice. 'We're on the verge of a military coup, and you've decided to stop and clean the fridge!'

We arrived at the Hotel Mandarin laden down with three taxi-loads of office equipment and files and an assortment of personal effects that had been shoved into every available nook and cranny of dozens of boxes and bags and suitcases. The rather snooty porter who met us with his trolley at the marble-stepped entrance to the hotel looked at us and our belongings askance – our faces were flushed and wet with perspiration, our clothes grimy with the dust from the packing boxes.

'We're five-star refugees,' I whispered to Natacha as we boarded the lift for the fourteenth floor. The trolley, loaded to the hilt with bags and boxes, took up most of the space in the lift, although one or two elegantly dressed foreign guests managed to squeeze in with us. When a plastic bag full of my cosmetics and items from the kitchen crashed to the floor of the lift, Rosalie scrambled to retrieve them. One of the occupants of the lift glanced down at the stooped figure of my mother, frantically stuffing lipsticks and packet soups back into the bag, and sniffed disdainfully, raising a hand to her perfectly coiffed head.

In the middle of that scramble to pack up and leave, I had taken a phone call from the First Secretary of the US Embassy in Jakarta, Gary Gray, who was phoning from the police headquarters in Dili. He described the scene unfolding before his eyes. 'There are people being herded in here from all over the place. They are waiting around for a bit and then being shepherded by the police and what look to be bands of militias onto the backs of trucks. I can't quite work out what this is all about, where they are being taken to. But we are talking thousands of people here.'

We were not yet to know that this rounding up of the population was the beginning of a large-scale, coordinated campaign of hostage-taking which would result in well over 200,000 East Timorese being forced across the border into West Timor.

The routine inside the embassy bunker was largely a continuation of that of the prison house. There was a gruelling daily round of meetings with the representatives of foreign governments and a number of the UN specialised agencies who, in the face of the humanitarian crisis looming in East Timor, were planning a massive relief effort and were coordinating this with Xanana and other CNRT leaders. Food was to be dropped from aeroplanes at strategic points where large numbers of internally displaced people were known to be seeking refuge from the violence. But the most urgent priority was to bring an end to the killing sprees and the organised destruction of public and private property that the Indonesian military claimed it was at a loss to halt. As many foreign governments commented, it was difficult to see how this could be the case when Indonesia had 12,000 troops and 8000 police deployed in the territory.

From Washington, President Bill Clinton issued a statement stressing that if Indonesia failed to restore security, future US financial assistance to and military cooperation with Indonesia would be suspended. At the APEC Summit hosted by New Zealand, world leaders gathered and spoke in unison about the need for Indonesia to seek external help in restoring peace. To our great satisfaction, Australia went out on a limb and offered to lead a multinational force to help provide security in East Timor. The problem was that the Indonesian parliament was not due to ratify East Timor's 'separation' from Indonesia until November 1999; external military intervention launched before then would be taken as an 'invasion' of Indonesia.

There were moments of intense personal anguish in those days of September. It was by now difficult to be in direct phone contact with our East Timorese friends and colleagues because the telecommunications infrastructure had been destroyed by the militias. We became increasingly dependent on the eyewitness reports of groups of Timorese and foreign members of the clergy who were fleeing the chaos and heading to Jakarta. The difficulties of communication inside East Timor, plus our inability to corroborate information and reports we were receiving, meant, inevitably, that some of the stories of deaths we received were based on hearsay alone.

One afternoon in the bunker, news reached us that Father Domingos Soares, alias Father Maubere, had been murdered by militias. He was one of the most legendary of the members of the Timorese clergy, a hardworking and devoted supporter of the independence cause, and someone whom both Colin and I had trained in the use of electronic communications over the years. Colin was there in the bunker that afternoon as I read the piece of paper announcing Father Maubere's death.

After the days of tension and hard work, I was unable to control my emotions any longer. I sobbed long and hard into Colin's shoulder, thoughts and memories of the small man – the earnest expression he wore as he sat bent over his laptop, the easy laughter he shared with members of his congregation – surfacing and resurfacing in my mind. Xanana, who witnessed the spectacle, berated me afterwards for my weakness, reminding me that I needed to set an example of emotional fortitude to my Timorese colleagues and the five Los Palos boys who were struggling to come to terms with the absence of news from members of their families.

I was inclined not to believe it when I heard that Xanana's father himself had fallen victim to the militias' thirst for the blood of anyone associated with the independence cause. After all, the story of Father Maubere's death had turned out, thankfully, to be untrue. But when the news of Xanana's father's death came from two different sources, I had to change my tune. I felt sick to my stomach. How would Xanana take the news? How would he stand up to the pressure and the demands on him if he was consumed with grief for his father?

Later that same day, a meeting with members of a UN Security Council mission was scheduled and I knew that it was important that Xanana be clear-headed and strong to argue the case for an international force with them. If and when Habibie and his generals caved in to the pressure, it was going to be necessary to have the support of the Security Council to pass a resolution enabling the establishment of a peace-keeping force.

I decided to put on a brave face and keep the news of his father's death from Xanana until after the meeting with the Security Council mission. The day was nothing short of torture for me. I intercepted each and every visitor to the bunker, imploring each one not to make mention of the news or to offer condolences to Xanana. One of the visitors to the embassy that day was Dr Ana Gomes, who, noticing the toll my personal mission was taking on me, how tired and thin I had grown, embraced me warmly and urged me to be strong.

That evening, I was steeling myself for the terrible task I had before me. The day's meetings over, Xanana was slouched in a lounge chair in front of the television that the embassy staff had kindly rigged up for us so that we could follow coverage of events inside East Timor. The Los Palos boys had just polished off the hamburgers I had bought for their dinner and were also focussed on the TV. From the back of the room where I was sorting through some papers I kept my eyes trained on the TV screen, hoping beyond hope that there would be no mention of the death of Xanana's father. But suddenly, there it was. Juan Federer, in Darwin, was interviewed on the BBC bulletin, citing sources inside East Timor as the origins of the rumour. I rushed to Xanana's side. He sat very still; his face betrayed not the slightest hint of emotion. When he felt my hand on his shoulder, he turned to me and said, 'If it is true, it's not unexpected. I accepted from the beginning that my family were likely targets of this mayhem. I only hope that if it is true, he went quickly.' I was a little taken aback by Xanana's hard-nosed realism. But then again, anything less would have made bearing up under the weight of the brutality of the situation untenable.

Popular outrage at what was happening in East Timor reached its peak. Demonstrations, vigils and protest actions drew crowds of thousands of concerned citizens in countries all around the world. The helpful staff of the British Embassy came and went discreetly from the bunker, offering whatever assistance we required and handing us reams of fax paper containing the messages of solidarity, of congratulation and of commiseration, from governments, organisations and individuals across the planet.

Some of the most moving pieces of correspondence came from ordinary citizens of Indonesia. One Indonesian man wrote to express his wish that East Timor's independence would bring peace and prosperity to the nation's people and that its leaders would actively reject the 'false and hollow' development paradigm pursued by Suharto and his cronies. Another writer, a woman from Surabaya, said:

> It is no wonder that your people opted for independence when the other choice was to continue to be bullied by the henchmen of a colonial power, disguising its intentions with the name 'development' whilst plundering the land of its natural and cultural resources. The same thing is happening in West Irian and Kalimantan. So is it any wonder that the people there grow restless? Sir, it is no exaggeration to say that the quality of life for the average Indonesian is deteriorating at a fast pace. We don't feel secure anymore anywhere in this country. Criminality is rampant thanks to the impoverishment of the majority of the Indonesian people. Surabaya where I come from is overflowing with pedi-cab drivers, former farmers who can no longer make a living in the countryside, and laid-off workers. Robbery and street assault are common and pick-pockets have perfected their techniques in original ways. The police turn a blind eye or, in some cases, collude with the criminals. So what do we ordinary citizens have to hope for?

As I read the letter, I felt a wave of intense sadness wash over me. The Indonesian people were, it seemed, destined to remain shackled for some time yet to the poverty and corruption that were the legacy of the Suharto years. The East Timorese people at least had the light of hope and the anticipation of something better to guide them through the difficult years ahead.

Also flooding in were petitions and poems and a barrage of emails from around the world imploring Xanana to refrain from returning immediately to East Timor 'since you would be putting your life and your country's future at risk'. Instead they asked him to travel to New York and to urge the UN to intervene to prevent further bloodshed.

I was in a taxi on the way to the airport to see my mother off to Melbourne when Habibie announced that Indonesia would seek the assistance of an international force to restore law and order in East Timor. Back at the bunker, the relief was palpable. Tears of joy were shed, embraces exchanged, and Xanana laughed for the first time since his release from prison. By now, too, we had received confirmation that Xanana's father was in fact alive and well – along with his mother, he was being sheltered by a group of nuns in their convent in Dili.

On the evening of 18 September, a day before the Interfet forces departed Australia for Dili, Xanana, our colleagues and I boarded a Qantas flight from Jakarta to Darwin. By taking up residence in the British Embassy, Xanana felt that he had exchanged one form of incarceration for another, and there was little to be achieved by remaining in Indonesia when the ongoing threat to his security meant that he was seriously limited in his movements and contacts with East Timor. Moreover, outside the British Embassy there were now daily demonstrations against Xanana. They were clearly being orchestrated by the same ultra-nationalist groups that had been angered by the prospect of foreign intervention on 'Indonesian soil'. Xanana was uncomfortable with the knowledge that his presence in the embassy had the potential to become an irritant in Britain's relationship with Indonesia.

And so, having once again dismantled our office and the piece of life we had created for ourselves in the embassy and Mandarin Hotel, we set off for Australia. Xanana, Indonesian Justice Minister Muladi and the Australian and British ambassadors all donned bulletproof vests before making the half-hour journey to the airport, such was the level of political instability and uncertainty at that time. The wait in the VIP lounge of Sukarno-Hatta Airport seemed interminable. With the weight and padding of the bulletproof jacket, Xanana looked a little better fed than he actually was and, as he sipped coffee with Muladi on the comfortable sofa, I thought to myself that an uninformed onlooker could easily have mistaken them for business partners discussing their latest joint venture.

We didn't quite know what to expect at the other end of our flight. The government of the Northern Territory (NT) had been informed of our imminent arrival in Darwin and arrangements had been made to receive us. A request had been made that there be no media present at Darwin Airport and that Xanana be granted at least some days of reprieve from the rigours of the past weeks before those of the new phase we were about to enter began. So upon arriving at the airport in Darwin, we were collected at the tarmac by officials of the NT government and bundled into a light aircraft. Where we were headed was a little sketchy, but by then we were too weary to care much. As the little plane taxied out onto the runway, we saw the Hercules and other military aircraft that were about to be deployed by the Australian armed forces in East Timor. The sight of military hardware had never made me feel so happy.

Our landing on the airstrip at our destination sent up a cloud of red dust that continued to swirl about our heads as we struggled off the aircraft clutching our copious hand luggage. Two plain-clothes police officers and a man in a park ranger's uniform helped us load our things into the back of a waiting Land Rover. We had reached the pristine paradise of the Cobourg Peninsula, some 200 kilometres northeast of Darwin.

'You'll be safe and peaceful here,' said the man from the NT Parks and Wildlife Commission. Indeed, just the sight of the huge expanse of blue sky and the familiar Australian flora was already causing my tension to melt away. 'This is the Gurig National Park,' he went on, 'and we manage it jointly with the local Aboriginal custodians. No one gets into the park without a permit. So just relax and enjoy yourselves.'

We were driven to two small wooden cabins nestled between a cluster of tea-trees and eucalypts. The way the flyscreen door to the cabin creaked and slammed shut with a bang reminded me of holiday houses from a carefree past, now distant in time and memory. We spread ourselves out over the two cabins and then joined in one for a plate of pasta and a bottle of white wine that someone had thrust into Paula's hands at Darwin Airport along with a bag of groceries.

But I could think of nothing but rest and so, after a mouthful or two of spaghetti, I curled up on the sofa and gave in to the irresistible urge to sleep. I woke a short time later to see Xanana taking my photograph with the little pocket camera someone had given him and Paula crouched on the floor, struggling to make the old TV in the corner of the room cooperate and give us some news about East Timor. I have to admit that I was quite pleased when she did not succeed and we were all forced to head off to bed with our heads filled not with images of buildings burning and people fleeing, but with the sound of crickets and the roar of the ocean.

We were woken the next morning by the sharp bite of the sun streaming through the windows. I had slept so heavily and so peacefully that my head felt pleasantly numb. There was nothing better to revive it than a dip in the rich turquoise of the ocean we had gazed at with longing from the aircraft the day before. Like a band of noisy teenagers on school camp, we all walked single file behind Sean, the police officer, and headed for the beach. It was only a short walk, but by the time we had wended our way through the scrubby bush to the thin strip of golden sand, we were breathless and impatient to launch ourselves into the sea. Xanana and I stripped off on a rocky outcrop at one end of the beach and called to the others to join us. Tito let out a whoop as he catapulted himself into the gentle milky waves. Xanana smoked a cigarette as he sat on the edge of some rocks and dangled his toes in the shallows of the sea where barramundi and coral trout were known to make their homes.

With my video camera I captured the expression on his face as he finally waded out into the crystal clear depths and then propelled himself forward in an exuberant bellyflop. I realised then that this was the first time Xanana had felt the caress of the sea in twenty years. Being a fairly typical Aussie when it came to sun and surf, I found it difficult to imagine any greater privation. We dived and larked about and delighted in the combined effects of the water, sun and salty air on our bodies and spirits, the only sound the screech of a seabird gliding overhead and the shouts of joyful laughter of our frolicking friends. Back on his rocky perch once more, Xanana drew hard on another cigarette and, exhaling, breathed out to sea: 'Now this is freedom.'

Later that day a representative of the NT Chief Minister, accompanied by Andrew Ladley, the UN Mission in East Timor (UNAMET) legal advisor, flew in to discuss details of our reception and accommodation in Darwin. He looked a little taken aback when Xanana stated that he needed to return to Darwin and be on the job within the next day or two. It seemed that an apartment had been rented to house our sizeable delegation but it had not yet been furnished. Xanana did his best to reassure the man that being fresh from prison, he would not be offended if the apartment lacked a few amenities or even, for that matter, a bed.

'For eighteen years the soil and leaves of my pátria were my mattress,' Xanana said. The conversation then turned to other matters, including Xanana's short- and longer-term plans. Did he intend to stay in Darwin long? Would the CNRT be establishing a semi-permanent base in Darwin? Xanana explained that whilst his wish was to be able to get back to East Timor as soon as possible, he was unable to give a precise date for his return. He explained that it was indeed very likely that the CNRT would establish a presence in Darwin, but again precise details would need to be the subject of consultations with other members of the council.

Apart from this meeting, the two days we spent in the national park were blissfully free of official engagements of any kind, and we made the best use of the short time available to us to recover our strength and bathe the emotional wounds of the past weeks and months in the salty waves of the ocean.

Back in Darwin, we settled into the three light and airy apartments prepared for us by the NT government. Cesar and Tito shared one spacious two-bedroom apartment with Xanana and me, with the rest of our team spreading out over the remaining two. It was such a pleasure to be able to unpack, to stock the fridge of the fully equipped kitchen, to hang clothes in a wardrobe in the knowledge that we could dispense with the suitcases for the time being.

As it turned out, this comfortable feeling of being, finally, rooted somewhere was to be short-lived. The CNRT was steadily regrouping and establishing a base for itself in premises supplied by the NT government. In a bare but spacious office located on the fifth floor of one of Darwin's central shopping malls, Xanana held meetings with fellow CNRT leaders and members on a response to the humanitarian crisis in East Timor, and made plans for a delegation of technically minded East Timorese to travel to New York and Washington to present development priorities to the UN and the World Bank. Naturally, it was felt to be important that Xanana lead this mission.

And so, within days of arriving back in Darwin, plane tickets were purchased and suitcases packed once again in preparation for our departure for New York. Our few short days in Darwin had been filled with meetings with the evacuated staff of UNAMET; consultations with representatives of around twenty international NGOs to plan and coordinate their emergency response; interviews with the Australian and international media; and a visit to the site where hundreds of East Timorese refugees were temporarily housed. The effect of the extensive media coverage of East Timor's vote for independence and its tragic aftermath was a phenomenal outpouring of sympathy and solidarity from people and organisations around the world.

It was only to be expected that, for many, Xanana was the most obvious person to whom the multifarious offers of material assistance and advice should be directed. He was the human face of East Timor's awe-inspiring struggle and victory. In practical terms this meant that the buzzer on the door of our Darwin apartment rang day and night, and that there were never fewer than about five or six guests sitting around our kitchen table. If our physical surroundings lent themselves to indulging a fantasy of normal life as a married couple, the practical political demands of the situation certainly did not.

The hectic pace of our Darwin days had taken the edge off the relaxed state of body and mind in which we had returned from the

Cobourg Peninsula. By the time we boarded the Qantas jet at 7 am on 25 September, Xanana was grey with exhaustion.

Sometime later that day – or perhaps it was the previous one, given our flit across the International Date Line – Xanana and I found ourselves eating boiled lollies in a VIP lounge in Los Angeles. To help pass the time while we transited in the plush Admiral's Lounge, I interviewed him on video.

'What should be arriving any minute now?' I asked.

No response, and a look of mild irritation cast in my direction.

'What did you leave in Sydney?'

Still no answer.

'You left it,' I said.

Finally Xanana said, 'Passport.'

During the trans-Pacific flight we realised that Xanana had left his Portuguese passport under a pile of newspapers in the lounge at Sydney Airport. He was as yet unseasoned in international travel and had no experience of handling travel documents. The customer service officer on the flight had telephoned ahead to LA to inform them of the mishap and request that the passport be put on the next flight leaving Sydney for LA. It reached us just in the nick of time before we were called to board our flight to New York.

We arrived in New York at 11:30 pm. What seemed to be the entire New York Police Department was assembled at the door of the plane. Other American Airlines passengers must have wondered who this tired little man in his faded, holey violet polo shirt was and how he could warrant such a motorcade of limousines and noisy flashing police cars. A convoy of screaming sirens guided us to our hotel.

The Kimberley was a small, boutique-style hotel, with olde-worlde furnishings and a lift that creaked and shuddered. Clearly Paula, who had travelled ahead with Natacha a couple of days earlier, had worded up our hosts about Xanana and my relationship, as we were accommodated in the same room. I tried to shoe-polish the red NT dust off my black sandals before falling into a jet-lagged heap on the bed. Xanana was not so lucky. Constancio

Pinto, the CNRT representative in the United States, was understandably anxious to spend some time with him. And there were others, too – I don't remember who they were, but they stayed too long and it was close to 4 am by the time Xanana was able to call it a day.

I was furious when, at 7:30 am the following morning, I found Xanana hoeing into his tenth sweet from the complimentary gift basket that had been deposited on the bench of the suite's little kitchenette. I cleaned up the wrappers strewn all around and warned him that he wouldn't make it through the day's important meetings on so little sleep. 'I just couldn't drop off,' he said through a mouthful of Turkish delight. He was trying desperately to prise open the window in the lounge room so that he could lean out and puff on a cigarette. From the lobby to the suite's bathroom, there were little white placard reminders that smoking was not permitted in the hotel.

We were conscious that this was a state visit – a first for East Timor – and the schedule for our four or five days in the United States was jam-packed. There were meetings with the UN Department of Peace-keeping Operations, the President of the UN Security Council and Kofi Annan. Paula and I managed to slink off sometime during the first day to invest in some cool-weather gear at Macy's, as autumn in New York was positively nippy for anyone used to the humidity of Jakarta and Darwin, and needless to say we were without coats.

Xanana, José and members of the technical team that had been formed in Darwin caught up with Madeleine Albright at the Waldorf Hotel. They impressed upon her the urgent need for Indonesia to disarm the militias and to collaborate with the UN High Commissioner for Refugees (UNHCR) in guaranteeing the repatriation of the hundreds of thousands of refugees still languishing in border camps in West Timor. With Kofi Annan, the Timorese discussed the CNRT's draft timeline for the transition to independence and a proposed structure for the transitional authority that would stand in for government until a Timorese-led one was democratically elected. At that moment, with the country still smouldering, the idea of democratic elections seemed an academic proposition, too distant in the future to be real.

We all did battle with our jet-lag during the long, coffee-less meetings at UN headquarters. During the lunch break the following day, the delightful Portuguese Ambassador, António Monteiro, whisked Xanana and me away in his big black embassy sedan to Bloomingdale's to buy Xanana some new clothes. In a continuing comedy of errors, the suits Xanana had left on our LA-bound plane still hadn't materialised. It was important that he look the part for the press conference at the UN, at which Xanana and José Ramos-Horta would speak, later that day. There was jazz playing in the menswear section of Bloomingdale's as Xanana tried on a selection of dapper suits and the Portuguese Ambassador explained to the sales assistant that any alterations would need to be done within the hour.

Back at our hotel room, Xanana was on edge as he went over the notes he had prepared for the press conference. He paced the hotel room and chain-smoked, having decided that it was worth risking dishonourable expulsion from the hotel in order to be able to indulge his habit. 'Cry-sis, not cree-sis,' I corrected his pronunciation from the kitchenette, where I was making him his fifth cup of coffee.

There was something about the sight of Xanana at the press conference – looking a little nervous and stumbling at times over the English text in front of him, with the blue UN flag on the wall behind where he and José sat – that brought a tear to my eye. Here he was finally, addressing the press and some member countries of that hallowed institution that had featured for twenty-four years in the hopes and dreams of freedom of the East Timorese people. Xanana and José spoke and took questions from journalists on the plight of the refugees and of East Timor's commitment to the development of a democratic system of government and the normalisation of relations with its giant neighbour, Indonesia.

We took an early morning flight to Washington DC on 29 September, and were put up at the Portuguese Embassy, which doubled as the residence of the ambassador. It was drizzling with rain when we arrived, but the grey sky did nothing to detract from the beauty of the old colonial building. We stayed in a room with yellow floral quilts and were attended by black servants in pinafores covered with lacy white aprons. It felt like something straight out of the antebellum south. Diplomatic security service personnel, with their earpieces and wires, lurked around the residence and added an American cops-and-robbers flavour to the bygone-era unreality of the whole escapade. The following day at the World Bank, Xanana impressed upon a conference hall packed with finance ministers from around the world the huge needs of his tiny country.

The sense of unreality continued when Xanana, José, Paula, Natacha and I were taken on the Portuguese government's private jet across the Atlantic to Lisbon. Xanana had never been to Portugal, and there was a formidable welcome awaiting him. It was as if he was a national hero, not the leader of a people whose homeland lay on the opposite side of the globe. People lined the streets from the airport all the way into the city to greet him. The Portuguese people, like so many around the world, had reacted with dismay and anguish as the images of East Timor's recent nightmare reached them in their homes and workplaces, and Xanana's visit provided a focus for their feelings of solidarity and sympathy with the people of their former colony.

Our three-day stay under the blue skies of Lisbon was another gust in the whirlwind of our transatlantic adventure. From Lisbon, our comfy little jet carried us across the water to Ireland, which loomed emerald and shrouded in a light mist of rain as we descended into Dublin. I had always had a 'thing' about Ireland – perhaps it was the calling of my ancestry, the coursing of some Irish blood in my veins – but had never visited, so the day and a half we spent flitting between meetings with the Prime Minister, the media and an audience with the President was a kind of torture for me. I would have liked nothing better than to 'defect' and spend a week exploring Dublin, testing it against the impressions and fantasies forged in my imagination. But that wasn't to be.

From Dublin we were whisked away to London where, between meetings with Foreign Secretary Robin Cook, and the requisite pressing of the flesh in front of 10 Downing Street, we strolled through Hyde Park, stood goggle-eyed and shivering in front of Buckingham Palace, and snapped some pictures under Big Ben's imposing tower. As Xanana ambled along the banks of the River Thames, raising his camera to capture the play of light on the magnificent parliament buildings or the look of delight in the faces of fellow gobsmacked tourists, he commented on how good it felt to be anonymous here, to be momentarily just another visitor on a stroll across London Bridge.

We arrived back in Darwin on 6 October. Soon after that, Abdurrahman Wahid, alias Gus Dur, stepped in to replace Habibie as President of Indonesia. The almost blind Muslim cleric and leader of the National Awakening Party (PKB) had visited Xanana in Cipinang in late 1998 and expressed his solidarity with the struggle of the East Timorese people. The two had developed quite a rapport. We were all a little astounded by his resounding victory in the presidential elections, but at the same time were hopeful that his personal friendship with Xanana would serve as useful leverage in efforts to restore peace to East Timor and some semblance of friendly cooperation to its relationship with Indonesia.

On 25 September 1999, the day Xanana and I had set off on our historic visit to the United States and Europe, Sister Celeste Carvalho, the young nun who had befriended me on my very first visit to Timor, set off by car from Baucau for Los Palos in the company of another Canossian sister and some other members of the clergy. Along the way the vehicle was intercepted and its passengers brutally murdered. Some say the Indonesian army was responsible, others a group of knife-wielding militia.

I still cry when I think of her, when I recall that afternoon on the beach at Baucau, her tiny frame, the pressure of her slender arm linked through mine as she guided me gently through my life's first Timor journey.

Chapter sixteen

HOMECOMING
October–November 1999

THE FACT THAT Australia had taken the lead in heading the international force that brought peace to East Timor was tremendously satisfying for me. Finally, defence of the lives and rights of innocent East Timorese was government policy, not just the demand of activists and concerned members of the public. Finally, the geopolitical tide had turned, and to be a friend of East Timor was no longer to be a hopeless idealist, but a defender of freedom and democracy.

Back in Darwin after our trip to the US and Europe, Xanana itched to return to East Timor. After seven years of exile from his *pátria*, he was understandably anxious to get home. An even bigger consideration for Xanana than his own longing for his homeland, however, was the knowledge that his people needed him there, both to help heal the still-fresh wounds of their bodies and souls and to restore their confidence in the future.

On the television in the CNRT office in Darwin, we watched the images of Australian soldiers being embraced by the grateful residents of Dili, others disarming bands of sorry-faced militias to the shouts, cheers and jeering of delighted onlookers. We saw buildings gutted, some still on fire and others smouldering. Dili, a once pretty place in spite of the prominence of corrugated iron and cement blocks in the more modern Indonesian structures, looked charred and war-torn. We saw bewilderment and fear still lurking in the faces of the few residents who had stayed or straggled back to the town to take a look at what remained of their homes. Children picked through the ashes and rubble of torched shops and office buildings.

A number of meetings with members of the Australian special forces (SAS) were held at the CNRT office and other discreet rendezvous points around Darwin. One of the officers in charge of coordinating the plan for Xanana's return to Dili was Steve, a tall, muscular young man with an angular jaw and a serious air. For the meetings with us he dressed in civilian clothes in order not to draw attention to his sensitive mission. Although Dili was, by now, relatively secure, there were still groups of militia on the loose, and therefore it was felt to be prudent not to give anyone other than Xanana's closest confidants too much prior warning of his intended arrival in the capital . . . just in case someone was preparing a hostile welcome. Steve communicated Xanana's wishes and concerns back to his boss – Australian Major-General Peter Cosgrove, the Interfet Commander – in East Timor, and finally an action plan was agreed upon. On 20 October 1999, Steve handed us a detailed, to-the-minute schedule of Xanana's movements from the moment he set off for the military airbase in Darwin the following evening.

And so the next night, after a day at the office spent carefully avoiding any reference to his plans, Xanana dressed himself in the Falintil fatigues he had brought with him from Jakarta and stood at the front door to our apartment, waiting to be collected by Steve. He was in high spirits and joked about with the Los Palos boys, all of whom, bar Tito, were to make the journey with him. I had pleaded with Xanana to be allowed to accompany him, unable to bear the thought of missing out on this moment of tremendous personal significance to us both, not to mention its historic and political importance. But he told me he needed to be sure that the conditions on the ground were sufficiently stable first and promised to call me to join him as soon as he was sure that it was safe.

Tito looked a little downcast and dejected as he watched his four friends placing their bags by the door of the apartment. Xanana had only managed to convince him to stay behind by making him feel that he was being entrusted with an important mission, that of taking care of 'Mana Kirsty'. Poor Tito. And so, after slapping the young man on the back and entreating him once again to 'look after your sister for me', he turned to me and kissed me on the mouth. 'I'll call you,' he said, turning his uniformed back on me and disappearing through the door. His voice resonated in my brain as I realised with regret that I hadn't found the words to say something meaningful or poignant, and nor had I even told him to be careful. 'I'll call you.' It was as if he was just heading out to the pub for a bite to eat or setting off for a long weekend away!

But call me he did, and much earlier than I had expected. The following afternoon I left CNRT early to do some shopping on the way home. It was a relief to leave the office; a group of irate journalists had converged on the place when they learnt of Xanana's surprise return to East Timor and Natacha was under fire for not having warned them.

'Xanana is my boss, not you,' she defended herself. 'My first duty is to him, you have to understand.'

I was in the frozen goods aisle at Woolworths, buying something to cook for Tito and me for dinner, when my mobile rang. There was static on the line that made Xanana's voice crackle as he whispered, 'I feel like I am in another prison here.' There was no time to ask him what he meant. 'The army people will be in touch with you. Come tomorrow.'

Earlier, in the CNRT office, I had watched with a huge lump

in my throat as the six o'clock news broadcast the images of Xanana addressing a jubilant but emotional crowd of many thousands of people gathered in front of the governor's palace in Dili. 'We proved to the world and to ourselves that we could do it!' he had shouted through tears of his own, as below him the people cheered and raised their fists in a mixture of triumphant joy and intense sorrow. Xanana's presence there not only had the effect of reaffirming the people's pride in their awesome victory, but it also reminded them of their sacrifices, of all they had lost in the weeks and months just past.

I added a few cans of sardines, a jar of vegemite and a packet of apricot muesli bars to my trolley – how did one shop, what did one buy in preparation for life in a devastated war zone? – and was heading for the checkout when my mobile phone rang again. This time it was a young officer named Peta, from the Army Liaison Department.

'Can you be ready to leave from your place at 5 am tomorrow?' she enquired.

'Ah, sure, no problem. The address is – '

'Don't worry, I already have it from Steve. So I'll see you at 5 am then.'

That night I packed my suitcase, informed a handful of my CNRT colleagues of my plans, rang Mum to do the same, and handed over a number of odd jobs to Paula and Natacha, who were a touch concerned that I was heading off so quickly, but at the same time glad that I would be with Xanana.

I pored over my personal possessions, deciding what to pack. It seemed that with the exception of the New York winter woollies, I would need just about everything. By pick-up time at 5 am the next morning I had had about two hours sleep. Tito chatted away excitedly in the back of Officer Peta Mitchell's small red hatchback as we drove to the airbase. Finally, at around 7 am, we were ushered out onto the tarmac of the airfield and invited to climb aboard the Hercules that would transport us to Dili. We were handed a pair of green, military-style ear protectors as we clambered into the belly of the huge aircraft and were instructed to strap ourselves into the seats, which were simple padded benches running down either flank of the plane.

Given that the only windows in the plane were a series of small portholes, it took my eyes a while to adjust to the dark and to be able to make out the other details of the aircraft's interior. Towards the rear there were piles of heavy-looking metal boxes, which looked as though they contained army supplies or rations, all anchored to the floor with ropes. As the plane's engines roared to life and we began to taxi, I noticed two pallets of Victoria Bitter beer amongst the provisions on board and, lying on top of them, fast asleep, an Australian soldier. The sight made me smile. I hoped that deep in the bowels of the plane, beyond the beer and rations boxes, our suitcases and other items of luggage had been stowed.

The only other passenger on board was the Interfet canteen lady, Meredith. It was her first overseas mission and she was looking forward to the challenge. An hour and a half later, the mountains and plains of East Timor were coming into view below us, and Tito and I were unable to resist the temptation of unstrapping ourselves from our seats and gazing through the smoky perspex of the windows. I felt a lump forming in my throat as I caught a glimpse of the brown hills sloping down into the three lakes of Taci Tolu, then Dili, a patchwork of black and grey ruins, entire neighbourhoods reduced to rubble. But it wasn't the sight of the destruction that choked me up; rather, it was the happy thought that this land I was about to arrive in, this country that had so thoroughly consumed my time and thoughts for as long as I could remember, now belonged to the East Timorese. And it was this knowledge, not the work of the militia and the TNI, that transformed the landscape in my eyes, making it appear unfamiliar and different somehow from the occupied land I had visited so many times in the past.

This transformation may have been more psychological than physical, but the changes to Dili's civilian airport were quite real. Khaki green canvas tents and awnings stood along the edges of the tarmac, and military trucks and cars zipped to and fro between these structures and the two or three aircraft dotting the airfield.

'Welcome to your new homeland!' I shouted at Tito over the roar of the Hercules' propellers as we descended the steps and headed instinctively for the only available circle of shade. It was only 9 am or so, but the sun was already fierce. Soon we saw a familiar face moving towards us. It was Matt, one of the British intelligence agents who had advised on security matters pertaining to Xanana's stay in the British Embassy in Jakarta. It was a little uncanny to see him again here. After the suave, clean-cut look of his Jakarta attire, I almost didn't recognise him sporting a military uniform with a dusty rifle slung over his shoulder.

It was a few years since my last visit to East Timor. As we were driven to the beachside compound where Xanana was being housed under SAS guard, I was struck by how militarised the environment was. UN tanks patrolled the streets and heavily armed peace-keeping troops stood guard on almost every corner. Bunkers had been fashioned from enormous white sandbags. From behind them, the watchful faces of soldiers from a number of nations peered out, their weapons at the ready should a threat of any kind rear its head. I felt a little as though I had entered the set of *M*A*S*H*. And yet, unlike the city under Indonesian occupation, fear was no longer evident in the eyes and bearing of the local population who strolled along the main thoroughfare leading from the airport into town. There was a sense that something heavy had been lifted, an uneasy feeling of normality and peace. The remaining Indonesian armed forces were very subdued; they were to withdraw completely in the weeks to come.

We were taken to a large, heavily fortified compound on the beachfront just west of Dili and a kilometre or two up the road from the Motael Church. The huge white building, which appeared to have been an office complex of some description, was one of the few that had escaped the destructive attentions of the militias. We passed through a gate reinforced with barbed wire and pulled up at the front door of the building, around the verandah of which sauntered a dozen or so soldiers, some bare-chested, some slouched against the front wall and nursing foil-covered plates. I guessed it was breakfast time. Some of them nodded politely as Tito and I passed with our luggage, but mostly they ignored us.

Before we had taken more than a couple of steps inside the front door, Steve was there beside us. After a few words of greeting and welcome, he guided us through to the rear of the complex, which was largely furniture-less and strewn with the soldiers' rucksacks and an assortment of army paraphernalia from torches, boots, sleeping bags and drink canisters to automatic weapons. Around a long wooden fold-up table in a back room were seated Xanana and three or four Falintil commanders, including Taur Matan Ruak and Commander Sabica. Xanana got up from the table where they were all hoeing into plates of tinned spaghetti and slices of white bread to greet me with a hug and a peck on the cheek. The circumstances permitted no more intimate expression of the delight we both felt at being together at last on East Timorese soil. Xanana introduced me to the commanders, whom I kissed warmly on both cheeks. Leandro Isaac, the CNRT member who had made the emotional call to me from the hills above Dili in early September, was also there. He looked a little gaunt and weary, but otherwise relaxed and happy.

A large map of Dili was attached to the wall with masking tape. As we all took our seats at the table and Steve assumed a schoolmaster's pose in front of the map, Xanana leaned over and whispered to me that he was planning to do a walk around Dili on foot the following day and that Steve was keen to plot out the route beforehand so that the Interfet boys could provide the best security possible. He was to be accompanied by journalists from the Portuguese RTP network and the BBC, who were amongst the small number of reporters who had ventured back into the country after the deliberate campaign of terror waged against the foreign media by the militias throughout September.

Later that afternoon, as the sun was sinking and the sky glowed a fiery orange, I proposed to Xanana that we take a brief stroll along the beach, just to relax and gaze at Timor's beauty, which was at its dazzling best at that cool and tranquil time of day.

'You're joking,' he whispered. 'I would have to take a platoon of these big Aussies with me. It would be no fun at all. That's if they would even permit me to do it.'

Then I understood what Xanana had meant when he had commented to me over the phone about being in yet another prison. Steve and his SAS men only had Xanana and East Timor's best interests at heart in offering this level of security, and Xanana was grateful for their presence and their efforts to be of assistance. Nevertheless, he scoffed at suggestions that there existed a generalised threat to his security inside East Timor.

Dinner was courtesy of Interfet: cold baked beans, two slices of processed cheese and a handful of dry biscuits. Bed was my camp mattress which put a centimetre of rubber between my bones and the hard tiles of the floor in the bare, windowless room I was allocated as my sleeping quarters. Not even the buzz of the mosquitoes or the boots of the patrolling soldiers kept me from falling soundly asleep, though.

The next morning we were taken in an armoured troop carrier to the point where Xanana would commence his walkabout. I had never seen such a monstrous contraption – except in war movies – let alone stepped inside one. Xanana had tried to insist that we travel in a regular army vehicle, but the SAS guys wouldn't hear of it. It was dark and airless inside and I noticed that Xanana leapt to his feet, as anxious as I was to breathe fresh air, as soon as the vehicle lurched to a halt. Goodness knows where we were. Outside the bright sun caused us to squint as we looked around and realised that we were in the part of the city that was once the bustling central business district. I had seen the pictures on the telly and prepared myself psychologically for the sight of the devastation, but I suppose I had not fully realised the extent of the damage – there was not a single building within eyeshot untouched by the violence. On either side of the tree-lined avenue where we got down from the troop carrier, the buildings that had once housed shops, offices and an Indonesian bank were empty shells. They had been looted first and then torched by the militias, their only contents now the charred remains of things that had been too heavy to cart off: a twisted filing cabinet, the skeleton of a metal book rack, the contorted spine of a rusty metal chair.

We began our march in the direction of the waterfront, the blue band of the sea like a beacon beckoning us away from that sad doomsday vision. A group of about five burly SAS soldiers had fanned out, forming a protective arc around Xanana. They stood with their weapons raised, their backs to Xanana and their eyes hawk-like, scanning the surrounding area from behind dark glasses. The BBC and RTP journalists and their respective camera operators were looking expectantly in our direction from the cracked and warped footpath, perhaps fearing to approach us in case someone had forgotten to inform Xanana's minders that their presence there had been authorised. Finally one of the soldiers motioned with a flick of his blond head to the journalists to fall in behind us as he and his colleagues quickened their steps to keep up with Xanana. Before we reached the corner, a block back from the beach, Xanana slowed down to take a closer look at the ruins of a two-storey building I thought I recognised as having been a bank in the past. He stepped into the wreckage, Leandro and I following behind him.

There was the sound of glass crunching underfoot, the acrid smell of burning still lingering in the air. The two cameramen scrambled over the mounds of crumbling cement, kicking up clouds of ash as they skipped and bobbed and lunged to find the best angle from which to shoot Xanana contemplating the nightmare he and his people had inherited from Indonesia. In spite of the forbidding presence of the SAS soldiers, a number of locals had gathered at the entrance to the building, anxious to catch a glimpse of their leader. Before too long a small crowd had assembled and Xanana responded to their calls and shouts of 'Viva Xanana' by stepping back through the rubble to squeeze their hands and kiss the wet cheeks of women and young girls. The soldiers tightened their protective circle around Xanana, scanning the faces of the growing number of bystanders for signs of malicious intent. They found only smiles of delight and looks of intense curiosity. Xanana then made his way up a flight of stairs littered with debris and shards of glass to the second floor of the building, the sweating cameramen hot on his heels.

It seemed that in the time it had taken us to ascend the twenty or so steps to the second floor and to venture out onto the wide balcony, half of Dili had gathered to witness this, only the second public appearance of their 'big brother'. Below us, filling the road in front and a good part of the promenade opposite the governor's palace, was a sea of upturned faces. Realising that he couldn't avoid addressing some words to them, Xanana stepped forward and raised an arm, which sent a wave of expectant silence over the crowd. His voice was low and soft when he began and the people below craned their necks and tilted their heads to hear him talk about how they should feel proud of their victory and of their courage in voting to defeat lies and oppression.

'They have left us with this, with nothing,' he said, indicating with his eyes the line of destroyed buildings he had just inspected. 'But we will refuse, as we did for twenty-four years, to be daunted by the difficulties before us – we will rebuild our city, our homeland, our lives!'

There was a thunderclap of applause, over which Xanana continued: 'We will show them that we are not dogs, but people, people with dignity and the will to start afresh, even with no rooves over our heads, no food in our bellies.' He was shouting now, his voice shaking with the anger and heartbreak he felt at seeing Dili, the city of his youth, reduced to ash and rubble. Rivulets of perspiration coursed down Xanana's face and neck.

The cameramen, having made the blackened balustrade their tripods, had the lenses of their cameras trained on Xanana's features as he regained his composure and concluded his address with a rousing cry: 'Viva Timor Lorosa'e!' 'Viva Timor Lorosa'e!' echoed the crowd, their fists punching the air above their heads.

I sank back into the shadows of the building, my eyes stinging with tears and the dust the soldiers' heavy boots had churned up. I wondered to myself what the SAS men made of this spectacle, whether they had felt the emotion of the moment, and were moved as I was. It was impossible to gauge their reaction. Their eyes were hidden behind the reflector glass of their shades, their faces set in an expression of determined vigilance.

Later that same day we boarded a helicopter painted in the green and camel shades of the soldiers' camouflage gear. A machine gun was mounted in the open window of the aircraft, and beside it crouched a young Australian soldier who didn't look older than about twenty. We were headed for Remexio, a village high in the hills south of Dili that was being established as the Falintil's mountain base.

So far only a handful of the Falintil companies that had previously been stationed in the Uaimori cantonment had relocated to Remexio. The plan was for others to follow. Nevertheless, this was Xanana's first reunion with many of the commanders he had fought with, and a huge welcome had been planned. As the helicopter circled above the small town, I saw a long white structure perched on a hilltop above a large expanse of green which resembled a playing field. On approach, the aircraft tilting and sending my heart into my mouth, I noticed that the field was dotted with the red berets of one hundred or more Falintil guerrillas. As we hovered low in preparation for our landing, the blades of the helicopter sent grass and leaves and dust swirling and spiralling about like a mini typhoon.

The half circle of men who formed the welcoming party twenty metres or so from the landing place were bracing themselves against the gusting wind, their hands raised to shield their eyes from its force. Steve and another soldier jumped out of the helicopter ahead of us and moved in the direction of the waiting reception committee. Two or three men in civilian dress and a priest in a pristine white robe rushed forward to embrace Xanana. As they did, the Falintil trumpeters took their cue from a command shouted by the slight, bearded figure standing erect in front of them, and a military bugle call rang out. I hung back a little, preferring on this occasion to be a spectator rather than a member of the official party. This was Xanana's moment, and it was he that the people had gathered to ceremonially welcome back into their midst.

Lining the grassy way to the wooden dais were festoons made of the young leaves of the coconut palm, their pale yellow fronds curled back and secured to form a row of decorative Os. Some had a sprig of gorgeous pink-orange bougainvillea tucked in at regular intervals along the stem. The members of the reception committee fell away to join the guests of honour seated on the dais, and into their place moved two rows of elderly women bearing wooden drums and metal gongs. In front of them, draped in lengths of the traditional woven cloth known as *tais*, stood a young girl who looked up nervously into Xanana's face. From a wooden tray she took a brightly coloured *selendang*, or shawl, and Xanana bowed to allow her to place it around his neck. When he stooped to kiss her on both cheeks, her face broke into a shy smile and she lowered her eyes to the ground.

Then the old women began their fast rhythmical beating of their little *babadoks* and Xanana moved with them as they shuffled backwards, their bodies swaying to and fro in time with the resonating beat of the gongs. Half a dozen or so traditional elders joined the procession, some brandishing swords, which they waved above their heads as they hopped energetically from foot to foot, chanting words of welcome to their leader. They wore elaborate headdresses made from the colourful plumage of their prized fighting cocks, and around their ankles was the pale fur of goats. Their faces, pinched and leathery with age and years of hardship, were animated and gay, their lips parted in toothless, betel-red grins. The low ululating moan of the buffalo horn was a sombre counterpoint to the lively rhythm of the other traditional instruments.

The pageant carried Xanana in its colourful wake to the foot of the dais, where the thirty-odd assembled guests had risen to their feet. The bugle player was silent now, the slightly built parade commander having barked a military command or two that caused the Falintil troops to stand to attention. Their faces were frozen, staring straight ahead in the direction of the dais, as Xanana moved briskly along the lines of men to inspect the troops. I was not familiar with any of this military rigmarole, but was struck by the discipline and coordination of the soldiers. They had clearly been in training for days in preparation for this moment.

Having completed his inspection, Xanana returned to the simple podium erected at the centre of the dais and saluted as a long-haired soldier prepared to raise the Falintil flag. As it was hoisted slowly up the flagpole, a chorus of young girls began singing the Falintil anthem, and the guests instinctively raised their hands to their hearts. The harmony of their voices was hauntingly beautiful. 'With your blood and your bodies you protected us,' they sang. All eyes, even those of the dozen or so foreign journalists present, were directed upwards to the blue, green and white flag fluttering on the breeze high above us. The last note of the anthem hung suspended in the air for a second or two, followed by a moment of impossible silence while the troops, the guests, the crowds of curious onlookers, refocussed their attention from the flag to the statuesque figure of Xanana, his hand still raised in a stiff salute.

And then he addressed the men and women of Falintil, now standing at ease under the implacable sun. Through his tears he invoked the memory of their fallen comrades, recalling the difficulties of their lonely struggle, the long years of privation and hunger and death, the defeats at the hands of the enemy, the support of the people across the country which had sustained them in their battle against the indifference of the world and the superior firepower of Indonesia's modern army. The sound of stifled sobbing could be heard all around. I can't say whether it was the sadness of these thoughts or the sight of Xanana weeping out of control that sent tears of my own cascading down my cheeks. Although I was not alone in succumbing to my emotion, I felt the urge to hide behind my video camera. I raised the viewfinder to my eye and captured the mixture of pride and anguish in the lowered eyes of the soldiers. The gold rim of Commander Sabica's dark glassed glinted in the sun, his cheeks awash with tears.

Xanana swept a handkerchief across his face and concluded his address with an appeal; it was an appeal for the Falintil and for the people as a whole to be proud of their victory and of their courage, and to put these qualities in the service of peace and nation building in Timor Lorosa'e. 'We must not live in the past,' he cried. 'The future is ours and it belongs to us alone.' There was a euphoric cheer and then Xanana turned on his heel and began to move along to rows of guests, all of whom followed his progress with red and swollen eyes. Some he greeted with a smile and a playful slap on the back, others sobbed uncontrollably as he reached them. Some were so overcome that they virtually collapsed in his embrace, and it was only after whispering something, perhaps some simple words of comfort, that they could be persuaded to release their grip on him.

As Xanana reached a group of a dozen or so widows of fallen Falintil commanders, he motioned to me to join him. Perhaps he had intended to introduce me to them. Nevertheless, I found myself taking a step backwards as they gave themselves over to their grief, clinging to Xanana, their faces buried in his shoulder. The waves of sobbing and wailing had built an inviolable wall of grief around the mourning women. Xanana was wordless. Perhaps he knew that his presence was some salve for the wounds the women bore. It was a heartbreaking scene, and I marvelled at Xanana's ability to retain his composure and to offer comfort in the face of such raw anguish and emotion.

Once the day's official proceedings were over, we were ushered up the grassy rise beyond the field to the church, which was the long, whitewashed structure I had seen from the helicopter. The church residence was wedged between the church itself and a large meeting hall. It was spacious and comfortably furnished, the homely smell of a wood fire and food cooking reaching our nostrils as we entered. Our bags and other belongings had been heaped in the corner of a light, airy bedroom, which I presumed was the guests' quarters. One of Xanana's cousins, a resident of nearby Aileu, had been called by the local priest to help attend to our needs, the regular staff of the parish having fled the recent violence. Genoveva was a short, jolly-looking woman who engaged Xanana in some lively banter that I didn't understand as she helped us unpack our things. A little later, around the long wooden table stretching the length of the dining room, Xanana explained to her that we would be making Remexio our temporary base until such time as the CNRT established permanent headquarters elsewhere. The mountain air was invigorating, and the prospect of making Remexio home for the time being was pleasing. After a meal in which buffalo meat in a range of culinary styles featured prominently, we took a bath in the icy water that had been collected in a huge red plastic basin.

Just before dusk we returned to the field below, and this time the absence of formalities meant that Xanana was able to introduce me to some of his oldest and dearest Falintil comrades, some of whose names I recognised from the letters and reports that had passed through my hands over the years. The sombre mood of the military parade and speeches earlier in the day had been lifted and replaced with a carnival atmosphere. All across the playing field, circles of bodies linked at the arm formed spontaneously and the *tebe* dancing began. The *tebe* is more of a ritual than a dance, really, the chanting and stamping in unison serving to consolidate the members of a community. But best of all, it was a lot of fun. I had seen the *tebe* performed before, but never taken part. Xanana and I joined one of the first circles to form. There was much merriment and laughter as Xanana lunged and dipped, exaggerating the rhythmic movements of the other dancers and deliberately falling out of step with them. I quickly got the knack of the pulsing, surging rhythms and fell under the hypnotic spell of the chanting. Our spirits were buoyed, our bodies aching with exertion, by the time we got to bed just after midnight.

The following day, after a breakfast of butter cake and sweet, black Timorese coffee, Xanana spent long hours in conversation with individual members of Falintil and the CNRT. Xanana explained to them why it was important to him that the guerrilla companies spread over four separate cantonments be brought together in one. There had been a number of incidents of small groups of armed men straying from the cantonments and being disarmed, sometimes in the most humiliating fashion, by members of Interfet who were largely unable to distinguish between militias and guerrilla fighters. Interfet considered that it was only fulfilling its mandate as prescribed by the Security Council's resolution of 15 September, but the incidents had caused tensions between the foreign troops and the Falintil.

The establishment of a single cantonment would facilitate greater monitoring and control of the movements of the forces. However, it seemed that the conditions in Remexio were not in fact conducive to accommodating the roughly 500-strong Falintil force from the other cantonment sites. The vast majority of the public and private buildings in the area had been so thoroughly devastated that there was no possibility of providing the soldiers with adequate housing. Running water was also a problem. As for me, I spent the morning and much of the afternoon chatting with some of the CNRT members whose names and stories I had become familiar with throughout the months of our stay in Salemba. Maria Paixão told me how she, her husband and nine children had narrowly escaped with their lives as they stormed through a militia roadblock in Dili at the height of the post-ballot violence. A hint of the horror she must have felt at that moment flickered in her eyes as she spoke.

Later in the afternoon, the sky grew dark and a bank of low cloud enveloped the church complex. A light rain was falling as I set about rigging up the satellite phone that had been given to Steve by UNAMET in Dili for Xanana's and my use. Unfamiliar with the technology, it was dinnertime when I finally had the antenna positioned correctly to communicate with the nearest satellite. Within minutes, the phone rang. It was Andrew Ladley, the New Zealander we had met on the Cobourg Peninsula. 'Just wanting to keep the lines of communication open,' he said. On the one hand it was reassuring to know that we had a link to the world; on the other, I had been quite looking forward to the telecommunications black hole East Timor had fallen into.

Before bed I phoned Mum ('I'm fine, we're safe and happy') and Natacha ('We're fine, please send urgent supplies: a ream of paper, pens, notebooks, sticky notes, toothpaste and shampoo'). On the other side of the world in New York, the UN Security Council passed a resolution establishing the United Nations Transitional Administration in East Timor (UNTAET).

The next morning, Xanana was up at 4 am to make a reconnaissance visit to Aileu. He had heard that Aileu had fared relatively well in the post-ballot mayhem and that the town, located roughly fifteen kilometres southwest of Remexio, might be a more appropriate base for the Falintil. In addition, he was on the lookout for a building that might serve as the office of the East Timor Transitional Council, a CNRT structure made up of five or six members that would work alongside the UN administration throughout the period of the transition to independence, articulating the aspirations and priorities of the East Timorese people. He returned mid morning, satisfied that Aileu did indeed offer the basic conditions for the establishment of Falintil's headquarters, and a relocation plan was devised there and then. When the Norwegian Ambassador to Jakarta turned up unexpectedly at the residence, Xanana wasted no time in proposing to him that the Norwegian government assist with rehabilitating a building in Aileu for the Transitional Council.

Xanana invited Steve, Leandro and Francisco Guterres to have lunch with us. Francisco, alias Lu'olo, was the Head of the Internal Political Front of the CNRT and the recently elected President of Fretilin. Next to the bulk and brawn of Steve, he looked positively tiny in spite of his proud bearing. With a map laid out before them, the four plotted an extensive homecoming tour that would give Xanana the opportunity to reconnect with people across the country. When I tried to help Genoveva clear the plates from the table, she whipped them out of my hands and ordered me to sit down again. I found it embarrassing to be waited on hand and foot and not to be allowed to contribute to the women's work in some way. Particularly since Genoveva and the other women of the house refused to join us for meals, preferring to stand against the walls of the dining room and engage in conversation with their guests from there. Was it because I was white, a guest, a member of Xanana's delegation? It seemed that the men experienced no such pangs of conscience and left the table just as soon as they had drained their coffee cups.

An hour or two later, Steve appeared in the doorway of the living room to announce that the 'helo', as he called the helicopter, was ready to take us to Poetete in Ermera district, the first stop on the first leg of our tour. Knowing that we would be back in Remexio within a couple of days, I packed only a small overnight bag, which Mario turned into a pillow on the twenty-minute flight to our destination. He and the other Los Palos bodyguards were painfully aware that with the deployment of the rifle-toting SAS men, their services were no longer strictly required. Nevertheless, Xanana did not have the heart to relieve them of their duties, so they would tag along with us, for now at least. Moreover, we had become firm friends and I found their presence oddly reassuring, giving me a sense of continuity with the recent past.

There were more jubilant scenes of welcome at the clearing on the outskirts of Ermera where our helicopter touched down. The Falintil cantonment here was built on the red earth of a dusty plain and nestled between stands of eucalypts. A length of blue UNHCR-issue plastic was strung between two flimsy-looking wooden beams to form a rudimentary shelter. The tarpaulin seemed to magnify the intensity of the sun's rays, creating a sauna-like effect for all who sought protection below. I left Xanana to explain his vision of the single cantonment to the assembled Falintil fighters while I handed Cesar a page ripped from my notebook and sweet-talked him into jotting down and translating the words of the most popular of the *tebe* chants for me:

O hele-le, o hele-la
O hele lao!
Kana mase olarinda

O hele-le, o hele-la
O hele lao!
Kana mase olarinda

O hele-le, o hele-la
Ami isin Maubere, klamar mós Maubere
[Our body is Maubere and so is our soul]

Suku lensu, desfiadu
Tau naran sá?
Tau naran Xanana ita mata dalan
[Sew a handkerchief or a tablecloth
And what name do you embroider it with?
The name of Xanana, our guide]

The people had looked to Xanana, their *mata dalan*, or guiding light, throughout the period of the resistance struggle. They continued to do so now. What a heavy burden the mammoth task of reconstruction that now lay before the nation was for one man to bear, I thought. Before Cesar had a chance to coach me in the singing of the tune, we found ourselves being herded back to the helicopter for our departure for Bobonaro and the third Falintil cantonment. The blast of wind from the helicopter's propeller provided some welcome relief from the humid, stagnant air of the camp.

I found the helicopter rides exhilarating for being a little hair-raising, but most of all for the bird's-eye view of Timor's beauty they offered: densely wooded forests on the slopes of rugged mountain ranges; grassy valleys dotted with the round, smoke-blackened rooves of the traditional dwellings; the dry beds of creeks and rivers snaking through the landscape like grey, car-less highways. In places the vegetation was tropical and rich, in others it bore a greater resemblance to the arid plains of Australia, silver gums and casuarina trees towering over tangles of low-growing scrub.

The traditional welcome in Aiassa, Bobonaro district, was followed by a cultural show that got underway at dusk. The *malae* (foreigners) were encouraged to contribute items reflecting their own cultural heritage. The mist started to roll in just as one of the Interfet soldiers treated the crowd to a couple of tunes on the bagpipes, one of them a reasonably competent rendition of 'Amazing Grace'. We could have been in the highlands of Scotland.

Xanana, though, was not permitted to indulge in any such fantasies of far-off places. The people were anxious to engage him in a dialogue about their problems. They spoke to him of their personal experience of the loss and destruction that had accompanied the ballot. They wanted reassurance that the Indonesian troops and the militias they had created would not return. They wanted to know what to expect now, what assistance would be provided by the UN, the international NGOs and the National Council of Timorese Resistance as they went about rebuilding their lives. Xanana appealed for calm and patience, explaining that the fight to free the land of oppression had been won, but that now it was necessary to free the people by restoring their ownership of their country and a decent standard of living. He explained the roles of the UN, the CNRT, political parties and civil society in the achievement of these goals.

Bed was a blanket on the floor of the Bobonaro police station, now occupied by Falintil and CNRT. It felt like poetic justice, given that many of the reprisals against members of the CNRT had been coordinated from this site. Just as I was snuggling up in my sarong, Steve called through the crack in my door to say that we were scheduled to leave at 8 am the following morning for Baucau.

At 6 am I woke to hear Leonel rooting around in my black satchel. 'Looking for a cake of soap,' he said with a guilty, sheepish little grin on his face. I helped him locate the toiletries and then ventured off to the former Kodim – or district military command – headquarters over the road. Xanana and the Interfet boys were already there and yawning around an enormous wooden table that had been laid out with plates of meat, rice and small sweet loaves of bread for our breakfast. Typically, the women who had been responsible for this impressive spread hung back in the shadows, now and then poking their heads around the door of the kitchen to catch a glimpse of Xanana and the other guests. I was surprised to see that the breakfast fare included cans of Coke and Indonesian Bintang beer. The Interfet guys justified their indulgence by stating that their consumption of the beer was part of their efforts to remove all traces of Indonesia from East Timor. As I tucked into my breakfast, a slightly rotund Australian soldier drew a chair up next to mine and introduced himself to me as Bob McCabe. He had been posted in Bobonaro to work closely with the Falintil inside the cantonment zone, and he was clearly well liked by them, as a number of the East Timorese soldiers patted him affectionately on the shoulder as they passed by.

There was a rousing send-off from the airfield. As the helicopter headed skywards, the people and soldiers down below waved so enthusiastically that they seemed to be oblivious to the hurricane force of the wind our aircraft generated.

We flew into Baucau at around 10 am and had morning tea at the residence of East Timor's second bishop, Dom Basilio do Nascimento. The boots of the Aussie diggers made a mess of the carefully polished white tiles of the foyer and dining room, but nobody seemed to mind. Over coffee and plates of warm fried *kulu*, or breadfruit, Xanana was tearfully reunited with some of the priests – Locatelli, João de Deus, Mario Belo – who had relayed items of correspondence back and forth between the Falintil and the resistance in the towns during the war. 'You were our lifeline,' Xanana told them. 'The church was always a kind of moral bulwark for the population in the most difficult moments of the struggle.'

Within an hour we were back on board the helicopter and

heading for Atelari, the fourth Falintil cantonment, located about thirty kilometres southeast of the town of Baucau in a dramatically beautiful valley. This was where the fighters from the Ponta Leste, the easternmost military zone taking in Los Palos, had gathered. While Xanana danced the *tebe* with a group of old women, to the laughter and cheers of the crowd, I took the opportunity to talk to the commanders – Renan, Aluc, Lere and Mau Nana – whom I had narrowly missed visiting in 1995. I think they found the reverence with which I treated them a little disconcerting. They all had about them a poise and a command of Portuguese that belied their many years of social isolation. Commander Aluc, the husband of Olinda, whom I had met during my 1995 visit to Los Palos, wore his red beret on a slight angle over his right eye. His high cheekbones and slender neck were accentuated by years of inadequate nutrition, but he nevertheless looked happy and, like the others, found it difficult to contain his joy at seeing Xanana.

After the early start and his exertions with the old ladies, Xanana was unable to stay awake through the evening's entertainment. We were guided to a hut which, in spite of its dirt floor, had been fitted out tastefully and elegantly with bamboo beds, a washstand and pretty lacy curtains over the windows. The hypnotic and repetitive rhythms of the *tebe* induced sleep immediately.

The next morning, I sat in on a meeting Xanana convened with the Falintil and CNRT cadres, where he spoke about how the year 2000 was to be devoted to meeting the immediate humanitarian needs of the population and of the importance of East Timorese participation in the country's reconstruction and development.

We headed back to Remexio at midday and it was a pleasure to be able to wash away the two days of accumulated dust and grime then change into something fresh and clean. The rest of the day was spent attending to a string of visitors, including the staff of the International Committee of the Red Cross and the Portuguese diplomatic and humanitarian missions. As the next day Xanana was scheduled to meet with Australian Defence Minister John

Moore and Major-General Peter Cosgrove in Dili, he had me type up a letter to the minister on my laptop which, after much fumbling and fiddling with cables and configurations, I was able to print out on a borrowed printer. Before bed, Xanana handed Lu'olo a business shirt and tie to wear to the meeting.

Xanana and I and our entourage strode out onto the airfield shortly after 9 am the following morning. The SAS boys had already fanned out around the two waiting helicopters, arms at the ready. When we realised Lu'olo was not with us, Xanana ordered a halt to our party's advance and called for someone to find him. Shortly after, he emerged from a hut at the end of the airfield, gestured wildly in our direction and then disappeared once again. I smiled to myself as I guessed at the reason for this delay in our departure. The soldiers and Xanana were getting jittery when he still hadn't materialised five minutes later. Lu'olo finally appeared and made a dash for the second helicopter and as he came into view I could see the evidence of the battle he had been waging with his tie. My first job upon boarding the armed personnel carrier when we reached Dili was to retie Lu'olo's troublesome neckpiece, with Xanana's assistance. He had never worn a tie before.

At the meeting with John Moore and Peter Cosgrove, Xanana urged the Australian government to further its already significant contribution to peace in East Timor by helping to train a future East Timorese defence force. According to Xanana's vision, the Falintil would form the core of the defence force and would be permitted to play an active role in the defence of the country, particularly in the vulnerable border regions. The response from the minister was lukewarm. He explained his department's view that East Timor needed a police force but that it would not be economically viable to maintain a defence force. The minister also questioned whether or not the UN would support the establishment of a parallel defence structure. As far as Xanana was concerned, apart from security in the long term being crucial, Falintil needed a role; they needed to be recognised for the part they had played in freeing East Timor.

The rest of that day was taken up with meetings with UNTAET and the World Bank. Mario Carrascalão, who had served as governor of East Timor in the eighties and early nineties, was at pains in both meetings to get the message across that the East Timorese would not be satisfied to be merely observers of the reconstruction and development process. 'We did that for twenty-four years,' he said. Back in Remexio, crowds of journalists and others seeking an audience with Xanana had gathered. I did my best with my limited means to impose a little order on the clamour, and drew up a tentative interview schedule that ate up most of Xanana's afternoon. The satellite phone rang constantly. Steve and the SAS boys had received care packages from home and they shared a can of Coke and a bag of crisps with me while we discussed plans for Xanana's attendance at the TNI withdrawal ceremony. Steve's information was that the ceremony would take place the following day, 30 October 1999, at 2 pm. So, when Andrew Ladley from UNTAET called, I reassured him that we would be in Dili by 12:30 pm.

My secretarial duties started early the next morning. Xanana took a phone call from the Portuguese President, Jorge Sampaio, at 7 am. He then moved into the meeting hall to preside over a meeting with the CNRT cadres while I tried to make sense of the conflicting advice I was receiving with regard to the timing of the farewell to TNI. Taur Matan Ruak handed me a written invitation to the ceremony that noted the start time as 9 am, and then at 10:50 am, Steve announced that the proceedings were to get under way at 11 am. It seemed that there was no possibility of getting to Dili in time. When Steve shrugged his shoulders and disappeared again, I presumed that the whole thing was off and returned to my telephone duties.

A couple of hours later I was taking a message for Xanana from an official of the Portuguese Banco Nacional Ultramarino when I heard the roar of helicopters landing on the playing field. As I walked out onto the verandah to see what was going on, I came face to face with an agitated Australian army officer. 'Where's

Xanana? UNTAET and the TNI delegation are waiting for him down in Dili. There's no time to lose.' From the doorway of the meeting hall, I gesticulated wildly in Xanana's direction until I was able to attract his attention. He quickly adjourned his meeting and within five minutes we were strapping ourselves into our seats on the helicopter. Throughout 1999, Xanana had spoken repeatedly about the desirability of the TNI being allowed to withdraw from the territory with honour and dignity and without loss of face. He recognised how culturally and militarily important this was. His presence at the ceremony was indispensable.

It was a stormy afternoon and the low cloud made it necessary to fly low to arrive safely in Dili. Crowds of UNTAET officials, including the Acting Special Representative of the UN Secretary-General, Ian Martin, and a number of high-ranking Indonesian military and civilian officials were waiting for Xanana inside the airport building. There was quite a crowd of Indonesian and other foreign journalists present. They had not been permitted to enter the building but were busy snapping photos of this historic occasion from the other side of the glass windows. A few of them tried to catch my eye, perhaps thinking that I had the authority to grant them access to the building and an exclusive interview with Xanana, who was wasting no time in engaging the Indonesians in some light-hearted repartee. The atmosphere was relaxed and cordial. Nevertheless, I couldn't help thinking that the thunderclaps and rain that accompanied the leave-taking were significant.

Andrew Ladley grumbled to me about Steve and what he described as the uncooperative attitude of the SAS men. I realised that I had been naive to assume that the UNTAET and Interfet were a close-knit and coordinated team. Perhaps it was the fact that Interfet differed from a peace-keeping force in that it was not, strictly speaking, answerable to the UN. Perhaps some of the other incidents of tension and miscommunication I was to note in the coming months reflected merely the difference between a military and a civilian approach to the life of a people and a nation.

We returned to Remexio by road, as the rain and heavy cloud

made it unsafe to travel by helicopter. Steve produced a bottle of Australian white wine that he had received from home and that night during our meal we drank a toast to peace and the departure of the Indonesian military. After dinner, Xanana had a meeting with an official from the International Monetary Fund (IMF) on the question of the currency East Timor was to adopt. Neither of us was well versed in the area of international finance and monetary questions, and it occurred to me that Xanana was desperately in need of competent technical advice in order to be able to debate and present well-informed opinions on these issues. My feelings of inadequacy were growing by the day.

The next day we set off for Baucau, the first stop on the second leg of Xanana's homecoming tour. We stayed overnight in the residence of the former district administrator, and the following morning Xanana was taken on a tour of the public facilities by his local CNRT colleagues. He was anxious to avoid a scenario whereby Dili became the seat of power and decision-making and the place where the country's resources were centralised. For that reason he was keen to set up the CNRT Secretariat in Baucau. He was a little dismayed, however, to learn that almost all the public buildings appropriate for the CNRT's purposes had been occupied already by the UN, Interfet or international NGOs.

At a meeting with the resistance cadres that dragged on until early evening, some members of CNRT articulated their discomfort with having to go cap in hand to the UN to request permission to make use of public property. There was a feeling that the Timorese were being treated like guests in their own land. Perhaps in response to these concerns, Ian Martin called on the satellite phone the following morning to request an urgent meeting with Xanana on the allocation of public resources.

This meeting, plus a series of others, took place in Baucau over the following two days. There was a consultation with the members of the World Bank's Public Service Working Group, a discussion on the social reintegration of Falintil with an expert from Washington, a meeting with a delegation from the UN

Development Program in New York. In the absence of a chief-of-staff – or a staff of any kind – I did my best in the course of these exchanges to take notes for Xanana.

On the one hand it was gratifying that Xanana and the CNRT were sought out actively by the UN and international agencies to provide their opinions and feedback on a range of important issues relating to governance, humanitarian assistance and legal frameworks in the period of the transition. On the other, it began to occur to me that there was something unbalanced, unjust even, about this partnership. The CNRT, unlike the UN, had few resources, human and material, at its disposal with which to support its participation in this process. Moreover, most of its members had very recently experienced the destruction of their homes and towns, many of them narrowly escaping the militia violence with their lives; many had no roof over their heads, let alone access to the Land Rovers, communications and office equipment that were available to UNTAET and the other international players.

The UN recognised that the CNRT had been the standard-bearer for independence and was the most broadly representative body in the country. However, various UNTAET officials explained to Xanana that as the CNRT was not a democratically elected party, the UN could not work with it exclusively and was obliged to work closely with any other organisation or individual it deemed able to make a contribution to the reconstruction of East Timor. UNTAET's mandate did not extend to providing support to the CNRT beyond the occasional use for urgent business of UN aircraft travelling between Dili and Darwin. It seemed that Xanana had no choice but to remain lumbered with me as his private secretary for some time to come.

Finally, with the flood of international visitors easing off momentarily, we were able to leave for our next destination. Viqueque was the first of roughly fifteen district and sub-district centres that we were to visit in the course of the next two weeks. At each destination, a colourful traditional pageant of the kind we had experienced in Remexio welcomed us. I never failed to be impressed by the people's resourcefulness. In spite of having lost virtually everything in the recent violence, communities scraped together the little they did have – food, traditional dress, decorations, musical instruments – to throw a party worthy of their beloved leader. In each place, too, Xanana devoted time to talking and listening to the people, giving them a chance to express their concerns and doubts. The heat, the pace of the journey and the intensity of the emotion encountered at each destination made it an exhausting trip. After a few days the SAS soldiers began to flag. Some of them fell ill and were forced to return to Dili. Xanana seemed to derive his energy from the people themselves, and we all marvelled at his stamina. In the heat the people would erect temporary shelters with a dais where Xanana could sit. Many times he stepped out from the shade of the shelter into the sweltering heat of the sun or the teeming rain in solidarity with his people.

Those days of non-stop movement and meetings afforded Xanana and I very little opportunity for quiet, private reflection on the significance to us both of finally being together in the ravaged but free East Timor we had dreamt of for so long. The months spent in Jakarta had taught me that my life with Xanana could never be just about the two of us. It was a fact that I accepted, sometimes a little more begrudgingly than others. The excitement and colour of the homecoming tour, and the feeling of privilege associated with being part of it, took the edge off any resentment I felt at not being able to savour the personal dimensions of our return 'home'.

By the time we reached Uatulari on the south coast I was craving a decent night's sleep, so I decided to forego that evening's *convivio*, or party, and retire early. As it turned out, I managed only a couple of hours of sleep given the decibel level of the music being pumped out by a crackling, squealing old PA system. The next morning, the sight of a drowning rat bobbing around in the blue plastic water tank in the bathroom dampened my enthusiasm for a hair wash. I settled for a sponge down instead and then sat down to fried banana for breakfast with Xanana. During the rare half hour we had to sit and chat calmly together, Xanana told me about an amazing old man he had met the night before. As was his habit, Xanana had invited members of the audience to raise their hands and put forward a question or concern for him to address. He found it a little sad and disheartening when time and time again those who raised their hands spoke of their anger and pain, and of their desire to see the perpetrators of the violence punished for their crimes.

Xanana responded by talking of the need for justice to be balanced with the need for reconciliation and peace. He noticed in the audience an elderly man whose arms and hands had been hideously disfigured. Although the man raised his withered hand at every opportunity, Xanana feared that the man would only add fuel to the fire by calling for the punishment of the person responsible for maiming him. Finally, so persistent was the old man that Xanana gave in and invited him onto the stage. To Xanana's surprise, the man spoke not of bitterness and revenge, but of the need to look to the future.

'Look at me,' he said, holding his twisted arms up for all to see. 'I am like this as a result of being tied up and tortured. This crime against me was committed many years ago. Like all of you, I used to want nothing better than to get back at those who did this to me. I went from being a proud man to a dependent wretch who needs help just to tie his shoes. But then, over the years I learnt something. Do you know what I learnt?'

The audience had fallen silent; all eyes were on the old man.

'I came to understand that whether or not I managed to have the perpetrators punished, whether or not I succeeded in killing them as I so wanted to do, it would not give me back the use of my hands. And therefore what was the point of screaming for blood! I urge you all to put behind you that which you can't change.'

There was a minute or two of silence while the old man returned to his place in the crowd. And then a cheer erupted and Xanana joined in applauding his wisdom and courage.

Our epic journey concluded with our arrival in Aileu on 15 November 1999. The Falintil in Remexio had by now relocated to their new cantonment. Genoveva was there to greet us in the large former residence of the *bupati*, or district chief, which was to be our home for the time being. The homecoming tour had been extraordinary for Xanana personally, and also for the people of East Timor, representing as it did the culmination of twenty-four years of long and bitter struggle. But the next year was to throw up many such moments, each of which seemed more climactic and significant than the last.

Chapter seventeen

OUT OF THE ASHES
November 1999–
14 April 2002

AILEU WAS A cool and pretty place and I relished the prospect of being able to unpack our belongings, get our loads of dirty washing soaked and set my computer and satellite phone up in the knowledge that they would not have to be disassembled again the following morning. We shared the house with the Los Palos boys and a handful of Falintil fighters who made beds of the sofas in the spacious living room. Our own bedroom had a cupboard and a desk on which to work. Best of all, the supplies I had requested from Darwin had arrived. Highlighter pens, notepads, paper, paperclips, yellow sticky note pads, even a plastic document tray and stapler. I now had the makings of an office with which to support Xanana in following up the tremendous number of issues and problems that began to arise almost immediately.

Within a day or so of arriving in Aileu, Steve and the SAS guys were replaced by half a dozen Brazilian military police, who would be responsible for Xanana's personal protection from now on. 'I hope they're up to the task,' said Steve as we thanked and farewelled him and his team. Appointed to head the Brazilian bodyguards was Bob McCabe, the endearingly rotund Australian soldier we had come across in Bobonaro. Bob was not as physically honed as his fellow SAS soldiers, but he was well endowed in the personality department. Xanana and I had liked him right away. Although communication between them was laboured, Bob appeared to be well respected by the Brazilians, who were professional but a little less intense in the performance of their duties than their Aussie counterparts.

Sergio Vieira de Mello, the Special Representative of the UN Secretary-General, arrived in Dili the following day and we prepared to receive him in Aileu. We had met Sergio briefly during our visit to New York a month or so earlier. The Brazilian diplomat radiated a charm and charisma that went deeper than the demands of his career. His trim, lightly tanned body gave an impression of energy and vigour. Xanana was pleased to be able to converse in Portuguese with the man who was to head the UN Transitional Administration in East Timor, Portuguese being the language he expressed himself in with the greatest ease. In the meeting, Sergio affirmed the UN's commitment to building a partnership with the East Timorese based on mutual respect and the common goal of preparing the people to manage their own affairs. Sergio was very clearly and understandably anxious to get his relationship with Xanana off to a good start, so he made liberal use of his winning smile that afternoon. Xanana, too, was at his charismatic best. Sergio invited Xanana to visit him at his office in the UNTAET headquarters in Caicoli, Dili, in two days time – but he was to get a taste of another side of his Timorese counterpart a little earlier than anyone had expected.

By the following morning, I was starting to get agitated. From the moment I had rigged up the satellite phone, its antenna cable snaking out the bedroom window to the roof of the house, it had begun ringing. The whole world, it seemed, needed to consult with Xanana on all manner of issues, from the return of refugees from West Timor, Xanana's winning of the European Parliament's

Sakharov Prize and CNRT use of UN aircraft between Dili and Darwin to the IMF's nervousness about CNRT's rumoured preference for the adoption of the Portuguese escudo and the resumption of diplomatic relations between Portugal and Indonesia. Moreover, Kofi Annan and the President of Portugal were wanting to speak to him urgently. When a call came through to say that the UN needed to reclaim the satellite phone – 'Its loan was an emergency stop-gap measure' – I didn't know whether to laugh or cry. The constant stream of visitors to the house was making it difficult for me to get five minutes alone with Xanana – not to engage in idle chatter, not to enjoy his company, but simply to convey to him the substance of all the phone calls I was receiving and to discuss what follow-up was required.

At 11 pm on the evening of 18 November, after the last of Xanana's visitors had departed, I was finally able to sit down with Xanana and go through the messages. At the end of a day of back-to-back meetings, he was on his last legs, and in no frame of mind to turn his attention to additional problems requiring answers. To make matters worse, he was coming down with the flu and so was inclined just to head straight for bed. I felt my blood simmering when Cesar knocked on the bedroom door to announce the arrival of two Falintil commanders who had a matter of dire importance to discuss with Xanana. 'This is getting beyond a joke!' I said, throwing my hands in the air and following Xanana into the living room.

The two men looked flustered. Commander Riak, a wiry figure with a shock of untamed hair, related that a group of around twenty Falintil soldiers from the Bobonaro cantonment had been in the process of relocating to Aileu when one of their trucks had broken down in Dili. Just as they were investigating an alternative means of transport, the Falintil men, who were fully armed, suddenly found themselves surrounded by about seven tanks and truckloads of Interfet soldiers, who proceeded to confiscate their weapons in a rather heavy-handed manner.

There was fire in Xanana's eyes as he listened to the story, and it wasn't just from the fever he was battling. 'Get Bob in here,' he barked to Cesar, who dutifully scampered off to call Bob from the adjacent house where the close personal protection team had set up camp. A few minutes later, Bob appeared, looking a little bleary-eyed and apprehensive.

Xanana related the incident to him and then announced, 'I want all Interfet out of Aileu tomorrow. And you can tell your superiors that tomorrow we will be making the trip to Dili to see Sergio in a Falintil convoy. Fully armed! Just let them try and disarm us!'

Having seen Xanana only at his diplomatic best until that point, Bob's face dropped and turned pale. He had come to know the soldiers from this particular cantonment well during his time in Bobonaro, and he looked genuinely distressed to learn of the indignity they had been subjected to. Whilst I understood Xanana's anger, it was difficult not to feel sorry for Bob. Needless to say, I didn't get through a single item on my list that night.

It was cold and misty at 5 am the following morning and getting out of bed was no easy feat. At 6 am we heard a helicopter land and knew for sure that it would be an Interfet official from Dili coming to mediate the conflict and try to dissuade Xanana from his action. Xanana refused to meet with the man and dismissed Bob's timid offer to accompany him with a wave of his hand. 'And remember, I don't want to see a single Interfet soldier here when I return.' He had one of the Falintil attach a holster and pistol to his belt. If the Interfet troops were to disarm his men, they would have to disarm Xanana, too.

The four-vehicle convoy moved off in the direction of Dili at around 6:45 am. I rode in the second vehicle, a green jeep, with Xanana. It was quite a sight to behold. The Falintil soldiers were jubilant. For the first time in history, they were able to make a public display of their pride as the nation's army of liberation, holding their weapons and their flag aloft and basking in the admiration of the people who ran from their houses and stared agog at the spectacle.

'Viva Falintil! Viva Timor Lorosa'e!' the onlookers shouted, raising their fists and cheering.

In the post-ballot period, Falintil had been prevented from going to the aid of the population in the interests of averting a civil war or at least Indonesian claims of one. Nowadays, their confinement to the cantonment sites meant significant hardship – far from their families, they had little means of support and, with the exception of a small amount of food supplied by the International Organisation for Migration, there was no external assistance. To add insult to injury, rather than being honoured for their role in freeing the country, they were being humiliated by the seizure of their weapons. This opportunity to parade through the streets and take over from Interfet in providing Xanana's security for the day was a salve for the wounds their honour had sustained. They were ecstatic.

Major-General Peter Cosgrove travelled to Dare to try to intercept Xanana and talk him out of continuing his march. But Xanana ordered our contingent to drive on and bypass the Interfet commander. A little further down the road, in Lahane, our convoy pulled up to refuel. The Interfet vehicles that were part of Major-General Cosgrove's party drove on past us and formed a roadblock a few hundred metres ahead, almost directly opposite the dwelling where Xanana had been captured on 20 November 1992 – seven years ago almost to the day.

Major-General Cosgrove alighted from his vehicle and made his way up the hill to the green jeep. 'Mr Gusmão, I appeal to you to please not continue with this action.'

Xanana, staring straight ahead, answered him: 'In my country we do not negotiate on the side of the road. I will talk to you at the UN compound, which is where we are heading.'

The roadblock meant that we could proceed no further by car, so Xanana ordered his men out of their trucks. They continued their march on foot, the Falintil soldiers forming a protective circle around Xanana. The Interfet convoy followed close behind at walking pace. I skipped ahead to where I could get the best view of the action and filmed on video the gathering crowds, the excited shouts of 'Viva Falintil', the looks of wonder and pride in the faces of the people, many of whom were seeing Xanana and his men for the first time.

The people must have asked themselves what it was that had prompted Xanana's descent to Dili and this apparent show of force by Falintil, but they seemed not to care; they were happy just to be granted this rare opportunity to catch sight of the men who had kept their dream of freedom alive for twenty-four long years. By the time we turned into the street heading west in the direction of the UNTAET compound, what had begun as a sombre military march had turned into a carnival. Foreign journalists had gathered at the entrance to the UN complex, looking even more bewildered than the locals as to the meaning of this noisy, colourful commotion. At its epicentre was Xanana who, with uncharacteristic brusqueness, strode purposefully past the group of waiting UN officials and headed in the direction they indicated to him.

Inside Sergio Vieira de Mello's cool, air-conditioned office, Xanana outlined the incident while I gratefully gulped down two plastic cups of water which a woman who must have been Sergio's secretary proffered. After the heat and exertion, my clothes were wet through with perspiration. A few minutes later, we were joined by Major-General Cosgrove, who wore a look of tired exasperation. Xanana shook his hand, and the three man sat together to thrash out their concerns.

'Your men are the saviours of our people, General,' said Xanana. 'But please don't forget that the heroes are my men, the Falintil.' Xanana's expression was hard and unsmiling. 'I will not accept that they be treated like armed bandits or petty criminals.'

Major-General Cosgrove then explained that the incident involving the men from Bobonaro had been a misunderstanding and that in future greater attention would be given by Interfet to establishing the true identity of any armed groups found outside the cantonment sites before action was taken to deal with them. Xanana was satisfied with the undertaking and the two men shook hands. There were no hard feelings.

Xanana had had over twenty years as a guerrilla commander during which to hone his judgement about when to take a stand. On this occasion it was a keen political instinct he displayed, based on his familiarity with the people, his strong sense of dignity, and his knowledge of what the limits were. Once they had been reached he did not vacillate; he was clear and unswerving. At other times when less was at stake, he was more accommodating and reconciliatory.

Once the air had been cleared between the two commanders, Sergio discussed with Xanana the mechanism for East Timorese participation in the structure and decision-making processes of the UN transitional administration. The UN Security Council's resolution of 25 October had granted fairly sweeping powers to Sergio as the Transitional Administrator – Xanana joked with him that he was East Timor's new 'governor' – however, given that UNTAET's principal role was to prepare the East Timorese for self-government, it would have been ludicrous to exclude them from playing a role in the day-to-day decision-making.

The idea of a transitional council proposed by the CNRT was not acceptable to the UN, as it was composed exclusively of members of the CNRT. UNTAET insisted that its Timorese partner body include all those East Timorese groups committed to a peaceful, democratic way forward, including the political parties, the church and special interest groups. The discussions that day in Dili were to lead to the establishment, a week or so later, of the National Consultative Council (NCC), which began its work in early December.

Back in Aileu, preparations were being made to receive the US Ambassador to the United Nations, Richard Holbrooke. Xanana had finally succumbed to the flu and fever he had been battling for days, so I did my best to supervise the construction of a platform where the welcoming ceremony would take place while warding off the hordes of visitors and journalists so he could recover in bed. By now, Paula had sent us a satellite phone of our own and, between administering cold and flu tablets to the ailing commander, I set about configuring it and my laptop so that I could once again send email.

In those first difficult weeks, as much energy was spent on sorting out the Timorese relationship with 'the internationals' as on attending to the multitude of internal problems, including that of Falintil's unacceptable living conditions. There were a few ruffled feathers in the ranks of the international NGOs to smooth over.

In the course of the final days of the homecoming tour, Xanana had met with representatives of a large number of international medical and humanitarian organisations in Manatuto, the town of his birth. He had received numerous reports of the failure of some of these agencies to deliver their assistance through the existing resistance structures, which were generally well suited to the task of gathering information on the needs of the people and ensuring that material aid reached the most needy sections of the population. Some communities felt slighted by the NGOs' apparent lack of trust in their judgement and superior local knowledge. And so in Manatuto Xanana had delivered a blistering attack on the NGOs, stating sarcastically that the East Timorese people might as well take a holiday and leave the task of responding to the needs of the population to the international organisations.

In a subsequent meeting in Aileu with the UN's Office for the Coordination of Humanitarian Affairs (responsible for coordinating the activities of the relief agencies), Xanana affirmed the gratitude of the East Timorese for the NGOs' assistance, adding, 'But if your intention is truly to help our people, then you must listen to them, respect them and treat them as equal partners, not as passive recipients of your aid.'

Within a few days, we were again packing our bags in preparation for a visit to Jakarta. Xanana and the members of his delegation – Avelino, Taur Matan Ruak, José Ramos-Horta – were keen to offer an olive branch to Indonesia. They recognised how important the relationship with East Timor's gigantic neighbour was going to be, especially from a security point of view. With the wounds still so fresh, Xanana went to make peace, to reaffirm the Timorese wish to foster the best possible relations with Indonesia at every level, and he was received as a quasi-head of state by President Abdurrahman Wahid and his government. Given the strong feelings among some segments of Indonesian society about East Timor's independence, there was some anxiety within our delegation about security. But Xanana insisted that there be minimal personal protection provided; he thought it would send the wrong message to our hosts. This trip was expressly about building confidence.

On our return to East Timor, I was sad to have to contemplate relocating yet again. When Xanana was appointed a member of the National Consultative Council, it became impractical for us to live in Aileu. As much as we could in two weeks, we had put down roots there, and I was not happy about returning to the heat, dust and mosquitoes of Dili. Accommodation was scarce there, with Dili's few intact buildings straining to house the influx of UN personnel and NGO workers. So we moved into a former bank official's residence in the seaside suburb of Lecidere. We shared a large two-storey building with a handful of CNRT members from the diaspora who, like us, were homeless.

The bare essentials of an office were set up in one of the three buildings that formed the complex. Here, around a long, fold-up table, Xanana conducted his meetings on the tremendous range of initiatives and projects that were being generated by East Timor's partners – foreign governments, the UN, NGOs and individuals of goodwill – in the complex task of rebuilding. The Timorese had their work cut out just responding to the strategies and action plans of others, leaving them little time and energy to devise their own.

At times I had the impression that the donor-driven machinery of the UN and the international community was speeding ahead like a high-powered locomotive that, in keeping with its own unrelenting schedule, barely had time to stop and take the Timorese on board. The Timorese were grateful for the support that was being extended to them by the international community, but at the same time, it was difficult for them to feel that they were participating in the rebuilding effort on an equal footing with their benefactors. There was a yawning gap between the experienced and resource-rich donor institutions and East Timorese organisations such as the CNRT, whose members had come together for the first time and were grappling with trauma and the immediate personal needs of their families as well as trying to assert themselves in the new and perplexing landscape of aid, donors, trust funds and UN bureaucracy. At times I felt like shouting out: 'Stop, slow down! Just let these people deal with getting their family members home and a roof over their heads. Just let them breathe a little, let them reflect on the past before you drag them into your complicated plans for the future.'

To add to the stresses, the relationship between the Timorese who had lived abroad for most of the last twenty-four years and those who had remained in East Timor was not always smooth sailing. Many of those who had stayed and conducted the struggle under Indonesian occupation resented the presence of their compatriots, who returned from Portugal, Australia and other countries with a range of language and technical skills that equipped them well to work with the donor community. Those who had remained in the country felt strongly that they had a superior knowledge of the needs of their people and the social and political complexity of their country. The cultural divide separating the two groups also presented significant challenges. Those who had spent a large chunk of their adult lives in Australia or Portugal found it difficult to adapt to a society and culture which, with the overlay of Indonesian-influenced habits and attitudes, was in many ways unrecognisable to them.

Xanana found himself in an unenviable position. He had to balance his need for the technical skills and experience of the diaspora Timorese with his reliance on the contacts, networks and savvy of the members of the local front for activities requiring popular mobilisation. It was a delicate and ongoing juggling act.

In mid December we found ourselves hopping on and off aeroplanes once more. This time our destination was Strasbourg, France, where Xanana was awarded the Sakharov Human Rights Prize. During the elegant lunch hosted by the President of the European Parliament in his honour, Xanana saw snow fall for the first time in his life. On the way home, he put in an appearance at the Tokyo Donor's Conference where the icy winter failed to cool the enthusiasm of the donor countries for contributing to the rebuilding of the brave new nation. At the meeting, donors pledged US$520 million for the country through the transition period.

Back in Timor, Xanana's father died on 24 December, casting a pall of gloom over our preparations for Christmas. Xanana was deeply saddened by the fact that his responsibilities to the nation had not allowed him to spend more time with his father following his return to East Timor. I, too, regretted that the opportunity to come to know the man who had been such a formative influence in Xanana's younger years was now lost to me. At least Xanana's mother, sisters and brother had the comfort of his presence during their shared grief. My mother arrived to spend the holiday season with us. I was sorry that her first visit to East Timor was dominated by sorrow and mourning, but happy that the preparations for the funeral became the focus of a series of family gatherings that enabled us both to get better acquainted with members of Xanana's family. The doubts I had harboured about how I would be accepted by them were put to rest: I was welcomed with open arms. Xanana's parents and each of his six sisters had suffered because of their blood relationship with the Falintil commander. Armandina, his youngest sister, was interrogated and humiliated by the Indonesian military following Xanana's capture in 1992. They all knew that their son and brother was the likely first president of East Timor, but at this moment of family grief they needed him to fulfil his role as eldest son in leading and organising the mourning rituals.

Having ushered in the new millennium with a flourish of public appearances and a huge party organised by UNTAET, we then took a brief but happy holiday on the Mornington Peninsula in Victoria. Back in Dili, we began to crave a little more privacy than our living conditions afforded. Some mornings we would wake up to find a group of five or six guests sitting around the communal dining table, each ready with a litany of problems to discuss with Xanana over breakfast. There was often a similar scene at the other end of the day. Not even Bob and the Brazilians were able to impede the constant flow of guests in and out of our accommodation.

Like everyone else, we were living out of suitcases and boxes, each of which contained fragments of our life in its various phases over the past six months or so – media releases, notes of meetings, plastic plates and cutlery, letters, name cards, packets of noodle soup. My brain was beginning to feel as cluttered as our tiny, unfurnished room looked. And so we began house-hunting. Given that close to eighty per cent of all public and private property had been destroyed in the post-ballot violence, there was hardly a glut of rental accommodation available. And so when we stumbled across a house painted blue in the heart of the central city suburb of Bemori, we negotiated the rent with the owners and moved right in.

The house was in a quiet area and was reached by a narrow alleyway, through the middle of which ran an open gutter that carried all manner of rubbish and sewage. The fact that vehicles entering the alley had to straddle the filthy drain and back out if they met a car coming in the opposite direction would, we hoped, deter some of our would-be visitors. Though it wasn't a pleasant house to live in – it leaked, it was dark and airless, and it was full of mosquitoes – I considered us fortunate to have a place to call home.

Before we had a chance to settle in and meet our neighbours, we were off on another whirlwind trip, this time to Asia. The voyage, sponsored by UNTAET, took us to Thailand, Malaysia, China, South Korea, the Philippines and Singapore in the space of less than two weeks. It was an opportunity for the East Timorese to boost their profile in Asia and build the foundations of future regional cooperation. It was beginning to irk me that I was still in charge of Xanana's agenda and loaded with the duties of private secretary. I wanted to pass some of the responsibility to others, so when it was suggested that Cesar join us on the trip to gain some experience of international diplomacy and gradually take on the role of appointments secretary, I endorsed the idea wholeheartedly. Cesar embraced the challenge with typical cheerfulness.

As had been the case in Indonesia a month or so earlier, Xanana was received at each destination as the future leader of East Timor. Although he was happy and proud to represent his country and people, he continued to insist that he would not run for president, in line with the commitment he had made to himself and the Falintil fighters that he would never seek high office when freedom came. In each city our hosts pledged generous assistance to the reconstruction process in the form of training, technical assistance and financial contributions. China granted the CNRT aid to the value of US$3 million for the purchase of agricultural equipment and a further amount for development of the fisheries sector, both of which would be vital to the country's eventual self-sufficiency in terms of food production.

It was at the end of an exhausting day of official engagements in Manila that I finally plucked up the courage to use the home pregnancy test kit I had purchased in Singapore. Since we weren't yet officially married, we had been accommodated in separate rooms in our hotel. I had mixed feelings about the prospect of being pregnant, partly because of my awareness of the heavy load of work and responsibilities that lay before us, and partly because we had not yet had the luxury of time and space to think about marrying. If I was pregnant, how would such a thing be viewed by the East Timorese people? And so, with some trepidation, I knocked on the door of Xanana's suite and, in his opulent marble bathroom, conducted the test. When the odd little plastic contraption presented the colours that meant 'positive', we stood and looked blankly at one another for a time.

'I'm not sure that now is the right time,' said Xanana.

Whilst I shared his misgivings, a part of me knew deep down that there would never be a right time and, feeling a little hurt by his lukewarm response, I returned to my room where I had every intention of crying myself to sleep. An hour or so later, Xanana called me to his room. He had had time to think things over and there was a gleam in his eyes as he talked about what it would be like to be a father again. I knew that everything was going to be all right. The baby I was carrying had been conceived on our holiday in Australia.

The early part of 2000 was dominated by a series of high-level visits to East Timor, beginning with the Portuguese Prime Minister and President. Following close behind them were UN Secretary-General Kofi Annan, and the President of the World Bank. Indonesian President Abdurrahman Wahid visited in late February. My view from the podium erected in front of the Governor's Palace of thousands of people cheering in response to Xanana's shouts of 'Long live the Indonesian people, long live the Indonesian President' was such proof of the magnanimity and courage of the Timorese people that I felt quite overcome with pride and emotion.

Following the Indonesian visit there were a spate of militia attacks in the border region, which led to speculation that the prospect of better Indonesia–East Timor relations had disgruntled some within the militia groups and sections of the Indonesian military. Xanana intensified his efforts to bring the remaining refugees home, engaging key militia leaders in a series of meetings along the border in the hope of encouraging them to release their stranglehold on the camps.

Between attending official receptions and dinners for our many venerable overseas guests, I read up in earnest on the stages of pregnancy and, together with Cesar and our other CNRT colleagues, attempted to impose some order on Xanana's erratic schedule. I continued to be frustrated in my efforts to throw off the private secretary mantle and devote more time to developing my own activities. There was no money to pay a CNRT member to fill the role of personal assistant, so by default I remained the first point of contact for most people wishing to speak with Xanana. Cesar had embraced the world of foreign relations with such gusto that he had decided he wanted to be a diplomat. By now a GSM network had been set up, and my mobile phone seemed to ring day and night.

Almost half East Timor's population were young people. I found it disturbing to see so many unemployed or underemployed youths on the street, with no chance of an education or of participating in reconstruction projects that required skills they didn't have. Even recreational activities beyond the occasional soccer or volleyball match were denied them. I decided to set up a reading room. I wanted it to be a place people felt comfortable to visit, not daunted by, so a library wasn't the answer. I wanted to create a place that would promote a love of reading and foster pride in the culture and fighting spirit of the people of my new home.

Xanana and I were gathering crate-loads of books and other reading materials on each visit we made abroad. It seemed ridiculous to me that these books and documents were gathering dust and mould in our house in Bemori when they could become a source of information and inspiration if they were made available to the public.

I found an appropriate building – a beautiful Portuguese colonial structure which, in Indonesian times, had been the office of the Dharma Wanita, an organisation of the wives of civil servants – and convinced the Le-Ziaval youth cultural group to manage the facility. The Xanana Gusmão Reading Room was born.

With the help of an Australian volunteer sponsored by Australian Volunteers International, Xanana's personal collection of books, documents and videos in English, Bahasa Indonesia, Portuguese and Tetum were catalogued and displayed on bookshelves we made ourselves. The money the Norwegian government had approved for an office for the now-obsolete transitional council (proposed by the CNRT and rejected by the UN) was instead put towards repairing and sprucing up the beautiful, well-appointed building, which would be Dili's first – and, for the time being, only – public reading room. On the walls we hung some of the photographs, paintings, awards, medals and other memorabilia that filled the rooms of our house – including the one soon to be transformed into our baby's nursery.

In March another huge goodwill trip – this time to the Nordic countries and Angola, Mozambique and South Africa – was put on Xanana's agenda. Although I had never visited Africa before, I decided to pass up this trip and visit Melbourne, where I had my first antenatal check-up. There were financial as well as biological imperatives behind this visit: neither Xanana nor I had a source of income, so I needed to make arrangements to rent out my flat so that we at least had the rental payments to sustain us in Dili. So, between shopping for baby paraphernalia, Rosalie and I packed into boxes the clothing and odds and ends that belonged to another seemingly distant phase of my life. It was just over a year ago that I had headed for Jakarta, but so many extraordinary things had happened since that I found myself gazing at my possessions with a peculiar detachment: it was as if they belonged to someone else. At the end of our respective trips, Xanana and I met up in Darwin. Before he left for Finland, I had insisted that he set aside one day en route to Dili to accompany me to my ultrasound appointment at Royal Darwin Hospital. It was there that we met for the first time the healthy, wriggling, alien-like creature that was rapidly turning into our baby boy.

In Dili, there were complaints that the infant nation's growth was not on as healthy a course. The people had so far experienced few tangible improvements in their standard of living: unemployment was high, foreign investment minimal due to the absence of a long-term legal framework, and the presence of highly paid UN officials and NGO workers was giving rise to a dual economy. Criticism levelled at UNTAET and foreigners generally increased in response to the obvious differences between the standard of living of the Timorese and that of 'the internationals'. The Timorese worked largely as drivers, security guards and interpreters in an administration dominated by foreign experts, many of whom were working on fixed-term six-month contracts. Before they could grasp the complexities of East Timor's reality, they were replaced by others fresh from the post-conflict zones of Kosovo and Bosnia. 'Timorisation' – putting greater responsibility and decision-making power in the hands of the East Timorese – was the catch-cry of the day.

UNTAET responded to the criticism by restructuring and broadening the composition of the NCC to include representatives from each of the thirteen districts as well as from youth groups, women's groups, the church and NGOs. Its name was changed to the National Council (NC). One of the first regulations it adopted established a Transitional Cabinet, made up of four East Timorese and four UNTAET representatives.

Xanana and I married in July. It was a simple wedding presided over by two priests – Father António da Costa, the Vicar-General of Dili, and Father Rafael – at Dare, the seminary in the hills behind Dili where Xanana had gone to school. Xanana's sister, Armandina, helped dress me in the *tais* I had chosen for the occasion and decorated my hair with my favourite flower, the frangipani. It was hard to feel elegant with my seven-month pregnant belly straining against the traditional outfit, and I joked with my mother and friends that I was not a blushing but a hot-flushing bride. We didn't want to make a big fuss about the wedding, so it was a very small ceremony, attended by just a few family members and close friends. The basketball match afterwards on the court next to the chapel provided our guests with some entertainment. Though being married didn't really make any difference to the way Xanana and I felt about each other – or to the way we lived – our relationship had now been given the official stamp.

My mother and friend Sarah decorated my old Datsun Bluebird with flowers and ribbons for our drive back to Bemori. The local kids were excited and joined us on the verandah for lollies and slices of wedding cake. Our ensuing trip to New Zealand wasn't a honeymoon, it was an official visit, and I took on the role of Xanana's personal secretary yet again.

With the exception of a Mozambican economist who was funded by the UN Development Programme to advise Xanana, he continued to operate without paid staff – the CNRT's basic office running costs were covered by a grant from the Portuguese government. The perennial problem of finding time to discuss the requests for meetings, interviews, book prefaces and letters of endorsement continued to haunt me. At the end of a long day of dealing with a multitude of problems and studying the drafts of regulations the NC was charged with giving feedback on, Xanana had little patience for the irritating questions and requests I bombarded him with on behalf of others. Sometimes, when he was really tired, it was a case of shoot the messenger – I was the one who bore the brunt of his exhaustion.

In addition to the phone calls and emails clamouring for attention, there were also paper letters that the embryonic postal service was finally managing to deliver to destinations in Dili. Post offices around the world had no record of a country called 'Timor Lorosa'e', and presumed that it was still part of Indonesia. So parcels and letters frequently arrived after a delay of three to four months, having been diverted to Jakarta. Nevertheless, answers still needed to be provided to individuals and organisations from around the world, some of whom wanted just to express their solidarity with East Timor, and some of whom wanted to know how they could be of use to the country in its hour of need. Sometimes I would have loved to turn my back on the mountains of correspondence, but I was concerned that silence would be interpreted as ingratitude or indifference, and I was keenly aware that East Timor needed all the friends it could get.

Xanana refused to entertain the possibility of taking on a personal assistant – in addition to the funding question there was the delicate matter of who would assume the role. If it were a Timorese from the diaspora, as it almost inevitably would have to be because of the English and Portuguese language proficiency required, Xanana risked hurting the feelings of his faithful comrades who had never left East Timor.

A month or so before I was due to give birth, I put my foot down. When Xanana returned home one evening from a reception in honour of the Hong Kong philanthropist Eric Hotung and presented me with a white foam box containing a slice of cream cake from the dinner, I barked, 'What I need is a life, not a dessert!'

As was the case every day, a line of people waited at our gate to see him. Even though it was 11 pm, he escaped my tirade by retiring to the verandah to deal with the visitors' concerns. I was furious! Why was it that everyone else's problems were always so much more pressing and important than my own? Why did my lack of administrative support not warrant serious thought and attention?

I sat seething at the kitchen table. The generator was roaring on the back verandah so there was no point turning on the television in the adjacent living room. And so, as I waited for Xanana to conclude his meetings, I studied the documents and other items he had plonked down in front of me. Amongst them was a lighter someone had given him as a memento. It had emblazoned on one side: *Serviço nacional de bombeiros* – the National Fire Brigade of Portugal. In spite of my anger, I chuckled to myself. What an odd choice of souvenir for a fire brigade, I thought. I suppose pyromaniacs keep firefighters in business, just as wars and humanitarian disasters keep aid workers and UN bureaucrats in a job, I mused.

Eventually, when the guests were gone, I asked Xanana how he thought I was going to be able to deal with the private secretary role once we had a baby to look after. 'It's not as if I'm asking you to take me out to the movies once a week or anything,' I protested. 'All I want is for you to open your eyes to what I am struggling to cope with and get me – no, you – some proper support. It isn't appropriate that everyone from Sergio Vieira de Mello to prime ministers and presidents have to be in touch with your wife to make an appointment to speak to you.'

Finally, my plea bore fruit. Xanana agreed to advertise for the position of personal assistant and to use the money from a human rights award he had won to finance the salary of the incumbent.

At the CNRT National Congress in August, Xanana was re-elected president. I invited the Aboriginal band Yothu Yindi to be part of the celebrations marking the first anniversary of the vote for independence. Much of the final month of my pregnancy was spent running to and fro between meetings of the organising committee, finding funding to transport an adequate sound system for the band from Darwin, and working out where the band members would sleep. The huge and noisy Independence party on Dili's foreshore was a fitting way of remembering and honouring both the courage the people had shown in voting for freedom a year before and their forbearance ever since.

At 1 am on 30 September 2000, I woke to discover that I was alone in bed. As was his habit, Xanana had fallen asleep on the couch in front of the soccer again. As I hauled my heavy frame upright from the bed to retrieve him, a gush of water escaped from between my legs . . . and didn't stop until I reached the living room. I was overtaken by a mixture of excitement and pure panic. When my shouts of 'A agua está a sair [the waters have broken]' finally roused Xanana from his slumber, he was off the couch in an instant and heading for the door to wake the Brazilian bodyguards to take us to the hospital.

I had decided to have my baby in Dili, in spite of the fact that the conditions of the national hospital were obviously inferior to those of a modern, fully equipped hospital in Australia. It was important to me that my child be born on East Timorese soil, in the country of which he would be one of the newest citizens. At almost 11 pm on 30 September 2000, Alexandre Brian Sword Gusmão came into the world. Rosalie, who had waited anxiously outside the delivery room throughout the labour, found herself being hugged and congratulated by one of the beefy Brazilian bodyguards when my baby's cries were finally heard. There was no pain relief, but Xanana stayed by my side throughout the whole excruciating business, nicking out only once in a while to puff nervously on a cigarette.

In addition to five live chickens, Alexandre's arrival on the scene brought a shower of traditional gifts in the form of baskets of mangoes, red rice and lengths of beautiful East Timorese woven cloth. Seeing the pleasure which Xanana took in Alexandre was just as rewarding as my own enjoyment of his presence in our lives. In spite of his unmerciful schedule, Xanana made time each day to bathe and dress his new little son. Alexandre was a joyful symbol of the new life being built around us. But first and foremost he was the product of the difficult love we had nurtured through times of adversity and momentous change.

At home in Bemori I had collected a vast array of mozzie-zapping implements: citrus incense sticks, lemongrass candles, every kind of spray on the market, various insect repellents and, my favourite, a tennis racket–shaped tool that electrocuted my new mortal enemy. It gave me tremendous satisfaction to hear the sound of a mosquito being frazzled on the wires of the racket. I spent an hour or so every evening just swatting mosquitoes around the Bemori house to reduce the risk of Alexandre catching malaria or dengue fever. Xanana must have thought that motherhood had completely unhinged me. He found the sight of me swinging my racket wildly about in the air, chuckling with glee every time I successfully zapped another mosquito, very amusing. 'You haven't had dengue fever,' I said, defending my eccentric behaviour. 'It's called maternal instinct.' Our house had narrowly escaped being torched by the militias in September 1999 but it suffered gaping holes in the roof and in a number of the ad hoc extensions. The rain gushed into the kitchen during the monsoonal downpours and the dust seeped into all the crevices. It was impossible to keep the mosquitoes out or to keep the house properly clean.

In October Xanana was voted in as the Speaker of the National Council. Without the support of an extended family network, the evening routine – feeding, bathing and putting Alexandre to bed – fell to me. I wanted Xanana's extra pair of hands to help me with some of the demands of the new baby, but it was impossible. He arrived home from the CNRT office late in the evenings, only to deal with the people queuing to see him at the gate.

At the tender age of six weeks, Alexandre was taken on his first overseas trip, to Australia, where Xanana was awarded the Sydney Peace Prize. We watched our baby grow and develop against the backdrop of the huge and significant steps the young East Timor was taking in the direction of independence and democracy. Almost every week a new institution or initiative was inaugurated, and Alexandre accompanied us to the receptions and parties organised to mark these landmarks, like a tiny mascot of East Timor's infant nationhood.

Alexandre ate his first solid food on the day in early February 2001 when the Falintil became the new East Timor Defence Force; he had begun making 'blah blah' noises with his tongue – a precursor to speech – at about the time it was announced that elections for the Constituent Assembly would take place on 30 August 2001. This body, a successor to the National Council, would draft a Constitution for an independent East Timor and would have some legislative responsibilities.

In March I found myself nursing Alexandre on the verandah of our house in the company of a couple from Suai. They were the parents of a girl called Juliana dos Santos, and the pain of her story was written in the faces of the stick-thin and poorly dressed couple who sat before me. They told me how their daughter, nicknamed Alola, had been brutally kidnapped from the Suai church by a militia leader on 6 September 1999. Minutes before she was taken by the vice-commander of the Laksaur militia group, their thirteen-year-old son, Carlos, was murdered inside the church along with about 200 others, including the priests who had made their desperate phone call to Xanana in Salemba on the night of 5 September 1999.

Juliana's mother, Maria, shook, and tears streamed down her gaunt cheeks as she recalled how her fifteen-year-old daughter was paraded by her captor, Igidio Manek, through the town like a war trophy, before she was finally bundled into the back of a car and driven away. The family had not seen Juliana since, although they had learned from returning refugees that she was now living across the border in Betun, West Timor, with her captor and the three other women he had taken as his 'wives'. A month or so earlier the family had received a note scribbled on a page ripped from an exercise book. The envelope also contained a crumpled and faded photograph of the baby Juliana had borne to Manek in November. The note, written in a hand the family did not recognise said, 'I am living well and have plenty of money. Once the UN withdraws from East Timor, the militia forces will seize the territory back from them.' These were not the sentiments of a new mother and it was clear that Manek had written the note himself.

I had to do something. I empathised with the sorrow and desperation Juliana's parents felt at having lost both their children, and at the same time I was well aware that their horrific tale of loss was one of very many. But was my inability to do something for every grieving family a reason to turn my back on Juliana and her parents? I decided to make a concerted effort to have Juliana reunited with her family. If, in this, I was able to draw attention to the plight of others, it would not be in vain for the larger population. And so I began lobbying the Indonesian government to allow Juliana to at least meet with her parents in conditions that permitted her to express her will freely.

In response, the Indonesian authorities claimed that Juliana had signed a statement admitting to being happily married to Manek. She also had no wish to return to East Timor, they said. It soon became very clear to me that there was a host of malignant forces and broader interests working against Juliana's return to East Timor. Juliana was a key witness to one of the worst atrocities following the 1999 ballot, a case in which not only Manek but senior members of the Indonesian military were implicated. So said a number of credible reports and eyewitnesses. Manek was to be indicted for crimes against humanity by the UN Prosecutor for his role in the church slayings. Any testimony that Juliana was able to supply confirming his participation and that of members of the Indonesian armed forces could have grave consequences for Manek and the military brass concerned. Moreover, there were suspicions that Manek had had a hand in organising the bloody attack on the UN office in Atambua in September 2000, resulting in the murder of three foreign staff of the UNHCR. Again, Juliana was uniquely positioned to confirm whether or not Manek had indeed plotted the attack and with whose backing.

In late March I travelled with Juliana's aunt, Domingas, to Geneva, where we testified before the fifty-seventh session of the UN Human Rights Commission. It was from Domingas' arms that Juliana had been snatched by Manek on that fateful day. The text of the statement that I read on behalf of Juliana's family included these moving words:

> We, the parents and family of Juliana dos Santos, present this testimony with sadness in our hearts and with none of the joy which is felt by so many of our fellow countrymen at having achieved our hard won freedom.
>
> As her family, we are powerless to do anything to bring her back from West Timor, and so we wait, hopeful that one day we will again see her smiling face and kiss with love the child born to her as a souvenir of her woman's suffering, of her fate as a pawn of war.
>
> We call upon the Commission on Human Rights to press for the independently monitored processing and return of East Timorese refugees held in West Timor against their will, with particular attention and sensitivity addressed to women and children victims of sexual violence.

Six-month-old Alexandre was laid down to sleep on the floor of vast conference halls in the decidedly baby-unfriendly UN building while my friend Margherita Tracanelli and I ran off endless photocopies of the documents relating to Juliana's case with which to petition the commission's delegates. Nappy changes and breastfeeds were performed on the floor of the Delegates' Lounge, where we informally lobbied the heads of country delegations to pressure Indonesia on Juliana's case and the cases of the other East Timorese hostages who remained in the militia-controlled camps of West Timor.

As a result of my lobbying and participation in a round of bilateral negotiations between the government of Indonesia and UNTAET in Bali in May 2001, the Indonesian government agreed to facilitate a family reunion between Juliana and her parents just inside Indonesia, in the village of Mota-ain. After weeks of complicated negotiations, the details of the reunion were agreed upon and Juliana and her baby son, Carlos, met with her mother and father in the Mota-ain police station. It was a brief, emotional meeting. Around the small, impersonal building of the police station were gathered between sixty and seventy armed Indonesian soldiers and a handful of nervous-looking Indonesian Foreign Affairs officials from Jakarta. They looked resentful of the fact that as a result of my campaign, they had been dragged to this remote backwater, all for the trifling matter of one young woman's future. Nobody was surprised when Juliana announced that she wished to remain in West Timor. She had undoubtedly been subjected to intense psychological pressure, if not explicit threats, by Manek prior to the family reunion. As she was guided, prisoner-of-war style, by two women police officers to a waiting vehicle, Juliana's mother collapsed in a faint on the steps of the police station.

I resolved not to give up on Juliana. But in the meantime, whole chapters of East Timor's history were being written within the space of months, and Xanana's position at the centre of just about every new development meant that I was guaranteed a bird's-eye view of the action. On 9 June 2001, the CNRT disbanded, having successfully fulfilled its objective of contributing to the process of transition to independence. It was a sad day for Xanana, who had made consolidating the role of the council as a broad platform of national unity the focus of his work to that point. The following month he established the Association of the Veterans of the Resistance as a means of supporting and voicing the aspirations of those who had conducted the resistance struggle in villages and towns across the country. He was elected as the association's president on 17 July 2001.

With the elections for the Constituent Assembly looming, pressure was mounting on Xanana to state unequivocally whether or not he would run for the presidency. The presidential elections were not due to take place until some time in 2002, however the people were anxious to know who the preferred presidential candidate of each party was before they voted for their representatives on 30 August 2000, as they were accustomed to the Indonesian electoral system, in which the parliament chose the nation's president. Although the Constitution that would determine how East Timor's president was voted in had not yet been written, everyone seemed to believe it would be by a direct ballot. And so, wishing to reassure the people and guarantee stability and calm for the elections, Xanana finally agreed to end the speculation and convened a meeting at the Dili Gymnasium on 25 August. Thousands of people and scores of local and international journalists crammed into the airless stadium to hear Xanana speak.

'I never harboured personal ambitions of my own, particularly since I had sworn on the blood of my fallen soldiers and in the presence of the guerrillas under my command that I would never claim any rewards for myself, out of respect for the tremendous sacrifices made by all East Timorese. It was always in this spirit that I endeavoured to serve as best I could the country and its people. It was always this principle that guided me in my actions, and I endeavour to continue to be true to this ideal today.'

All eyes were on Xanana. You could have heard a pin drop as he continued.

'I declare here and now that I will accept to be nominated by the parties to the office of President of the Republic of Timor Lorosa'e.'

A cheer went up before he had even completed the sentence. It was some minutes before the applause and excited chatter subsided and Xanana was able to continue.

'I wish to put an end to speculation on this subject. I am conscious that I am not the best person for the job. It is true that I have begun to feel tired as a consequence of twenty-five years of heavy responsibility. I always nurtured the dream that after independence I would have time to cultivate pumpkins and breed animals. And hope should never die.'

As we struggled back to the car through the crowds, Alexandre squirming in Xanana's arms, I called to my husband, 'I don't like your chances.' He looked at me a little puzzled, perhaps thinking

I meant that I didn't fancy his chances of winning the presidential elections. 'The pumpkins,' I explained. 'I don't like your chances of becoming a pumpkin farmer just yet.'

It had become painfully obvious to us both that Xanana would not avoid the role that he had already been cast in for many years. For as long as I had known him, Xanana had resisted all suggestions that he was the obvious leader of an independent East Timor. His pledge to the dead Falintil fighters was not insincere or the clever ploy of a politician. It was heartfelt. The fact that popular pressure had caused him to go back on his promise to them and to himself saddened him . . . and me. I recalled the first time I had heard Xanana cry. In July 1994 he had sent an audiotaped message to José Ramos-Horta in which he responded to José's suggestions that he was destined to be the nation's first president – the sound of his weeping as he recalled those who had died for freedom and his oath to them had put me in a melancholy frame of mind for days. Indeed, so profound was the impact of his tears on me that I believe it was on that day that I knew I had fallen in love with Xanana Gusmão.

Once again, on 30 August 2001, the eyes of the world were focussed on East Timor. After we voted for the Constituent Assembly in Manatuto, we flew by helicopter to a number of centres around the country to observe people casting their votes. As had been the case two years earlier, the people displayed a tremendous democratic consciousness, with a voter turnout of roughly ninety-three per cent. Alexandre, now a robust and healthy eleven-month-old boy, was lovingly pinched and pampered by the crowds at each destination. As expected, the Fretilin party won the lion's share of seats in the new assembly. Twenty-two of the eighty-eight elected members of the assembly were women.

When Alexandre turned one and was looking as if he could start walking any day, we decided that it was time to move house. The thought that our young son might be led by his curiosity into Bemori's infamous open drain was a little frightening. And besides, I was getting tired of putting my arsenal of mozzie-zapping devices to the test. Xanana began house-hunting. It was October by the time he chanced upon the house in Balibar, a hillside village some ten kilometres south of Dili. It was late November by the time the house was made habitable and we were able to move in. The house was small, poky even – but being cool, light, airy and virtually mozzie-free, it was perfect luxury to me. Not even the twenty-minute drive to Dili detracted from the charms of our new abode, which included a majestic view of the island of Atauro and the hills and coastline east of Dili.

We were in Oslo, Norway, attending a donors' conference and the hundredth anniversary celebrations of the Nobel Peace Prize when I became aware that I was pregnant again. It was December 2001, and with presidential elections scheduled for April and independence to be declared in May 2002, it was bound to be another challenging and busy year for the fledgling nation and for our young family.

The presidential election, the third and last UN-organised election in East Timor, took place on 14 April 2002. Xanana's only rival was Francisco Xavier do Amaral, the former Fretilin president who now headed the ASDT (Timorese Association of Social Democrats) party. A few days after the vote it was announced that Xanana had won 82.7 per cent of the votes. If our fate hadn't been sealed long before this, it certainly was now.

Chapter eighteen

BALIBAR
20 May 2002 and beyond

AFTER THE SPECTACULAR and moving Independence celebrations at Taci Tolu, I arrived home in Balibar in the early hours of 20 May 2002 with a president for a husband and a new role of my own. Nothing could have prepared me for the dramatic changes that have occurred in my life since I first began to dabble in matters Timor-related almost twenty years ago. I have gone from being a language student and activist to the first lady of the poorest country in Asia, and a wife and mother in a country very different from the one I grew up in.

In spite of my long experience of living and working outside Australia and of preparing others to do the same, I still find myself doing battle regularly with my cultural baggage. East Timorese society is hierarchical and ageist, and I often find behaviour reflecting these different values jars with me and the egalitarianism of my Australian roots and upbringing. Nevertheless, I enjoy friendships with East Timorese from all walks of life and feel that I have been warmly welcomed by the citizens of my new homeland in spite of my non-Timorese heritage. Perhaps my long history of involvement in the country's struggle to achieve independence has contributed to people's perception of me as, first and foremost, an East Timorese – and an Australian only by birth.

With my new role has come a tremendous change in lifestyle. Nowadays, whenever I set foot outside my home I am accompanied by a small retinue of bodyguards. Whilst neither Xanana nor I feel that our security is threatened inside East Timor, personal protection is just one of those things that comes with the job. Although I sometimes lament the loss of my ability to be anonymous and spontaneous in daily life, I have to say that the women and men who make up my security team double as excellent babysitters and I am very grateful for the many odd jobs they do for me. Having household help is not something that has ever sat comfortably with me. It is something I have had to learn to get used to. But the fact is that without the team of loyal and hard-working women who assist me at home, I wouldn't be in a position to pursue a single interest or activity outside the domestic sphere. As a public figure, even a simple shopping expedition becomes an exercise in public relations. Smiling and meeting and greeting whilst pushing a shopping trolley around a supermarket is an art I am still perfecting.

Regardless of the peculiarities of my situation, in many ways the dilemma I face today is that of every working mother worldwide: that of juggling my responsibilities and duties as a wife and mother with the demands of a job and the broader expectations of society.

I gave birth to my second son, Kay Olok Sword Gusmão, in the maternity wing of Dili National Hospital in the early hours of 11 August 2002. A typical day in my life consists of balancing time spent with my two children with fielding requests for meetings with journalists and other visitors to East Timor, handling applications for assistance from widows, students, schools and women's groups, negotiating customs clearances for containers of school supplies and donated goods from around the world, and attending meetings of the many organisations and projects of which I am a patron. I have become quite adept at balancing a baby feeding at the breast in one arm and taking calls on my mobile with the other.

There is so much still to be done to restore the most basic services to the East Timorese, to rebuild essential infrastructure – every area is a priority, and the renewal of one sector depends on the recovery of another. The needs of the people are overwhelming and Xanana and I grapple with them at a personal level each day, as well as in our official capacity as public figures.

The patience and resilience the East Timorese developed through the years of resistance to Indonesian rule continue to be put to the test as the nation's leaders grapple with the huge and complex task of rebuilding. Xanana speaks often of the need of the East Timorese to acquire a new sense of nationalism. The patriotism that guided the people in their struggle against foreign domination is no longer relevant. Today nationalism demands of East Timor's leaders, civil servants and members of the public a commitment to working selflessly to defeat a new enemy: that of poverty and ignorance. For the first time in history, the responsibility for winning this battle on a national level is in the hands of the East Timorese.

Under Indonesian rule, the East Timorese were effectively excluded from senior management positions in both the public and private spheres. Civil servants were not encouraged to be creative, to take the initiative; nor was any sense of civic duty engendered. 'Non-government organisation' were dirty words, and only a handful of local, tightly controlled NGOs existed. Today civil society is being challenged for the first time to contribute actively to the building of East Timor's democracy, so the learning curves are sharp. Despite this, many important advances have been made, and the East Timorese are genuinely committed to strengthening democracy and ensuring that the tears and blood of the past were not shed in vain.

Ironically, the forging of East Timor's independence on the rubble of a violent past has highlighted its dependence. The country relies heavily on financial and technical assistance from abroad and will continue to do so for many years to come. The rebuilding process is one to which many countries, individuals and organisations wish to contribute, and dealing with these diverse players and their different, sometimes conflicting visions represents a challenge in itself. And yet East Timor is lucky to be blessed with a huge number of brave, talented, wise and dedicated friends, some old, some new, but all full of respect for and goodwill towards the East Timorese people and all representing a source of wealth and experience.

My efforts to bring Juliana dos Santos home to her family in Suai have been unsuccessful. Indeed, she remains in West Timor as I write. I continue to explore with Juliana's family ways to resolve her case, but I am all too conscious of the psychological and political dimensions of her predicament. She is a pawn in a much bigger game. Her personal story is in many ways a symbol of the plight of her homeland, which for twenty-four years was enslaved by the powerful interests of others with military might on their side.

One of the most disturbing things I have found about working on Juliana's case is how it highlights the social vulnerability of women in East Timor. I decided to establish the Alola Foundation to keep Juliana's tragic story in the public eye and to draw attention locally and internationally to the problem of sexual violence as experienced by the women of East Timor. Given the absence of government support for my work, the Alola Foundation has become a vehicle for me to respond to a wider set of issues of national importance.

As a mother of two small children, tackling the high maternal and child mortality rate is also a priority for me. I am involved with a number of government-sponsored campaigns aimed at improving the health of mothers and children, and promoting breastfeeding and immunisation across the country. I established the Klibur Susubeen Inan Nian ba Kosok Oan (National Breastfeeding Association) in February 2003. The lives of a large number of newborn babies could be saved each year in East Timor if exclusive breastfeeding were practised. Many babies die of malnutrition and gastrointestinal infections caused by the preparation of breast-milk substitutes in unsanitary conditions.

Much is demanded of women in East Timor. They are expected to contribute to the social and economic life of their families and communities, and yet they are accorded little acknowledgement and granted very little power in public and political life. As in many countries, women and girls are a priceless and under-utilised resource in East Timor. They could contribute to so many areas of the life of the nation, and yet too often unequal access to education and employment, financial dependence on men, and traditional social and religious mores mean that the country fails to benefit from their skills, wisdom and nurturing instincts. Unequal gender relations within the family and traditional patriarchal values and customs also contribute significantly to the high incidence of domestic violence. Fear, lack of confidence in the justice system, a lack of knowledge of victims' rights and limited support services all play a part in the fact that a large number of cases of domestic violence go unreported. Nevertheless, violence within the home is the single most reported crime in East Timor today.

With so many problems, big and small, it is all too easy to forget to be thankful for the absence of the fear, intimidation, oppression and military excesses of the past. I am occasionally reminded of those dark, difficult years when, in the course of my daily life, I stumble across the asylum-seekers, guerrilla fighters and student activists with whom I once fought against the world's indifference. Nowadays these same people are government ministers, senior officials in the defence force and members of parliament.

As president, Xanana's role is much better defined and the parameters of his responsibility are much clearer than they were when Alexandre was a baby. He has staff who handle requests for meetings and all the other day-to-day business that once fell on my shoulders. Whilst people don't expect to have quite the same access to the president of the country as they did to the president of the CNRT, there are always long queues of people outside Xanana's office and he continues to find it difficult to say no. And I still occasionally find myself slipping down to the office in the early morning to correct or print out a speech that Xanana is due to deliver later that day.

We have little time to enjoy one another's company or that of our children, to delight in Alexandre as he attempts to get his tongue around the three languages he hears each day, and to feed Kay Olok his first solids. He likes pumpkin, and Xanana, who is not about to give up on his pumpkin-farming dream, often says that he will personally cultivate the vegetables we serve up to our children of the future. Having young kids in our circumstances helps keep us grounded and focussed on the future. I am convinced that it is good for Xanana's sense of perspective that at the end of a day of dealing with affairs of state, he is obliged by Alexandre to spend time in front of the Wiggles and *Sesame Street*.

It is ironic, but at times Xanana and I look back on the early years of our unusual courtship, the difficult Cipinang prison years, with a degree of nostalgia. It seems that back then there was more time and space in our lives for thinking, reflecting, and indulging romantic fantasies and personal dreams. The long road we have travelled since then has brought us to the realisation of many of those dreams, and this fact is a source of tremendous happiness. But the loss of our personal 'freedom', which has come with liberation of the country, sometimes weighs heavily upon us. At the end of each exhausting day it is my children who affirm my knowledge that every sacrifice involved in marrying the father of a nation was a sacrifice worth making. After all, they embody all the hope, promise and potential that is our home, Timor-Leste.